Basics of Economic Geography

About the Author

Prof. Dr. Kanan Chatterjee obtained her B.A. (Hons) (1967) and M.A (1969) Degree in Geography from University of Calcutta. She was also awarded Ph.D. (Arts) Degree from University of Calcutta (1977). Dr. Chatterjee started her teaching carrier as lecturer in Geography by joining North Bengal University, West Bengal in 1976 and University of Calcutta, Kolkata in 1979. The areas of her interest are Social and Economic Geography. Prof. Chatterjee was awarded UGC Emeritus Fellowship in 2013. She visited countries of Europe (1996) and USA (2013) for academic exercise. Prof. Chatterjee conducted a number of research projects – UGC Major Research Projects, DRS etc. A number of research scholars were awarded Ph.D. degree of University of Calcutta under her supervision and guidance. She has contributed a large number of research papers in peer-reviewed journals of national and international repute. Prof. Chatterjee edited and authored a number of books in various fields of Geography. She is a life member of various learned national and international bodies.

Basics of Economic Geography

Prof. Kanan Chatterjee
Emeritus Fellow
Former Professor
Department of Geography
University of Calcutta

CONCEPT PUBLISHING COMPANY PVT. LTD.
NEW DELHI-110059

ISBN-13 : 978-93-5125-175-0 (H.B.)
ISBN-13 : 978-93-5125-176-7 (P.B.)

First Published 2015

Published and Printed by

Concept Since 1974

Concept Publishing Company Pvt. Ltd.
A/15-16, Commercial Block, Mohan Garden
New Delhi-110059 (India)
T: 25351460, 25351794, *F*: 091-11-25357109
E: publishing@conceptpub.com, W: www.conceptpub.com
Editorial Office: H-13, Bali Nagar, New Delhi-110 015, India.

Cataloging in Publication Data--*Courtesy:* D.K. Agencies (P) Ltd. <docinfo@dkagencies.com>

Chatterjee, Kanan. author.
Basics of economic geography / Prof. Kanan Chatterjee.
pages cm
Includes bibliographical references and index.
ISBN 9789351251750 (HB)
ISBN 9789351251767 (PB)

1. Economic geography. I. Title.

DDC 330.9 23

Dedicated

to

my mother

Late Indu Prova Chakraborty

Prelude

Since the extent of economic development is an important index of over-all growth in a country, the progress and consequent expansion of economic geography provide an interesting subject of study. An attempt has been made in this study to show how far the resources and expansion of economic activities can be considered rational from the point of view of economic viability. Basic components of economic geography have been explored by taking into consideration the changing trends, the study of which is by itself a lively topic of investigation at the present time.

Considerable study has been made by several workers in this field, but basic issues in economic geography has hardly been studied in depth and an interdisciplinary approach towards the investigation of problems relating to the economic growth and development has not been attempted. Hence, a geographical-cum-economic analysis of the same has been carried out and with this as background the possibilities have been spelt out. Geographers are engaged in planning resources and their utilization and have shown their importance in national and international agencies that deal with the study, inventory and administration of natural and human resources. To work out strategies in the management of resources application of technology is obviously required.

This work will evoke considerable interest amongst the reading public in other disciplines of commerce, economics, agriculture etc. The intention here is to bring out a text and reference book. Institutions, teachers, students and research scholars may find that it covers their course contents in one way or other. It is hoped that the publication will generate desired enthusiasm and thinking in this field.

Prof. Kanan Chatterjee
Emeritus Fellow
Department of Geography
University of Calcutta
West Bengal

Acknowledgements

The author wishes to thank the University of Calcutta, Kolkata, West Bengal for providing her with infrastructural facilities for the publication of this book. Appreciation is also extended to her research scholars especially Sri Utpal Khara for their co-operation and help in pursuing the publication work.

Contents

List of Tables

List of Figures

List of Plates

List of Abbreviations

APEC	—	Asia-Pacific Economic Cooperation
ASEAN	—	Association of South-East Asian Nations
BoP	—	Balance of Payment
DGTD	—	Directorate General of Technical Development
DIC	—	District Industries Centre
E-commerce	—	Electronic commerce
EEC	—	European Economic Community
EERM	—	European Exchange Rate Mechanism
EP	—	Export Promotion
EPZ	—	Export Processing Zone
FDI	—	Foreign Direct Investment
FERA	—	Foreign Exchange Regulations Act
FTZ	—	Free Trade Zone
GATT	—	General Agreement on Tariffs and Trade
GDP	--	Gross Domestic Product
HYV	—	High Yielding Variety
ICAR	—	Indian Council of Agricultural Research
IMF	—	International Monetary Fund
IRDA	—	Insurance Regulatory and Development Authority
IS	—	Import Substitution
ISPs	—	Internal Service Providers
JGSY	—	Jawahar Gram Samriddhi Yojana
JRY	—	Jawahar Rozgar Yojana
METI	—	Ministry of Economy, Trade and Industry
MITI	—	Ministry of International Trade and Industry
MRTPA	—	Monopolies & Restrictive Trade Practices Act
MRTS	—	Mass Rapid Transport System
MSMEs	—	Micro, Small and Medium Enterprises

NAFTA	—	North Atlantic Free Trade Area
NICs	—	Newly Industrializing Countries
NIEO	—	New International Economic Order
NSSO	—	National Sample Survey Organization
OCBs	—	Overseas Corporate Bodies
OECD	—	Organization of Economic Cooperation and Development
OPEC	—	Organization of Petroleum Exporting Countries
PPP	—	Public Private Participation
SEZs	—	Special Economic Zones
SNA	—	System of National Accounts
TRIMPs	—	Trade Related Investment Measures
TRIPs	—	Trade-Related Intellectual Property Rights
UNCED	—	United Nations Conference on Environment and Development
UN	—	United Nations
WTO	—	World Trade Organization

CHAPTER 1
Economic Geography
Scope, Content, and Objectives

1.1 Definition, Scope and Content

Geographers define geography in several ways. Some believe that the way man lives in a place is greatly influenced by landforms, climate and soils. A few believe that human activities are determined by geographic factors. In spite of differences of opinion, all geographers will probably agree that geographical study may well include an examination of spatial patterns of on the surface of the earth. Spatial pattern and their variation have profound significance in human life.

Geography analyses and explains variations in activities over space. Economic Geography is the study of the spatial variation of activities related to production, exchange and consumption of goods and services. Whenever possible the goal is to develop generalizations and theories to account for these spatial variations. This definition was given jointly by Hartshorn and Alexander. Prof E.W. Zimmermann pointed out that "Economic Geography deals with the economic life of man with relation to environment." According to Dudley Stamp, "Economic Geography involves consideration of the Geographical and other factors which influence man's productivity, but only in limited depths, so far as they are connected with production and trade".

In pursuit of its aims, the economic geographer answers to three questions (a) where is the economic activity located? (b) What are the characteristics of the economic activity? (c) To what other phenomenon is the economic activity related? The first question relates to the location. Map provide the answer to the question "where". If no such map exists, the Geographers will have to construct one because maps are basic tools and are essential in understanding of real relationship. The idea of pattern or distribution may facilitate the concept of location. A pattern is arrangement of an element over the surface of the earth. The world pattern of population, for example, reveals some densely populated areas in China and India, some areas of less density in U.S.A. and Russia and some sparsely settled areas in North Africa and central Australia. The second question decides the significant characteristics of the economic activity and their description. For example, what are the characteristics of tea plantation that distinguish the regions devoted to it? How many areas do the plantation farms occupy? What kind of buildings are on them? How much tea is produced? In what respects are these regions different from rice or wheat growing areas? Careful observation of the various aspects will enable the geographer to distinguish the tea producing regions both from regions of contrasting activities and from other regions of tea production. Then in terms of these characteristics a geographer finally decides where to draw the boundary of the distinctive region of his map. In answer to the third question there are four ways to investigate the relationship. [A] One useful approach is through an analysis of cause and effect. [B] Some geographers concentrate on relationship with physical and cultural phenomena. [C] An alternative approach is to consider relationship within a region and those between regions. [D] Finally, some geographers prefer to study relationship in terms of co-relationship.

Different types of economic activities like primary, secondary, tertiary, quaternary and quinary are included in this subject. Besides these, detailed study on different industrial activities, locational theories, developmental policies etc. are dealt with. Transport and communication, trade and commerce emphasize on economic development of a country. Now study on multi-dimensional aspect like economic inequality or disparity, unemployment, poverty, urbanization related with industrialization etc. also enter into periphery of economic geography.

1.2 Objectives

Different points of view are held as to the meaning, approach and objectives of the subject. Economic Geography deals with the problems of making a living. It belongs more to the field of human than to physical geography. Special emphasis is laid on economic production and trade. According to Ellsworth Huntington, " Economic Geography deals with the distribution of all sorts of material, resources, activities, institutions, customs, capacities and types of ability that play a part in the work of getting a living. Farming, manufacturing and trade are the main methods of getting a living. Hence, Economic Geography combines three main phases—agricultural, industrial and commercial—but mining, lumbering and fishing must also be considered. Economic Geography, like other branch of Geography cannot be separated from physical geography. Its main problem is to discover ways in which the distribution of physical conditions influences the distribution of the methods by which people satisfy their needs for food, clothing, shelters, tools and other products."

The study of the manner of the exploitation of the earth's resources and the limits set by physical environment is the proper scope of Economic Geography. According to Jones and Darkenwald, "Economic Geography deals with the productive occupations and attempts to explain why certain regions are outstanding in the production and exportation of various articles and why others are significant in the import and utilization of these things."

In this study of interdependence of production emphasis should be given upon the degree of human initiatives and the nature of physical forces enacting to shape certain life pattern. They should be studied as a comprehensive system of interaction between man and nature. It is not only content with the analysis of the present pattern of production and productive occupations, it also studies their dynamics. Global resources pattern change not only in response to increasing knowledge, improved skill and techniques but also, perhaps more, in relation to changing socio-political scenario. Thus, Economic Geography is much embracing subject. It not only aims at the understanding of different natural phenomena but also takes cognizance of racial traits and customs, advantages of an early start, availability of capital and labour, accumulated technical knowledge and skilled managements, stability of Governments, Governments' aids or hindrances in the form of tariffs, subsides or urbanization schemes and so on.

Economic Geography investigates the diversity in basic resources of the different parts of the world. It tries to evaluate the effects of physical environment upon the utilization of these resources. It studies differences in economic development in different regions or economy of the world. It also studies transportation and trade resulting from this development.

The problems of economic resources have become more complex today with millions of starving and unemployed. Population disparity in the state of economic well-being and competitive attitude of many countries give rise to socio-economic problems. Economic Geography also aims at revolving such problems by better and efficient utilization of limited resources through rational, systematic, scientific and long-term planning. Economic Geography serves as an essential tool for reducing and finally eliminating world society's disparity gaps by scientific study of their economic resources, modern needs and cultural heritages.

1.3 Approaches to Economic Geography

Among the several methods of studying Economic geography, the four most important approaches are:

(a) Regional Approach
(b) Systematic or Community Approach
(c) Activity Approach
(d) Principal Approach

(a) ***Regional Approach:*** In considering this popular approach, the world, a continent or even a country or a state may be divided into geographic regions. The basic advantage of this approach is that it gives a better and comprehensive knowledge of the different parts of unit, their relationship to each other and to the units as a whole.

(b) ***Systematic or Community Approach:*** This approach provides a systematic description and interpretation of the distributional pattern of individual resources or commodity (e.g. wheat, rice, tea) or an industry (e.g. Iron and steel industry, cotton textile). As observed by W. Smith "it analyses the whole sequence of their development and catches them or their march to progression or retrogression."

(c) ***Activity Approach:*** This approach aims at dividing man's basic economic activities into three categories—Primary, Secondary and Tertiary; Primary activity is connected with nature and includes agriculture, forestry, fishing, hunting etc. Secondary activity depends on the process of converting the primary products into more usable ones like all branches of manufacturing industries. Tertiary activity sets up a link between primary and secondary activities such as trade and transportation.

(d) ***Principal Approach:*** In this approach generalizations are made about man and his environment on the basis of analysis of facts at a specific time point. Generalizations like "plains invite occupancy, mountain repel settlement" are made. This approach enhances the clarity of reasoning and depth of analysis. All these approaches have their own merits and limitations. Any single approach is therefore incompetent to give a complete picture of the economy of a country or a region.

1.4 Innovation in Economic Geography

Economic geography emphasizes spatial interaction among places of production and consumption. Understanding as economy requires that the fundamental economic activities as production, consumption and distribution be treated as integrated parts of a system. Economic geography, as a field of study, focuses on the flows in the economic activities of distribution. Economists are interested in the aggregate such as national totals. The supply and demand for goods or services are markets. Government policy can affect the economic characteristics of a place or region or it can directly modify patterns of spatial interaction. Innovation may be defined by technological upliftment and theoretical advancement as well.

A review of research in Economic geography and planning would be incomplete without the consideration of recent developments, research techniques and tools employed by regional planners. There is a strong case for experimenting with the application of techniques like multiple factors analysis, grouping techniques such as nearest neighbor techniques, cluster analysis to problems in spatial planning.

The review of the work done by the Indian Geographers in the field of Economic geography reveals that few geographers have been able to free themselves from the theories of industrial location and produce a really geographical analysis of locational aspects. However, the contributions of some Indian geographers are pleading for a careful planning of industrial location with distinct regional bias refreshing expectations.

Location Theories: The major work on industrial location theory has been carried out by economists attempting to analyze location into the main body of economic theory. Location is concerned with spatial relationships and this has also attracted the attention of numerous geographers. The theoretical approaches are by Ricardo, John Heinrich, Von Thunen (1783-1850), Mill, Smith (1966) etc. The analysis is structured around different approaches of industrial location theory.

(a) The least cost approach (Weber-1909, Hover-1948), (b) Market area analysis (Losch 1954), (c) recent theorists Isard *et al.* (1956) in particular have attempted to remould the Loschian approach into a more profit-maximizing approach. Loria, an Italian, suggested that industrialist seek locations that give them maximum profits considering both markets and costs in 1884, (d) modernization theory is one of the leading theories of economic development. Two models are drawn from modernization: (i) The model of the demographic transition; and (ii) The model of sectoral shifts—primary to secondary to tertiary that take place with economic growth. The basic premise of modernization theory is that historical processes are predictable and hold into the future. The past experience of some countries can be used to predict the future experiences of other countries. With respect to the demographic transition, some countries can expect a decline in their population growth rate in the future because other countries have experienced such declines in the past, sectoral shifts can be expected in some countries because they have already happened in others. The most comprehensive version of modernization theory is presented by W.W. Rostow (1978) in his description of the five stages of economic development. The first stage is 'Traditional Society' characterized by limited technology, an economy consisting of primary sector activities and low levels of capital investment. The second stage establishes the 'Precondition for Takeoff'. These preconditions come about because of increased agricultural productivity. The productivity improvements in agriculture ultimately provide output surpluses that can be sold. These earnings become the capital surpluses needed for infrastructural development which in turn improves productivity in the economy because it serves to integrate the regions of the developing country. The third stage of development is called the 'Takeoff' and as the name implies it is period of rapid economic growth. It is brought about in response to the demands of a single growth demand of labour and capital. The single growth industry has a multiplier effect on the whole economy. The fourth stage is the 'Derived to Maturity'. At this point, the economy is broadened as the production processes that were once employed only in the dominant growth industry are now used in other industries. The final stage of development is that of 'high mass consumption' in which manufacturing becomes oriented toward the production of consumer goods and the service sectors becomes the dominant one in economy.

As historical account, Rostow's version of modernization theory is a very interesting one. It provides particular years when different countries entered the various stages of development and describes particular events that were pivotal in the progress of national economic conditions. It describes particular events that were pivotal in the progress of national economic conditions. Its general applicability as a theory of development with respect to currently developing economics is questionable, however, if only because the relevance of eighteenth and nineteenth century European history appears to be rapidly declining in the contemporary global economy. The decade of the 1980s has shown that the path of economic growth and progress is not as smooth and predictable as modernization theory implies.

Agricultural technology and diffusions: It is difficult to define technology. Sometimes, it is considered to simply as applied science, implying that produces developed in laboratories constitute technology when they are used in the more practical situations of the outside world. The word is used as a synonym for a set of techniques. Terms such as primitive technology and modern technology imply ways of doing things in historical context. Computer technology implies the general use of computers as a set of tools and automotive technology indicates the set of techniques that are used in building motor cars and trucks. The term agricultural technology implies a whole series of techniques and processes that are linked by their applications to a particular type of production. In general, agricultural technology consists of a series of tools and techniques that effectively enhance the two major factors of agriculture production, land and labour, or even provides substitutes for the ways that cause agricultural productivity to increase. Not all technological advances in agriculture are embodied in machines. Advances in irrigation and drainage practices, are improvement in agricultural technology. Mechanization was in fact the primary area of technological change in agriculture from about 1800 to 1930, since that time scientific changes seem to have been more important than engineering changes. The development of chemical fertilizers and pesticide, for example, is the result of increased knowledge of biochemistry. Biotechnology is being used to improve agricultural productivity in a number of ways. All technology has some geographical source from which it spreads to other places in a form of spatial interaction called spatial diffusion. Diffusion is actually in temporal process as well as spatial one, contagious diffusion is marked by distance decay. Actual implementation of an innovation takes more time, but knowledge of the innovation is a necessary first step in its diffusion. Distance is less of a barrier to the spread of information in hierarchical diffusion.

New Agricultural Strategy and Green Revolution: Since the mid 1960s, the traditional agricultural practices are gradually being replaced by modern technology and farm practices in India and variable renovation is taking places in our country. As a result of new agricultural strategy, area under improved seeds has gone up from about 15 million hectares during 1970-71 to nearly 75 million hectares in 1995-96. The new varieties are of short-term duration and consequently, instead of growing one crop, two crops and sometimes even three crops are grown. In the case of wheat, unprecedented enthusiasm has prevailed among farmers in Punjab, Haryana, Delhi, Rajasthan and western Uttar Pradesh for the New Mexican varieties like Lerma Rajo, Sonara 64, Kalian and P.V. 18 and a situation developed in which the demand for the seeds by the farmers exceeded the supply. But in the case of rice, the new varieties like TN1, IR8, ADT17, which were tried and found successful on a laboratory scale could not be successful applied on the field.

Traditional agriculture relies heavily on indigenous inputs such as the use of organic manures, seeds, simple ploughs, primitive agricultural tools, bullocks, etc. Modern technology, consists of chemical fertilizers, pesticides, improved varieties of seeds including hybrid seeds, agricultural machinery, extensive irrigation, use of diesel and electric power, etc. Since 1966, the use of modern agricultural inputs has increased at a compound rate of 10 per cent per annum in contrast to the traditional inputs rising at the rate of only one per cent per annum during the same period. Industries supplying the modern farm inputs are growing at a rapid rate. Massive programmes of farm mechanization and irrigation have also led to an increase in the consumption of electricity and diesel in rural areas.

Increased agricultural production in a certain region would produce secondary and tertiary effects. For instance, the availability of more food in the country would decrease dependence on food imports and thereby releases scarce foreign exchange resources for other sections of the economy. Similarly, increased production of commercial crops would lead to the expansion of agro-based industries.

Achievement of the new agricultural strategy include: (a) boost to the production cereals, (b) increase in production of commercial crops, (c) significant change in crop pattern, (d) boost to agricultural production and employment, and (e) forward and backward linkages strengthened.

The new agricultural technology has made the subsistence farmers market oriented. The farmers are dependent on the market for the supply of inputs and for the demand of their output. Modern technology has definitely proved its superiority over the traditional technology only in those areas where appropriate conditions prevail only in certain selected areas. There is a requirement for the evolution of a low cost technology which can be adopted by all small farmers and which can use and exploit the local resources. A study of this aspect of economic activity is an area that requires exploration.

1.5 Recent Trend in Economic Geography

Economic Geography of the world changed a lot in the last 25 years. During this period, the World economy mushroomed in size and complexity. At the same time, greater independence among nations added new dimensions to the World system. Major new work forms emerged as the post-industrial economy revolutionized the job market. The propelling force in economic growth became information and technology in the place of traditional raw materials and smokestack industries. New forms of management and organization develop to shape and lean these changes. The World becomes particularly aware of Japanese business practices in the 1980s. The most visible and influential institution associated with business activity remained the multinational corporation, much larger than before. Governments became more actively involved in promoting economic development.

World inflation rates accelerated in the 1970s, an energy crisis emerged and a crisis of finance gained momentum as the disparities between the developed and developing countries increased in the mid-1980s. Several newly influential groups of countries became important in the global market place. These included the Organization of Petroleum Exporting Countries (OPEC) block, the Newly Industrializing Countries (NICs), the Organization of Economic Cooperation and Development (OECD) group and the European Economic Community (EEC).

World trade became a crucial factor in the development process. More and more goods were 'international' in the sense that complex combinations of management, raw materials, technology, and semi-processed goods, from many countries interacted to create them. As the less developed countries climbed the technology ladder, they began producing products at home to substitute for previously imported items and eventually began exporting more sophisticated products as well. In turn, the more developed nations moved to knowledge-intensive activities such as electronics integrated circuits, robots, aerospace, telecommunications and biogenetics.

To finance this process, nations brought and sold one another's products at an accelerating and unprecedented pace. Unfortunately, aberrations in the process have declining activities in some nations. The more developed nations generally financed the expansion of activity in less developed areas by extending credit, leading to growing dependency on the major powers by the Third World countries.

The comprehensive measures called for in the NIEO (New International Economic Order) will dominate the agenda of economic geographers in developing countries throughout the world. The measure of NIEO are grouped under the five heading in the UN resolution-international trade, transfer of real resources, science and technology, industrialization and food and agriculture. The concern of economic geography in the 1990s and beyond must also include the heartland problems at a hierarchy of scales from local to global. The way in which economic geographers perceive these problems of growth and distribution reflects the development of the discipline over the country. Although a history of the subject is of interest for its own scale, it is also important if we are to understand the context in which economic geographers view the issues of current global concern.

Classification of Economies: The economy is the system of production and consumption, including the means of decision making and the allocation of resources in a particular country. Economic categorization can be made (A) by per capita propensity to exchange, (B) by level of economic development, and (C) by political-economic affiliation.

(A) Classification by per capita propensity to exchange: It can be approximately measured by (1) money income, and (2) real income. Money income indicates the average amount of money actually received by each member of an economy over a given period. The real income indicates the actual value of average money income of which he is member. Using this per capita real income as the master criterion, the world economies can be classified into three categories: (1) commercial, (2) commercial-subsistence, and (3) subsistence-with-some-commerce. This represents a declining order of propensity to exchange.

The commercial Economies account for nearly one-fifth of the world's people. The countries with the highest per capita propensity to exchange, nearly all of which are politically independent, are the manufacturing and commercial nations of NW Europe and their younger offshoot in North America, South Africa and Oceania.

Commercial-subsistence economies, involving about one-third of the world's population, are particularly conspicuous in Latin America, countries of West Asia, Northern Africa, Eastern Europe, Russia and the island nations of the Far East. Politically they tend to be either entirely or partially independent. Few of them are controlled completely by foreign capitals.

Nearly one-half of the world's people living under subsistence or subsistence-with-some-commerce conditions are found largely in the low latitude of Africa and in eastern and southern Asia. Recent world trends towards nationalism are affecting many of these countries. Among the large countries that contain the basic ingredients for raising their levels of economic activity are Communist China, India, Indonesia and Pakistan. They make up the lion's share of the world's most underfed, ill-clothed, ill-housed and yet rapidly multiplying inhabitants.

(B) Classification by level of economic development: Following this method economy can be classified in two levels of development (i) those which are economically and technically advanced, and (ii) those which are economically and technically underdeveloped.

A multitude of criteria have been employed to determine level of economic development. Of these, two appear to generalize the results– (a) the percentage of a country's labour force in agriculture, and (b) the per-capita gross national product.

Accordingly Chile, Argentina, Uruguay are placed into the underdeveloped category while Poland, Venezuela, and Kuwait are grouped into the technically advanced ones.

(C) Classification by political-economic affiliation: The degree of public and private ownership is the key features of economies under this category. Accordingly there are two types: (i) economies of subordinate affiliates, and (ii) economics of sovereign nations.

Economies of subordinate affiliates are controlled mainly by their mother countries, with the rigidity and degree of that control varying with the status of the dependency. There are two affiliates of non-communist countries and affiliates of communist countries. The first category includes colonies and overseas territories. All communist nations operating independently, namely Russia belong to the second category.

Among the world's sovereign states, ownership of the means of production and exchange is primarily public or semi-public. The USA alone stands as a major nation where private ownership is outstandingly championed. The non-communist European nations are characterized by government ownership and government policy is dominant in formulating and executing economic arrangements.

Although they contain less than one-third of the world's people, the technically advanced countries tend to dominate economic affairs, using their methods and instrument of scientific and technological know-how of capital accumulation, of a higher standard of living of outright political ownership.

Spatial organization of economic activities: Beginning in the 1950s, Economic Geography made new attempts in creating a theoretical approach and in building on the workshop economics and in relying heavily on quantitative methods to understand the 'spatial organization' of economic system. Spatial organization is the aggregate pattern of use of space by a society. It refers to the relative internal location of the elements in a spatial distribution: the location of each element relative to each other element and location of each element relative to all the other elements together.

In order to explain the spatial structure and national economic development, J. Friedmann suggested a simple model. The model shows the stages of spatial organization, a national economy passes through a primitive pre-industrial society to industrial maturity. The four stages in its progress are illustrated as—

(i) A spatial pattern of separate cities, each in an enclave isolated from the others.

(ii) At the time of incipient industrialization, the pattern is dominated by a single strong centre or core, surrounded by an extensive periphery.

(iii) The core-periphery situation is gradually transformed as strong peripheral sub-centres emerge alongside the single national centre. Inter-metropolitan peripheries now replace the previous national periphery. The sub-centres bring further resources into the national economy, thus enhancing the growth potential of the economy.

(iv) Finally, a functionally interdependent system of cities appears. Inter-metropolitan peripheries are completely absorbed and full integration of the economy is achieved, thus minimizing regional imbalances and maximizing the nation's growth potential.

CHAPTER 2

Concept of Resources and Economies

2.1 Meaning of the term 'Resource'

The word 'resource' means something of value or usefulness. In the early days, this value generally meant 'valuable'. Since economic value increases with scarcity, only the scarce commodities or substances were considered as resources. So, the "free resources" like sun light, air etc. were not considered as resources as these are not scarce. But in the modern world, a resource means something which is functionable in relation to human demand.

Two basic pre-conditions must be satisfied before something can be classified as a resource: (i) the knowledge and technical skill must exist to allow its utilization, and (ii) there must be a demand. For example, a fertile land is considered to be a resource as an agricultural land if people have the knowledge and technical skill to use that land for agriculture and if there is a demand for crops. Similarly, a person working in an organization is considered as a human resource because that person is able to satisfy the demand of the organization. It is, therefore, human ability and need which create resource value, not mere physical presence.

Zimmerman's definition (1933): According to the definition given by E.W. Zimmerman, the word 'resource' dose not refer to a thing or a substance but to a function which a thing or a substance may perform or to an operation in which it may take part, namely the function or operation of attaining a given end such as satisfying a want. For example, the existence of petroleum is not considered as a resource, but its functionability in relation to the human demand is considered as a resource.

Earth Summit resolution (1992): Earth Summit held at Ri-de-Janeiro in 1992 resolved that anything which may have some function not only to satisfy human demand at a given end but also to ensure preservation of biosphere should be considered as resource. So, everything required for the proper maintenance of eco-system will be resource and anything which may disrupt the system will be considered as resource if it is not economically utilized (like fishing). But filling up of the wetland may adversely affect the ecosystem of the area. So, from the environment point of view the wetland is a resource even it is not directly used by man.

Resistance and Neutral Stuff

Meaning of the word 'resistance' is opposite to that of resource. In other words, it has negative functionability and hence, it hinders the resource development process. For this reason, efforts for resource development also include resistance reduction.

Resistance may broadly be divided into two categories—natural resistance and man-made resistance. *Natural Resistance* means the resistance which occurs as a natural phenomenon. Flood, earthquake, cyclone, drought, etc. are known as natural resistances. These resistances are normally independent of any human influence. But human activities may induce some of these resistances. For example, flood can be induced by unplanned construction of dams and barrages and drought can be induced by deforestation and air pollution. *Man-made resistance* means the resistance which is created by man. It may be of two types, human resistance and cultural resistance. When the resistance is created by the size, growth and other demographic characteristic it is known as *human resistance*; for example, over-population, underpopulation, very high population growth etc. When the resistance is created by the cultural limitation or misuse of culture, it is known as cultural resistance; for example illiteracy, religious superstitions, war, etc.

Neutral stuff: According to Zimmerman (1951), a thing or substance remains 'neutral stuff' when either of the two conditions exists: (i) present knowledge and technical skill do not permit its utilization, and (ii) there is no demand for it. A neutral stuff is converted into a resource when functionability and utility are added to it. For example, petroleum had been a neutral stuff before its utilization started. Similarly, uranium deposit in the Meghalaya plateau may be considered as neutral stuff because presently available technical knowledge and skill do not permit its cost-effective utilization.

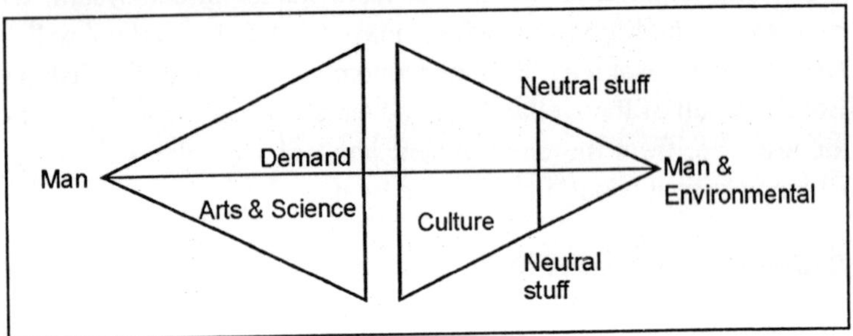

Fig. 2.1: Resource process from neutral stuff to resource (According to Zimmerman)

Nature of Resource

- **Dynamic of resource:** Nature of resource is always dynamic. Functionability of resource changes with the change of time and place and this change is activated by the change in demand and technology. For example, generation of wind power is caused by the increase in demand for non-polluting renewable resources and the development of technology to generate power from wind, dynamic of resource is identified by the changes in the quantity and quality of resources.
- **Component of resource development**. There are three components of resource development: nature, man and culture. **Nature** is considered as the 'store house' of all materials, some of these materials are 'free' resources which are available to man without any effort; for example, sunlight and air. Other materials remain as neutral substance and some of these neutral substances are converted into resources by making these neutral substances functionable. **Man** is the producer and consumer of all resources. Resource is created by the ability of man to satisfy his own demand. **Culture** is conditioned by the demand and ability of man. Man uses culture to convert neutral substances into resources and also to neutralize the resistances.

• **Availability of resource.** Availability of resource is viewed from two perspectives: Physical availability and functional availability. Physical availability is the quantitative measurement of resources. For example, total quantity of coal which is available from a coal mine is the physical availability of this resource. For fund (fixed supply) resource, physical availability increases with new discoveries and decreases with its use. Functional availability is the qualitative measurement which, in other words, means functional value. For example, functional availability of petroleum means its fuel and non-fuel uses. Functional availability may be increased without increasing the physical availability. For example, coal, in addition to fuel, may also be used as raw material for chemical industries. Similarly, by improving the methods of production, steel output can be increased to some extent without increasing the input of coal.

2.1.1 Classification of Resource

Resource may be classified into different types on the basis of different perspectives.

A. On the basis of ***durability*** or nature of availability resources may be classified into two groups:

(i) ***Fund or exhaustible resources*****:** this is not everlasting and exhaustible forever after use e.g., coal, petroleum, uranium etc.

(ii) ***Flow or inexhaustible resources:*** here supply of resources remains unchanged even after renewed use e.g., river water, sea-wave, sunshine, airflow etc.

B. On the basis of availability of ***frequency of occurrence***, resources can be classified into four groups: (i) Ubiquities, (ii) Commonalities, (iii) Rarities, (iv) Unique. Ubiquitous types of resources are found everywhere e.g., sunshine etc. and rest of three categories resources are called localized resources. Localized resources are available only in some places, e.g., petroleum, iron-ore etc.

C. On the basis of resources ***aspects,*** resource can be classified into three groups:

(i) ***Natural resources***—all the components of nature having functionability and utility, e.g., sunshine, water, forest, soil, minerals etc.

(ii) ***Human resources***—physical power and brain power of man comprise human resources.

(iii) ***Cultural resources***—different aspects of culture which contribute to the development of the society and which have positive functionability are known as cultural resources, e.g., education.

Table 2.1: Classification of Resources

Classification of Resources		
Basis of classification	*Types of resource*	*Examples*
A. Nature of availability	Flow	Sunlight, running water
	Fund	Coal, iron ore
B. Frequency of occurrence	Ubiquities	Sunlight, air
	Commonalities	Water, soil
	Rarities	Coal, petroleum
	Unique	Cryolite (found in Greenland)
C. Resource aspects	Natural	Land, minerals
	Human	Knowledge, physical ability
	Culture	Skill, education
D. Existence	Tangible	Trees, land
	Intangible	Human skill, knowledge
E. Ownership	International	Ocean
	National	Resource entire of a country
	Individual	Physical ability, health
F. Organic Nature	Abiotic	Iron, Aluminium
	Biotic	Fish
G. Stage of Development	Actual resource	Coal
	Potential resource	Biogas

D. In general resources are classified into two groups. On the basis of ***existence*** (a) material resources, (b) Non-material resources. Material resources are tangible substances, i.e., coal petroleum, iron ore, copper, water etc. Non-tangible resources are intangible substances, i.e., health condition, culture, ethics, freedom, environmental harmony etc. Material resources are freely bestowed by nature. Non-material resources are cultivated by human beings with the help of increasing knowledge. Material resources may again be sub-divided into two groups:

(i) **Organic resources** like forest, fish, livestock etc.
(ii) **Inorganic resources** like iron-ore, manganese, mica etc.

E. On the basis of ***ownership,*** resources may be divided into three groups:

(i) ***International or world resources*:** This is owned by global population, i.e., the total resources owned by all individuals and nations. The sum total of all material and non-materials resources comes under this category.
(ii) ***National resources*:** this is the sum total of resources of the inhabitance of the nation and resources of the nation itself.

***Individual resources*:** Both tangible, i.e., property, money, wealth and intangible resources, i.e., knowledge, wisdom, health etc. owned by any individual is known as individual resource.

F. On the basis of **organic nature**, resources may be divided into two groups:

(i) **Abiotic resources** comprise of non-living things (e.g., land, water, air and minerals such as gold, iron, copper, silver).
(ii) **Biotic resources** are obtained from the biosphere. Forests and their products, animals, birds and their products, fish and other marine organisms are important examples. Minerals such as coal and petroleum are sometimes included in this category because they were formed from fossilized organic matter, though over long periods of time.

G. On the basis of **stages of development**, resources are classified into two groups:

(i) **Actual resources** are those that have been surveyed, their quantity and quality determined, and are being used in present times. For example, petroleum and natural gas is actively being obtained from the Mumbai High Fields. The development of an actual resource, such as wood processing depends upon the technology available and the cost involved. That part of the actual resource that can be developed profitably with available technology is called a **reserve resource**, while that part that cannot be developed profitably because of lack of technology is called a **stock resource**.

(ii) **Potential Resources** are known to exist and may be used in the future. For example, petroleum may exist in many parts of India and Kuwait that have sedimentary rocks, but until the time it is actually drilled out and put into use, it remains a potential resource.

2.2 Approaches to Resource Utilization

2.2.1 Environmental Approach

The growing recognition that environmental considerations must be incorporated into resource utilization strategies is starting to have some influence on policy making and to take place. Environmental cost benefit analysis is applied to welfare economics. The basic methodology is first to identify and measure the environmental effects and secondly to translate them into monetary terms for inclusion in the formal project analysis. For example, if the afforestation programme is to be undertaken for a particular area, first the costs are to be calculated which will include the cost of planting trees, the land rent, the possible loss of revenue from that by any other use, the cost of personnel and the cost of infrastructure. After that, the benefits are to be calculated which would include the direct benefits like the forest products and indirect benefits like control of soil erosion, improvement in the quality of air, control of flood, probable increase in natural rainfall etc.

However, extending cost benefit analysis to incorporate the environmental impacts of projects encounters a number of problems:

(i) Physical estimation of environmental effects is often difficult.

(ii) As most environment resources are non-marketed common property goods, economic valuation of the services is not straightforward.

(iii) Little consensus exists regarding methods for monetary valuation of intangible environmental goods such as, the need to preserve unknown species for their intrinsic value.

2.2.2 Economic Approach to Resource Utilization

Economic approach is also another important aspect for resource utilization. In respect of limited amount and uneven distribution of resources it is responsible factors to proper utilization of resources. Resource accounting involves adjoining national income to register both the direct cost inflicted by environmental degradation and the depreciation of natural capital to allow for losses future production potential. By including the loss of future income through declining resources stocks and deteriorating environmental quality of the national accounts record; a clear picture is obtained for the national level of economy which would immediately necessitate the appropriate measure to check the discount rates. The appeal of such an approach is that it would rely on traditional economic tools and concepts, such as, marginal opportunity cost, to measure the total environmental cost of resource degradation and depletion. Designing macro-economic policies and incentives for natural resource management may in the long run provide the best potential for initiating policies based on the concept of sustainable economic development. At present, however, this approach has yet to be developed sufficiently for implementation as concise policy guidelines for Third World countries.

There are number of limitations of this approach in site of its appeal to economic policy markets:

(i) Measuring the stock of economic capital and its rate of depreciation in Third World countries is in itself a complicated task.

(ii) Some natural resources such as forest timber fish stocks are more readily counted as directed units whereas others such as soils and watersheds are not measurable 'stocks'.

(iii) Resource accounting only covers part of economic costs of environmental degradation.

2.3 Causes of Resource Depletion

1. Increasing population pressure: The size of population of the world increased from 1.6 billion in 1900 to 5.9 billion in 1998 and over the next 25 years it is expected to reach a size of 8.5 billion. This rapid increase in population creates pressure on the natural resources and demand for food increases. Most of these increases of population take place in the poorer countries. These increases have strained the abilities of economies in the developing countries to provide employment, to increase agricultural production and to make necessary investment for development. Although there is a downturn in the overall growth rate of population in the world, in some parts of the world it has been increasing at a significantly high rate.

2. Effect of consumerism: Consumption, especially of natural resources, is the focus of attention in the present world. With rise of standard of living in the industrialized countries and also in many urban and semi-urban areas of some developing countries, the demand for the consumer products records a steep increase during last 50 years. 'Basic needs' of these people have been gone up. People living in industrialized countries consume a large share of world's natural resources. Such consumption not only deprives us of resources needed for future development but also contributes to the world's environmental degradation. Fast decline of some fund resources may be inevitable.

3. Optimum approach to resource utilization: For a long time, natural resources have been viewed as the 'commodities' to be exploited for the fullest possible satisfaction within the shortest possible time. This approach has not only caused the rapid exhaustion of fund resources in some areas (like petroleum in south-eastern USA) but has also threatened the existence of self-renewable flow resources (like forest resource of some parts of Brazil).

4. Dependent on conventional fund resources: Consumption of natural resources are highly dominated by the fund resources. Steel, which is the back-bone of modern industrial civilization, is manufactured by using two fund resources, iron ores and coal. The three fund energy resources, namely, coal, petroleum and natural gas, account for 85 per cent of the total use of commercial energy in the world. Most of the important raw materials for industries are also fund resources. Increase in the consumption of all these resources leads to faster depletion.

5. **Rapid urbanization:** Rapid urbanization resulting from the growth of non-agricultural economy has enhanced the process of resources of resource depletion. Urbanization has caused high level of resource consumption, and it is also responsible for the degradation of natural environment. Dumping of urban waste affects not only the urban environment but also the adjoining rural areas in the form of contamination of soils in the agricultural lands and contamination of water.

6. **Environmental degradation:** Effect of expansion of human influence may take many forms. One such effect is the depletion of resource caused by the degradation of natural environment. The threat of global warming looms large on the future of resource use. Water pollution causes extinction of marine species and land pollution causes the loss of agriculture. Very existence of biosphere may be threatened by environmental degradation.

2.3.1 Conservation and Management of Resources

Conservation means to "preserve", "to retain intact or unchanged". Resource conservation is conservation of natural resources, plants, animals, nature, landscape resources and even the whole environment. The modern conservation movement was initiated by a concern about forest depletion and soil erosion in the USA in the 19th century. Among the types of conservation the first is the conservation of ecological and scientific values. Wildlife or nature conservation is basic to the maintenance of the scientific and ecological value of organic resources. Problems of wildlife conservation include the identification and management of endangered species. Closely related to wildlife conservation is that of wilderness preservation. The second is the conservation of biological values whose central theme is the concept of sustained yield. Sustained yield implies the maintenance of optimal production under a given level of use. Sustained yield in forestry, fishing and agriculture alike require that the rate of cropping does not exceed that of resource renewal. The third is the conservation of aesthetics values. Modern intensification of land use and expansion of outdoor recreation has stimulated increasing concern for the aesthetic value of organic resources. The problem basic to the conservation of aesthetic values is that of the perception of beauty. Conservation of aesthetic qualities tends to conflict which that of biological/economic values. The fourth is the conservation of environment quality. Modern conservation has become synonymous with the maintenance of environmental quality of which pollution control is the most crucial point. The main problems of pollution control are the establishment and maintenance of environmental standards.

Finally, it is to be noted that the conservation of resources and of environmental quality are very closely interdependent. With respect to the whole problem of curbing resource depletion and pollution, human do not lack the technical know-how. The main difficulty is that they have not yet learnt to cope with the national and international economic, political and social implications of ecosystem conservation.

2.4 Concept of Resource Adequacy and Scarcity: Limits to Growth

'The Limits to Growth' is a 1972 book about the computer simulation of exponential economic and population growth with finite resource supplies. Funded by the Volkswagen Foundation and commissioned by the Club of Rome it was first presented at the St. Gallen Symposium. Its authors were Donella H. Meadows, Dennis L. Meadows, Jorgen Randers, and William W. Behrens III. The book used the World 3 model to simulate; the consequence of interactions between the Earth's and human systems.

Five variables were examined in the original model. These variables are: world population, industrialization, pollution, food production, and resource depletion. The authors intended to explore the possibility of a sustainable feedback pattern that would be achieved by altering growth trends among the five variables under three scenarios. They noted that their projections for the values of the variables in each scenario were predictions "only in the most limited sense of the word", and were only indications of the system's behavioral tendencies. Two of the scenarios saw "overshoot and collapse" of the global system by the mid to latter part of the 21st century, while a third scenario resulted in a "stabilized world."

Purpose: The purpose of 'The Limits to Growth' was not to make specific predictions, but to explore how exponential growth interacts with finite resources. Because the size of resources is not known, only the general behaviour can be explored. The authors' state in a sub-section titled The Purpose of the World Model:

In this first simple world model, we are interested only in the broad behaviour models of the population-capital system. By behaviour models we mean the tendencies of the variables in the system (population or pollution, for example) to change as time progresses. A variable may increase, decrease, remain constant, oscillate, or combine several of these characteristic models. For example, a population growing in a limited environment can approach the ultimate carrying capacity of that environment in several possible ways. It can adjust smoothly to equilibrium below the environmental limit by means of a gradual decrease in growth rate, as shown below. It can overshoot the limit and then die back again in either a smooth or an oscillatory way, also as shown in Fig. 2.2. Or it can overshoot the limit and in the process decrease the ultimate carrying capacity by consuming some necessary non-renewable resource, as shown in Fig. 2.2. This behaviour has been noted in many natural systems. For instance, deer or goats, when natural enemies are absent, often overgraze their range and cause erosion or destruction of the vegetation.

A major purpose in constructing the world model has been to determine which, if any, of these behaviour models will be most characteristic of the world system as it reaches the limits to growth. This process of determining behaviour models is "prediction" only in the most limited sense of the word. These graphs are not exact predictions of the values of the variables at any particular year in the future. They are indications of the system's behavioral tendencies only.

The difference between the various degrees of "prediction" might be best illustrated by a simple example. If you throw a ball straight up into the air, you can predict with certainty what its general behaviour will be. It will rise with decreasing velocity, then reverse direction and fall down with increasing velocity until it hits the ground. You know that it will not continue rising forever, nor begin to orbit the earth, nor loop three times before landing. It is this sort of elemental understanding of behaviour models that we are seeking with the present world model. If one wanted to predict exactly how high a thrown ball would rise or exactly where and when it would hit the ground, it would be necessary to make a detailed calculation based on precise information about the ball, the altitude, the wind, and the force of the initial throw.

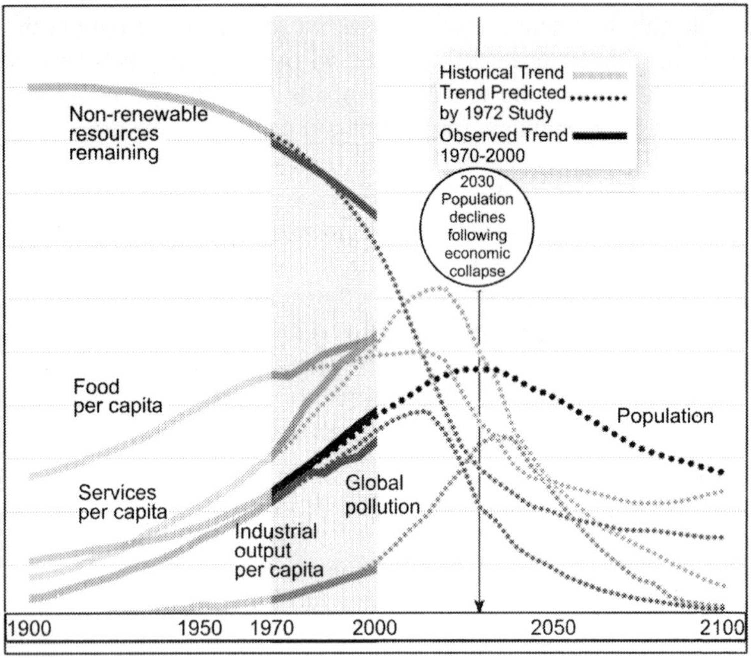

Fig. 2.2: Trend of variables (according to the limits to growth model)

2.5 Concept of Human Resource

Human resource is the most precious of all resources. Man plays the dual role of a producer or creator and a consumer or destroyer of resources. Man offers his/her labour primarily mental and secondarily physical when he/she creates a resource. He/she interacts with nature and builds up a cultural way of life. Culture lessons his/her physical labour he/she has a definite aim and purpose and thus he/she enjoys the benefits of advancing civilizations.

But the dual role played by the man in the overall scheme of resource development is not necessarily "*separated by time and space*". He/she gets joy out of creation, becomes rejected when he/she fails. In every stage of advancement in civilization man's role as a producer has been glorified. Man is essentially an element of nature but he/she is different from the other elements of nature because he/she has the capacity to think and act accordingly. Thus, he/she is not only the producer but also director, planner and aspirer. More he/she liberates himself/herself from strangle of physical labour, more he/she reaps the fruit of real wealth for the future. This seems to be predestined by his/her unique aptitudes. So, the role of man in the scheme of resource development should be evaluated from the view-point of mental faculty than physical labour wherein he/she is lagging behind. Maximization in production has primarily been achieved by man either by division of labour or through specialization.

Where increasing automation, man has freed himself more and more from physical labour and he/she specializes in production maximization and profit maximization. In order to withstand the higher degree of mental work, a man must be both physically fit and healthy. He/she should also be properly educated and trained. Thus, any scientific programme of resources development aims at the proper improvement of health and education.

Apart from his/her role as a producer or creator, man's role as a consumer is equally important in the scheme of resource development. It is indeed the human wants that boost the processes of production. Resources are developed only to satisfy certain degree of human wants.

Human wants can broadly be classified into: (a) Basic wants and (b) Cultural wants.

Basic wants include primarily the needs for food, clothing, shelter and thus are related with the material aspect of our life. But, human wants are never ending in nature. They do not cease to exist with the satisfaction of basic wants. Rather, it leads to greater magnitude of wants. We may thus conclude '*satisfaction of primary or basic needs simply results in the creation of greater human needs*.' So, not only want alone but also satisfaction that motivates man to act in the role of producer. Man's role as a consumer or destroyer of resource is no less important than that of the producer because satisfaction rests on himself. Actually, production and consumption of resource are integrated in an endless chain.

We must also consider the means of satisfying the wants. Means or ways must be in accordance with the ends which they usually serve. As the wants change, there must be change in the means of satisfying them. They must reflect the changes in social objectives which are also liable to change in accordance with the change in the political ideology. The aims of pre-revolutionary China were quite different from those of the Communist Period. Since the Communist Revolution, the Chinese resources are expanding very rapidly and are being utilized in much more productive ways. The entire process of resource creation in India underwent a radical change with the departure of the British colonial lords and with the establishment of a new welfare government in independent India. So, the satisfaction of individual desire and national desire constitute the end values to be achieved in the process.

We may conclude that man, in his dual role of producer and consumer, is the guiding factor in resource development. In emphasizing the dual role of man in the scheme of resource development E.M. Hoover remarked "*the study of human resource is vital from the point of view of economic welfare. It is particularly important because human beings are not only instruments of production but also ends in themselves*".

2.6 Idea on Sustainable Development

Introduction: Sustainable development is a noble and necessary aspiration. It is a visionary development paradigm. The term, sustainable development, was popularized in *Our Common Future*, a report published by the World Commission on Environment and Development (WCED) in 1987. Also known as the Brundtland report, *Our Common Future* included the "classic" definition of sustainable development: "development which meets the needs of the present without compromising the ability of future generations to meet their own needs". Acceptance of the report by the United Nations (UN) General Assembly gave the term political salience; and in 1992 leaders set out the principles of sustainable development at the UN Conference on Environment and Development (UNCED) in Rio de

Janeiro, Brazil, also referred to as the Rio Summit and the Earth Summit.

The definition of sustainability shows that sustainable development is a complex and multidimensional issue, which combines efficiency, equity, and intergenerational equity based on economic, social, and environmental aspects.

- **Main Dimensions of Sustainable Development:** As a general concept, sustainable development encompasses three fundamental approaches: economic, environmental, and social developments, which are interrelated and complementary. Traditionally, the concept of sustainable development involves three equivalent components: environmental, economic, and social development; as well as three dimensions of well-being, i.e., economic, ecological, and social, and their complex interrelations. In other words, sustainable development is a certain compromise among environmental, economic, and social goals of community, allowing for well-being for the present and future generations. Ghosh (2008) presents the concept of sustainable development as a geometric shape, i.e., a triangle encompassing three main areas: economic, social, and environmental. Of course, sustainability can be defined in relation to only one dimension (economic, environmental or social), therefore involving the sustainability of some economic systems, natural processes or social phenomena. It focuses on an impact analysis and does not identify a long run analysis. Also, as Pierantoni (2004) argues, in this case, sustainability might have different meanings and because of that it might include short-run or long-run strategies, as well as require indicators used for short-run effects, and other related to long-run effects. For the purpose of further analysis, it is useful to compare three interpretations of sustainable development (economic, ecologic, and social) found in contemporary literature. At the same time, it is necessary to understand, that the conformity and usage of which to perceive sustainable development is not an easy task, as the three proposed elements of sustainable development have to be equally assessed.

(1) **The economic** sustainability seeks to maximize the flow of income and consumption that could be generated while at least maintaining the stock of assets (or capital), which yield beneficial outputs. The main goal of implementation of sustainability principles

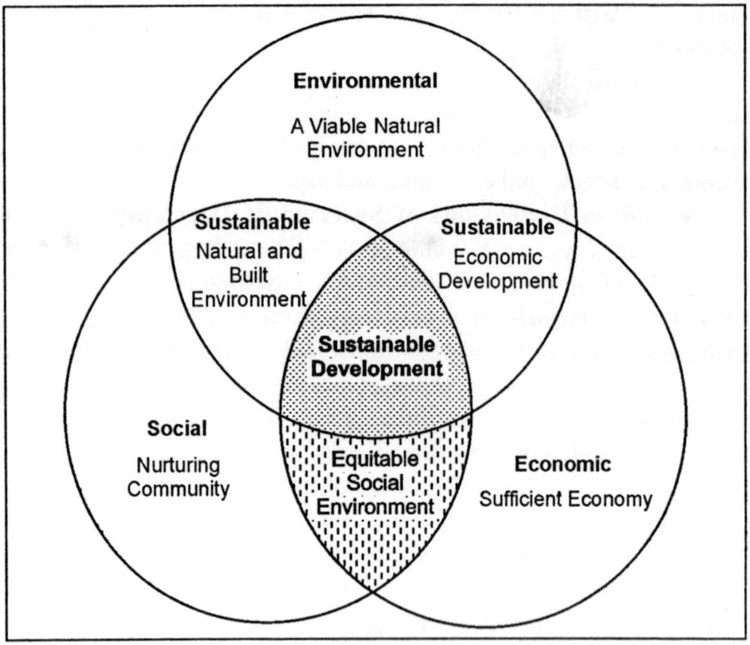

Fig. 2.3: General concept of Sustainable Development

is safeguarding of an optimal amount of general capital (or sum of different kinds of capital) for the future generations. Already in 1974, Solow analyzed the problem of an optimal distribution of capital accumulation among generations.

(2) **The ecological** approach to sustainable development pays most attention to stability of biological and physical systems. According to this approach, the primary task of economic development is to determine the natural systems limits for various economic activities. In this case, the vitality of sub-systems becomes essential in the critical view of global stability of the total ecosystem. Thus, the significance of preserving biological variety is emphasized here in order to secure balanced nature, elasticity of ecosystems at a global level and their ability to adapt to changes in biosphere, as well as ability to secure future possibilities. Referring to biological variety, it is worth noticing that it cannot be replaced by anything else. This fact gives us a strong argument against discount application in determining the value of biological variety. It is also important to

consider the significance of thermodynamic laws for the economic sustainability.

(3) Sustainability forces limitations upon the society's ability to exchange with the surrounding natural systems and upon the society's structure as well. People-oriented the social-cultural sustainability concept reflects the interface between development and dominating social norms and strives to maintain the stability of social systems. Social sustainability seeks to reduce vulnerability and maintain the health (i.e. resilience, vigor, and organization) of social and cultural systems, and their ability to withstand shocks. Socio-cultural sustainability requires at least the preservation of certain critical components of social capital, the latter being understood as the ability of the society to solve social, economic, and environmental problems, and to be active in forming the development of the whole system. Responsibility for the planet requires global solidarity and consolidation, based on systematic approach to the reality, holistic thinking, seeing the biosphere and humanity as one system, and global cultural basis. Sustainable development actually represents this shared responsibility. At the same time, the concept of sustainable development is a way to solve two different and sometimes conflicting groups of aims: "development-progress-growth" and "stability-safety-environment" (The Baltic Agenda 21, 1998). The corporate social responsibility for social-cultural sustainability is partly important too.

(4) Helm (1998) stated that the implementation of any policy depends on the institutional aspect – the importance and significance of institutions in the policy, and the competence of these institutions. For this reason, the implementation of the policy of sustainable development requires the evaluation of the organization (institutional) sustainability dimension, since effective, properly functioning institutions are essential for sustainable development in the realization of the social, economic, and environmental aims set by the society. The National Strategy of Sustainable Development (2003) also states that the assurance of the purposeful development, rational combination of departmental, regional, institutional, and group interests, and limitation of those interests for the sake of the general interests of the society are possible only in the presence of strong management on the state, regional, and municipal levels as well as clear inter-institutional division of functions. Estimation of

Sustainable Development requires the Germination on Institutional Level too. Institutional structuring of ecologically sustainable programs implies making normatively-oriented decisions on various levels of social institutions and organizations concerning alternative scenarios of development by combining various functional decisions that take into account the environmental requirements. The ignorance of institutional dimension and institutional capital is one of the biggest shortages of management of implementation of society sustainable development. Mauerhofer (2008) proposes a 3-D sustainability model for the evaluation of activity; the institutional aspect was introduced into the model as well as for a better reflection of the idea of sustainability.

We tend to think that the analysis of sustainable development should be based on the assumption developed by Jiliberto (2003), indicating that sustainable development is based not on the economic, social, ecological, or institutional dimension, but rather on their system as an integrated one. That system is not algebraic sum of the four (or more) systems but an entity or system to be identified as the starting point and converted into the object of analysis. One should take into account the fact that the need to identify relationships and indices is strong only when the multidimensional structure of sustainable development is applied, i.e., sustainable development of economies is analyzed together with environmental conditions that do not entail exhaustion of future generations' natural resources. In case on a one-dimensional interpretation, sustainability only involves specific problems in a certain dimension, and hence relationships with development in other fields may be very weak.

CHAPTER 3

Primary Economic Activities

3.1 Concept of Primary Activities

Primary activities are those related to the extraction of natural resources. They include age-old activities such as agriculture, hunting animals, gathering and collecting forest products, harvesting trees, extracting minerals and fuels from the Earth's crust, fishing in the rivers, lakes and oceans. All these activities yield raw materials for subsequent processing. Primary products may be named 'red-collar' workers due to the outdoor nature of their work.

Salient Features of Primary Activity

- It has been directly related with nature in terms of man and environment relation.
- It has been basically done for livelihood purpose.
- Physical abilities are more important than mental abilities.
- Generally family members supply labour force.
- Most labourers have been belonging to marginal category.
- Produced goods help to develop secondary activities, especially agro-based industries.
- These groups are collectively known as red-collar labour.
- Mostly underdeveloped and developing countries viz. most South-east Asian countries, African countries are involved with this activity.

MAJOR TYPES OF FARMING

3.2 Intensive Farming

- **System:** This type of farming is distinguished by the

relatively large amount of effort to produce maximum feasible yield from a given parcel of land. In other words, land is cultivated as intensively as possible to get the best possible return. Its results from scarcity of agricultural land where demand is high and supply is limited. It is found in the densely populated regions of the world. Relatively large numbers of people depend on small quantity of land resulting into small farm size and high yield rate. Intensive farming system attempts to optimize all the available inputs for farming. Even then, this farming system may not be cost efficient.

- **Major areas:** Intensive farming is most commonly found in the countries of South-east and East Asia. Some of the major countries are India, China, Bangladesh, Thailand and Indonesia. Farming is also highly of intensive type in Japan. Intensive type of farming is also found in Western Europe where the major countries are France, Germany, U.K and Netherlands. Although intensive farming is found in some developed countries like Japan in Asia and Western European countries, this farming is most common in the densely populated countries of developing economy.

Major Characteristics

- **Physical Environment:** Intensive farming practiced in tropical climatic regions; require high temperature and high humidity. The temperature should be fairly high at mean monthly of 25°C. Its farming areas need 200 cm annual rainfall for crops.
- **Small farm size:** High demand for agricultural land results into small farm size. Generally farm size may be inversely correlated with the productivity of land. Farm size tends to be smaller in the areas of high productivity because in that case even a very small size of agricultural land can support a family. In southern part of China average farm size is 0.3 hectare. In the lower Ganga plain region of India average farm size is 1.2 hectares.
- **High labour input:** Intensive farming is highly labour intensive in developing countries of the world. It is primarily due to the high degree of dependence on agriculture and relative scarcity of agricultural land. In the countries of monsoon Asia pressure of man on agricultural land is excessively high. But highly mechanized form of intensive farming is found in Japan and in the countries of Western Europe where agriculture is a much less significant occupation.

Plate 1: Labour intensive farming.

- **High yield rate:** Intensive farming is identified by its emphasis on maximum feasible yield from a given parcel of agricultural land. Average yield rates of wheat in France and Germany exceed 7,000 kgs per hectare.
- **Low per capita output:** In spite of high yield rates, per capita output of crops is low due to high man-land ratio. This may result into insignificant surplus or even deficiency.
- **Dependence on Environment:** Intensive farming in South and South-east Asia is primarily dependent on monsoon rainfall and fertility of alluvial soils. But high demand for agricultural land may result into the utilization of physically less favourable areas for agriculture.
- **Emphasis on food grain cultivation:** Rice is the most important type of crop in the intensive farming areas of Asia and wheat is most important in Western Europe. In South-east Asia, rice becomes the predominant crop due to very high internal demand. Other crops are generally cultivated in those areas where physical conditions are not suitable for rice cultivation.
- **Influence of Market:** In Asia, intensive farming is primarily consumption oriented. For example, about 5 per cent of the total production of rice is available for the international market. But in Western Europe intensive farming is more market oriented. For example, France is a major exporter of Wheat. Even then, it is much less market dependent than extensive commercial farming.
- **Cropping Pattern:** Since land is utilized as much as possible,

double cropping or multi-cropping is practiced wherever the opportunities are present. In lower Ganga Plain, two crops are common features in many areas (like *Aman* and *Boro*) and if conditions are suitable third crop (like *Aus*) is cultivated or some cash crops may be cultivated.

- **Significance of Animals:** Although cattle rearing by the farmers is a common phenomenon in South Asia, commercial use of animals is not much significant under this type of farming. Bullocks are frequently used for ploughing in South and South-east Asia.
- **Farming Technology:** Intensive farming in Asia is primarily based on the animate sources of energy which include muscle power of man and animal. Farming technology is generally traditional and labour intensive. But in recent years, modern technological inputs are gaining their ways into the agricultural systems. This is evident from the increasing uses of tractors, modern irrigation facilities, higher consumption of chemical fertilizers and greater uses of high yielding varieties of seeds.

3.3 Extensive Farming

- **System:** Extensive type of farming is identified by an abundance of agricultural land with a low labour input. Supply of labour is significantly greater than demand primarily due to low density of population and lesser significance of agriculture as an occupation. Yields per hectare may be low and land may be wasted, but farming is undertaken with minimum attention and in relation to returns. This farming system has a tendency to become mechanized and capital intensive.
- **Major Areas:** Extensive farming is more commonly found in the countries of low density of population and large areas of agricultural land. Countries with significant development of extensive farming are USA, Canada, Argentina, and Australia. In Canada and USA, extensive wheat farming involves high degree of mechanization and capital outlay is expended on vast quantities of land. This farming is also found in some parts of Asia which are sparsely populated and land is not much productive. North-western part of China and some part of West-Asia may be cited as examples.

Major Characteristics

- **Physical Environment:** Extensive farming practiced in temperate climatic regions requires medium temperature and medium humidity. The temperature should be fairly high at mean monthly of 20°C. Its farming areas need 50 cm annual rainfall for crops.
- **Large Farm Size:** Abundance of agricultural lands causes the farms to be large in size. On the drier parts of the Great Plains of USA an average farm size is more than 200 hectares. In other parts of USA an average farm size is 50 hectares. It is to be noted that large farm sizes are associated with two different sets of factors: (i) poor physical conditions like low soil fertility, arid climate etc., and (ii) higher standard of living (because increased wealth can be obtained from a large farm size).
- **Low Labour Input:** Extensive farming is practiced in the sparsely populated areas. As a result, agriculture is not labour intensive. Besides this, agriculture is not a dominant occupation in most of the areas which also causes low labour input. Relative scarcity of agricultural labour increases the labour wages.
- **Low Yield Rate:** This is caused by a less favourable physical condition as compared to the intensive farming areas and lack of efforts to optimize the factors of production. For example, in North America average yield rate of wheat is less than 2,500 kgs per hectare.

Plate 2: Mechanized farming

- **High Per Capita Output:** Although yield rate is generally low, low man-land ratio causes the high per capita capital output.

This may result into high amount of surplus production and for this reason; extensive farming has a tendency to be commercialized.

- **Environmental relationship:** Extensive farming is more commonly developed in those areas where physical conditions are not conducive to high productivity and as a result large farms are required to support the farmers. But in some areas yield rates have been increased through the technological input like irrigation and fertilizer. With the exception of these areas, influence of environment is manifested by low productivity.
- **Market Orientation:** Large farm size and low labour input may lead to the creation of significant amount of surplus production which makes the farming oriented towards the market. Low cost of labour and high return per unit of labour due to low labour input are the favourable conditions for the farming to be dependent on market. Influence of market on the selection of crops and the production patterns of these crops is quite significant.
- **Crop Selection:** Selection of crop is influenced by the environmental conditions and the demand pattern in the market. Wheat is a food grain cultivated under this farming. Winter wheat is cultivated in those areas where snowfall is either nil or insignificant during winter season. In other areas spring wheat is cultivated. Maize (known as corn in USA) is important both as food as well as fodder crop and normally cultivated in those areas where physical conditions are not much suitable for wheat cultivation. Normally in the drier areas food crops give way to fodder crops. Cotton is an important cash crop in USA grown under this type of farming.
- **Cropping Pattern:** Single cropping and monoculture are the dominant cropping patterns. These are primarily due to the low demand for crops.
- **Importance of Animals:** Animal farming becomes highly significant in the places of drier climate and great distance from the market areas. In the countries of southern hemisphere like Argentina and Australia, sheep rearing is an important occupation. In USA cultivation of fodder crops and rearing of animals go together in the drier western part which is known as extensive commercial mixed farming.
- **Farming Technology:** Large farm size and relative scarcity of labour tend to make this farming mechanized and in some cases

highly capital intensive. Modern technology helps to reduce the cost of labour which is much higher than intensive farming areas. Modern technology helps to reduce the cost of labour which is much higher than intensive farming areas. As a result of mechanization, farming is largely dependent on inanimate energy.

3.3 Subsistence Farming

- **System:** The word 'subsistence' means self-supporting or providing sustenance. In this farming, the producer lives directly on what he produces. So basically it is consumption oriented farming with little or no influence of market. Subsistence farming system becomes very important in those areas where population density is high; economic development is at a low level and a gainful employment opportunity in the non-agricultural sector is limited. Important regions of concentration are South-east Asia and tropical Africa.

Major Characteristics

- Subsistence farming mainly found in tropical climatic region in the world.
- Subsistence farm economy is more commonly associated with intensive type of farming.
- As the farming for the self-consumption, influence of market on production pattern is insignificant.
- Where growth of non-agricultural sector is poor and population growth is high, increasing pressure of man on agricultural land causes low per capita output and declining marginal returns from the land.
- Since the farming is not profit motivated and market dependent, there is not much effort to make the farming cost-efficient.
- Subsistence farming is dominated by small and marginal farmers and in many cases the farm sizes are below the limits of economic viability.
- Primary emphasis is given on the product of cereals like rice or wheat. Coarse grains are cultivated in those areas where conditions are not suitable for the cultivation of these two crops.
- Although technology is predominantly traditional, in some

areas modern technology is being introduced to increase the return from the agricultural land.

3.4 Commercial Farming

- **System:** Farming is identified as commercial when the crops are cultivated with the main objective of selling those crops in the market and earning profit. So, commercial farming is always market oriented and profit-motivated. Consumption of the products by the farmers, if at all takes places, is an increasing proportion of the total production. Demand patterns and price structure are the major determinants of production in this farming system. Farming is organized and an effort towards excessive production is deliberately avoided to maintain price stability because more supply as compared to demand may bring down the price.

Commercial farming is important in North America, Europe and Oceania. It is also significant in Argentina, Chile and portions of Brazil in South America. In recent years, commercial farming is gaining significance in the countries of East and south-east Asia.

Major Characteristics

- Temperate climatic areas are favourable for commercial farming.
- Population fed by commercial farming is normally non-farm population who lives in urban areas and engaged in non-agricultural activities.
- Commercial farming is more commonly extensive type and as a result most of the commercial farms are large and the trend is toward even larger farms.
- Minimization of the cost and maximization of the per capita output are the two most important objectives in this farming and to fulfil these objectives machinery, fertilizer and high yielding varieties of seeds are used extensively.
- Commercial farming is integrated with other allied activities and these include storage, processing, canning or packing, wholesaling and retailing of the products etc. all these activities generate employment and boost up the economy.

• Monoculture (using the farm land for only one crop) may be associated with commercial farming. This has the advantages of increasing efficiency and quality of produce (by means of specialist techniques, scientific innovation and labour specialization) while at the same time reducing the costs.

• Labour input in the commercial farming of the developed countries is low resulting into a low man-land ratio. This is primarily for the purpose of cost reduction and obtaining high per capita output.

3.5 Mixed Farming

• **System:** Mixed farming involves the cultivation of crops and rearing of animals in the same farming areas. Crops and animals occur in various combinations in different places, but the role of crops is particularly crucial in that they provide multiple roles as feed for animals, as cash crops and as food supplies for farm families. But the main source of revenue is livestock, especially beef cattle and hogs. Mixed farming is an important type of commercial agriculture in USA, Canada, Ireland, Ukraine, Russia, South Africa, Argentina, Australia, and New Zealand.

Major Characteristics

• Temperate as well as Mediterranean climate areas are suitable for mixed farming.

• A system of crop rotation is practiced in many places in which different crops are planted in successive years. Each type of crop adds different nutrients to the soil. The fields become more efficient and naturally replenish themselves with these nutrients.

• Crops are grown mainly to the internal demand of the farm. Fodder crops are more important than others. Different fodder crops are maize, oat and soyabean. Maize and soyabeans are also used as food crops. In USA, maize is known as corn and it is the most important crop under mixed farming. Corn is mainly used for fattening the beef cattle.

• Unlike commercial grain farming, mixed farming in North America and Western Europe primarily depends on the domestic market. High demand for livestock products (e.g. beef) in the big cities of these two continents is the motivating factor for the development mixed farming. But the mixed farming in Argentina, Australia and New Zealand is largely dependent on export.

- Modern method of farming are adopted to increase the productivity and to reduce the cost of production.
- Mixed farming in many places is developed in the sparsely populated areas. So, it is not a labour intensive farming. But skilled labourers are required for the livestock farming and these labourers are not always easily available.
- This farming generates the opportunities of employment both directly and indirectly. Indirect employment may include crop trading, meat processing and other allied activities.

3.6 Plantation Framing

- **System:** Plantation farming is a specialized type of commercial farming in which the crops are not indigenous to the locality. This farming is completely market-oriented and profit motivated. Organized plantation farming started in the tropical areas during the last part of 19th century under the influence of colonial economy. Tropical region provided the necessary physical environment for the cultivation of plantation crops and the labour was very cheap. Capital, technology and organization came from the temperate region. Initially the market was primarily located in the temperate region. But these situations have been changed to a great extent. At present plantation farming in many tropical countries is more dependent on the domestic market than the foreign capital has been replaced by domestic capital. Four most important plantation crops in the world are tea, coffee, rubber, and cocoa. Tea plantation is primarily concentrated in south and East Asia. India is the leading producer, followed by China. Outside Asia, Kenya is a major producer which now ranks 3rd in the world. Coffee plantation is very important in South America where Brazil is the leading producer followed by Columbia. Rubber plantation is primarily found in South-east Asia where major producers are Thailand, Indonesia and Malaysia. Cocoa plantation is most important in Africa where Cote d'Ivoire (formerly Ivory Coast) accounts for more than 40 per cent of the world's total production of Cocoa.

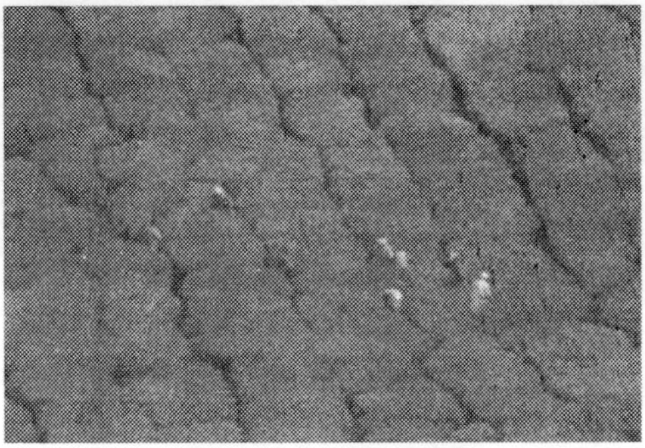

Plate 3: Tea cultivation

Major Characteristics

- Plantation farming is noticed in tropical climatic areas with high temperature, rainfall, and humidity required for planted crops like tea, coffee, rubber, and cocoa etc.
- Major plantation crops are not the food crops. So, this farming is totally dependent on market. Rise and fall in the demand pattern causes fluctuation in the crop production.
- Market areas are traditionally located not only outside the farming areas but outside the producing countries. Major market areas of plantation crops are located in North America and Europe. But, presently market areas within the producing areas are becoming significant; for example, India and China.
- Plantation farming in most of the countries of Asia and Africa originated as a part of colonial exploitative type of economy.
- Plantation farming is highly labour intensive and most of the works are done manually. This is caused by the availability of cheap labour in the major producing countries. Low cost of labour is the main reason for the continuation of the labour-intensive farming practices.
- Food grain farming is very important in these countries, as a result, plantation farms are traditionally located in those areas where soil are less fertile and general physical conditions are not very suitable for the cultivation of food grain.
- Chemical fertilizers are required in large quantities and modern irrigation techniques are widely used.

• Many of the population farms are the large estates. But in recent years contributions from the small growers have been increasing.

• Dualism is found in some regions where modern plantation farming continues side by side with traditional subsistence farming. This dual character of economic practice has also created a dualism in social condition.

3.7 Agricultural Regions—Concept, Delineation, Techniques

Agricultural regions are not the natural regions. They are defined in terms of agricultural elements, which are crop, livestock, farming

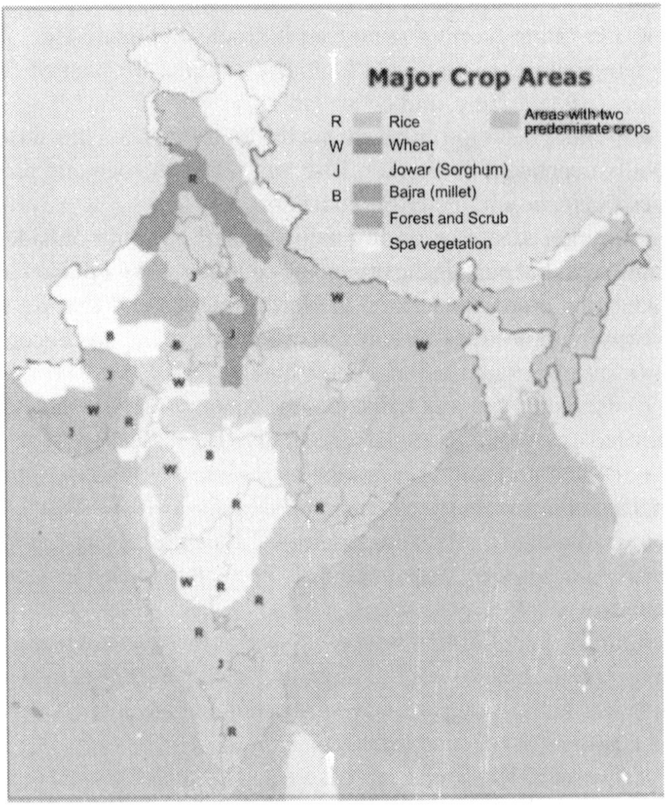

Fig. 3.1: Major crop areas in India

processes etc. The term agricultural region conveys that it is an uninterrupted area having some kind of homogeneity with specifically defined outer limits. Its homogeneity is determined by the use of certain selective agricultural features that are relevant to a regional interest.

A primary basis of agricultural regionalization may be the combination of crops and livestock which are raised. Further, the levels of agricultural productivity, extent of intensiveness in agriculture, degree of commercialization, degree of subsistence level, types of farming practices, diffusion of farm-technology may be considered as additional criteria for further subdivision within the basic regionalization.

An agricultural region involves two propositions—definition and delimitation. The definition takes into account structural attributes of agriculture, such as dominant crops, crop structure, crop and livestock association, farm processes, agricultural types etc. The delimitation involves drawing of maps in quantitative terms. There are various techniques which have been used from time to time for the delimitation of agricultural regions. These may be grouped into five distinct techniques: (1) normative; (2) empirical; (3) single element; (4) statistical (multi-element, new statistical and complex multi-elements); and (5) complete multi-facet (quantitative and qualitative).

3.8 Crop Combination

Agricultural geographers have worked out various statistical techniques which are an improvement on the other techniques. The new statistical technique for agricultural regionalization is a combination of two approaches: (a) cluster analysis and (b) combination analysis.

J.C. Weaver (1954) has pointed out three different lines in which crop-combination analysis may have more significance. Firstly, they are essential to an adequate understanding of individual crop geography, secondly, crop-combination in itself is an integrated reality that demands definition and distributional analysis; thirdly, such regions are essential for the construction of the still more complex structure of valid agricultural regions.

Weaver proposed this technique to establish crop, livestock or enterprise combinations involving both the qualitative and quantitative aspect of crop production, livestock husbandry and functioning forms of agriculture. The technique involves comparing the actual propositions of the grossed cropped hectare area occupied by different crops with abstract theoretical distributions' model wherein the gross cropped area is equally distributed amongst the different crops. The purpose is to establish the combinations where actual and theoretical distributions closely resemble each other. This situation arises when the standard deviation is the lowest. The least squares techniques may be adopted for the derivation of crop combinations. Jasbir Singh (1976) applied it in Indian situation. The least square technique suggests that theoretical 4 crop combination in enumeration unit is ideal where eleven crops are considered.

The least squares techniques may be regarded as an important algorithm for establishing combination of homogenous crop farming or livestock raising only in those areas where they are practiced as independent agricultural activity.

3.9 Crop Diversification

Crop diversification is a normal feature of stable agriculture and progressive farm management. This has been made possible by modern irrigation and the liberal use of fertilizers, HYV seeds, pesticides and mechanical technologies. Besides, there are other factors which force the cultivators to take crop diversification. First, vagaries of weather compel the cultivators to sow a number of crops or practice a variety of enterprises for there are operational holdings so as to get some return under adverse condition of weather. Second, rural life and the orthodox farm practices force them to obtain most of their domestic requirement from their holdings. Third, the agricultural experts are laying emphasis more of crop diversification for agricultural sustainability, maintaining soil health and gainful employment at farm throughout the year.

The choice of cropping system is dependent primarily on physical variable and secondly on technical and economic considerations, when physico-socio-economic conditions stimulate the growth of variety of crop, farmers obviously led to diversity of the agricultural pattern.

Crop diversification is important from the point of view of the steep rise of farm inputs. Consequently, each crop is bound to occupy only a small proportion of the arable land.

Many agricultural geographers have attempted to measure the indices of crop diversification and map them, normally, it is assured that if the number of crops grown in a unit is large, say about ten, each occupies only 10 per cent of the cropped area. It means that the cropped area is distributed uniformly among all the ten crops. In such a case, crop diversification is of a very high degree. In contrast, if a particular crop occupies 100 per cent of the cropped area, then there is no diversification at all. Here, monoculture or crop specialization is the rule. It may be inferred that lower the value of index, higher is the degree of crop diversification and vice-versa. In most parts of India, the number of crops grown varies from two to twelve. Suppose, in a regional unit, "A" there are six crops occupying 30, 20, 18, 12, 8, and 6 per cent of the cropped area respectively, and in the regional unit "B", three crops cover 67, 20, and 10 per cent of the cropped area respectively. The degree of crop diversification in the former place (A) is higher than in the latter.

Bhatia (1965) has covered a formula for measuring the index of crop diversification as—

> Index of crop diversification = (percentage of sown area under x Crops) / (Number of x crops)

Where 'x' crops are those crops which occupy 10 per cent or more of the cultivated area in a regional unit.

J. Singh (1976) used the formula in a modified form as—

> Index of crop diversification = (percentage of total harvested area under n crops) / (Number of crops)

Where, 'n' crops are those which individually occupy 5 per cent or more of the total harvested area.

The indices of crop diversification thus derived are mapped and exhibit a very significant spatial pattern of crop diversification in India.

3.10 Agricultural Productivity and Efficiency

Productivity as defined in economics and agricultural geography means output per unit of input or per unit of area respectively, and the improvement in agricultural productivity is generally the result of a more efficient use of the factors of production, viz. environment, arable land, labour, capital and the like, productivity, which may be industrial or agricultural, is a difficult theme, both in concept and in terms of measurement of its level. It is essentially a measure of the efficiency with which the inputs are utilized in production. The regional differences in agricultural productivity are the result partly of natural advantages of abiotic environment (soil and climate) and partly of farming efficiency as controlled by cultural ecology. Farming efficiency refers to the properties and qualities of various inputs and the manner in which these are combined and put to use for production. Increase in agricultural productivity is largely related to the choice of inputs, and their relative quantities, and the skill with which these are used in the production processes.

Several techniques adopted for computing efficiency in level of agricultural productivity per unit area per unit of time, or per unit of farm workforce, etc. are detailed below:

- Assessing the value of agricultural production per unit area.
- Measuring production per unit of farm labour or man-hour.
- Determining output in relation to input, or output-input ratio and profitability of farming measured in terms of the return for the sum total of human efforts or paid-out-cost in relation to the output (Khusro 1964).
- Expressing production of agriculture in terms of grain equivalents per head of population (Buck *et al.*).
- Considering output per unit area or yields per hectare after grading them in ranking order, thereby deriving the *ranking coefficient* (Kendall *et al.*).
- Giving weightage to the ranking order of the output per unit area with the percentage share under each crop (Sapre *et al.*)
- Using the carrying capacity of land in terms of population (Stamp, 1958 and 1967).
- Determining an index of productivity (Enyedi *et al.*).

- Calculating the index number of agricultural efficiency by expressing the unit area carrying capacity (in terms of population) of the component enumeration unit as a percentage of the per unit area carrying capacity for the entire region (Jasbir Singh, 1972 and 1974).
- Computing the crop yield and concentration indices ranking coefficient (Jasbir Singh, 1976).
- Involving the area, production and price of each cultivated crop in each of the constituent areal units of the region, and then relating out-turn in terms of money of the unit to the corresponding productivity of the region (Hussain, 1976).
- Delimiting agricultural productivity by computing the intensity and spread indices of three variables, i.e. (i) yield, (ii) grain equivalents, and (iii) cropping system (Singh, V.R., 1979).
- Assessing net income (farm business income) in rupees per hectare of cropped area or per adult-male unit farm family workforce (Khusro *et al.*).
- Weighted composite level of agricultural performance (Singh J., *et al.*, 1990).
- Crop productivity efficiency levels (Singh J., 1997) or crop productivity perception index.

3.11 Green Revolution of India

Between 1947 and 1967, efforts by the Govt. of India at achieving food self-sufficiency were not entirely successful. In a perfect case of Malthusian economics, population was growing at a much faster rate than food production. This called for drastic action to increase yield and the action came in the form of green revolution which took place during 1967-1978. It is a term applied to successful agricultural experiments in many Third World countries. It was most successful in India.

There were three basic elements in the method of the green revolution:

(a) Continued expansion of farming areas,
(b) Poly cropping in the existing farmlands,
(c) Using seeds with improved genetics.

The area under cultivation was not enough to meet the rising demand for food. Though other methods were required, the expansion of cultivable land also had to continue. So, the green revolution continued with this quantitative expansion of arable lands.

Ploy cropping was a primary feature of the green revolution. Instead of one crop season per year, the decision was made to have two crop seasons per year. The first crop was based on natural monsoon and water for the second phase came from huge irrigation projects. Dams were built and simple irrigation techniques were adopted.

Using seeds with superior genetics was the scientific aspect of the green revolution. The Indian Council of Agricultural Research (ICAR) developed new strains of high yielding variety (HYV) seeds, mainly wheat, rice, millet and corn.

The green revolution was a technology package comprising HYV seeds of two staple cereals (rice and wheat), irrigation and improved moisture utilization, fertilizers and pesticides and associated management skills.

Benefits of Green Revolution: The green revolution resulted in a record grain output of 131 million tonnes in 1978-79. This established India as one of the world's biggest agricultural producers. Yield per unit of farmland improved by more than 30 per cent between 1947 and 1979. The crop area under high yielding varieties of wheat and rice grew considerably during the green revolution. The production of millet and corn has also registered an increase. The green revolution also created plenty of jobs not only for agricultural workers but also industrial workers by the creation of related facilities such as factories and hydroelectric power stations. This improved the quality of life of the people in villages. India paid back the loans it had taken from the World Bank. This improved India's creditworthiness in the eyes of the lending agencies. India transformed itself from a starving nation to a food exporting country. The green revolution was one factor that made Mrs. Indira Gandhi and her party INC a very powerful political activity in India.

Shortcomings of Green Revolution

The green revolution, however impressive, has not succeeded in making India totally and permanently self-sufficient in food. Ever today, India's agricultural output sometimes falls short of demand. In 1998 and year of 2005 India had to import onions. Last year India imported sugar. The country has also failed to extend the concept of HYV seeds to all crops or to all regions. In terms of crops, it remains confined to food grains only. In regional terms, only the states of Punjab and Haryana showed the best result. The eastern Ganga Plain in West Bengal also showed reasonably good results but in other parts of India the results were not so impressive. The green revolution has created some adverse impacts on the environment. The increasing use of agrochemical based pest and weed control in some crops has affected the surrounding environment as well as human health. Increase in the area under irrigation has led to rise in the salinity of the land. Although HYV seeds had their plus points; it has led to significant genetic erosion. By the 1970s, the new seeds, accompanied by chemical fertilizers and for the most part, irrigation, had replaced the traditional farming practices in the developing countries. The green revolution cannot therefore be considered to be successful in all aspects.

3.12 World Agricultural System: Von Thunen's Model and its Relevance

The very first attempt to device a scientific theory explaining the location of an economic activity can be credited to J.H. von Thunen (1783-1850) of Germany. Both a scholar and a farm operator, Von Thunen formulated his famous theory on the basis of 40 years experience in managing an agricultural estate near the city of Rostock in Mecklenburg on the Baltic coast of East Germany.

His theory tries to account for the types of agriculture that will prosper around an urban market. The theory rests upon several assumptions:

Plate 4: Von Thunen

- There is an isolated area considering of just one city and its agricultural hinterland. Such an area could be called "an isolated state".
- The city is the market for surplus products from the hinterland and receives products from no other area.
- The hinterland ships its surpluses to no other market except its city.
- The hinterland has a homogeneous physical environment favourable to the production of mid-latitude plants and animals.
- The hinterland is inhabited by the farmers desiring to maximize their profits and capable of adjusting their type of farming to the demands of the market.
- The hinterland is traversed by only one means of land transportation. In Von Thunen's day this was the horse and wagon.
- Transportation costs are directly proportional to distance and are borne entirely by the farmers who ship all food fresh.

Given the above premises, different types of agriculture would develop around the city in discrete rings. The greatest distance from the city at which any given type of farming could be conducted depended on selling price at the market, production cost on the farm, and transport cost between the two. Any profit a farmer realized depended on the relationship of these three variables, as expressed in the formula—

$$P = V - (E + T)$$

Where,

P = Profit;

V = the value of commodities sold;

E = Production expenses (labour, equipment and supplies);

T = Transportation cost. Two principal themes of his theory are—

(i) The number of profitable options decreases with distance from the city market,

(ii) There is a minimum distance within which a farmer would not choose to produce a given commodity because some other commodity yielded a greater profit.

From these two principles, Von Thunen postulated that six concentric zones of agriculture would develop around the market city on an isolated state A as shown in Fig. 3.2.

Zone-I: The land nearest the market would be used to produce perishable items like milk and vegetables. These activities would be concentrated in the inner zone because of the slowness of transportation and the absence of food-preserving techniques.

Zone-II: This zone would be specialized in producing wood, with firewood in much greater demand than lumber. According to Von Thunen, forestry yielded greater returns to the farmer near the city than did any other type of production except milk and vegetables.

Zone-III, IV, and V: These areas would tend to be devoted to grains and other crops. With distance from the city the intensity of cultivation would decrease. This is indicated in the proportion of fallow land zero in zone III; 14 per cent in zone IV and 33 per cent in zone V.

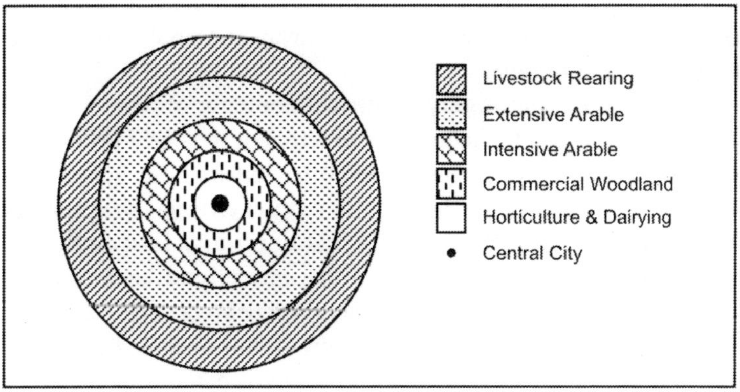

Fig. 3.2: Von Thunen Model (Land use pattern)

Zone-VI: This would be the region of livestock farming. Marketed products would be of two types: Livestock which could be driven to market, hence cutting transport costs almost to zero and cheese, which is not highly perishable and which is valuable enough to be able to stand higher transport costs.

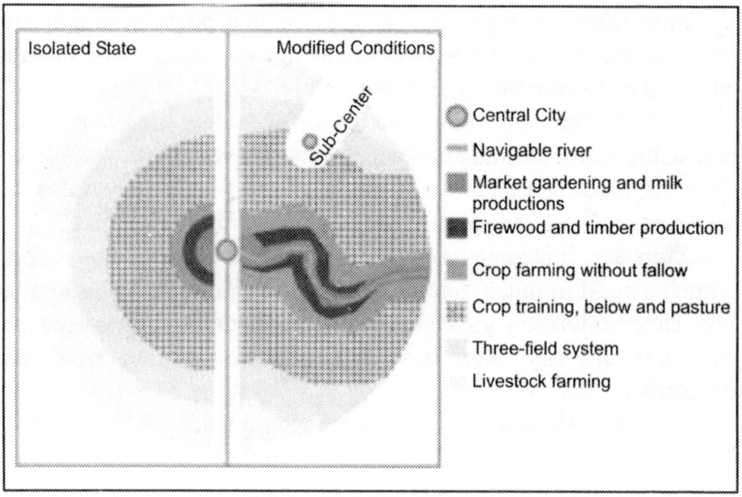

Fig. 3.3: Modified Theory of Von Thunen Model

Modified Theory: His theory would be modified by the presence of a navigable river and a smaller market city. Along the river land use pattern should be located in parallel way and small town created a micro business region.

Relevance: The highly empirical contents of Von Thunen's classical model can be understood in terms of the early years of his life and their influence on his location ideas about agricultural activities. His model drew heavily for econometric analysis upon his farm accounts and many of the assumptions. His model has demonstrated certain properties of the agricultural landscape and provided a framework for location theorist like Weber (1909), Hoover (1936 and 1948), Losch (1954), Dunn (1954) and Griffin (1973). Von Thunen's analysis is concerned with movement minimization in terms of cost, time and energy. Although the basic forces Von Thunen tried to explain in his theory are still operative, it is difficult to find examples today.

The ring model has been radically modified by changes in transportation characteristics, new technology's achievements (refrigeration) and the replacement of fire wood by certain substitutes (coal, gas, electricity etc.). Many of the needs of his time now seem obsolete. With improvement in transportation and reduction in transport cost, the radii of land use zones have become larger, but the concentric zones may still be recognized on a continental scale. At the small scale of farmstead and village, the ring effect still persists. Hence, the movement continues to be measured in terms of time and man-days rather than freight costs.

In the less developed and underdeveloped countries the conditions may still be similar to those of Von Thunen's isolated estate and there are several cases cited in geographical location where land use around a settlement is directly related to distance from the settlement. Moreover, the adoption of green revolution technology at all size classes, particularly in the intensively irrigated areas has disturbed the application of Von Thunen model in Indian context. His precondition was fully valid right up to the early decades of the 20th century. With changed conditions, the distance from the market is now only a cost factor. So, the classic Thunian agro-spatial model is no longer operative in its original format.

3.13 World Agricultural System—Agri-business

The issue of the global concentration of agri-business is crucial to the future of the food systems of developing (and poor, non-developing) countries. These countries have been a target of corporate investments from the outset of the industrial food system. This process has been uneven—at different times corporate investment has focused on one or another part of the food system. Today, this uneven and often uncoordinated foray of metropolitan corporate capital is still subjugating the agriculture and domestic food markets of many developing countries, particularly smaller, peripheral ones undergoing rapid urbanization, to the needs of global agri-business. For some of the larger developing countries, however, national capitalists are the principal force behind the emerging urban food system. In addition, the state has been playing a key role in the consolidation of the urban food system in certain emerging economies.

Foreign participation in the food industry was once typically concentrated in the more sophisticated food segments geared to the emerging urban middle class and to exports, primarily to wealthy countries. Because of lack of patent protection, there was little foreign private capital investment in the genetic inputs industry. Thus, the nascent private seed industry, especially maize, was restricted to the non-GMO (genetically modified organism) hybrid markets. Foreign direct investment was also largely absent until recently from the retail sector.

- ***Responses to Decreased Market Growth in Developed Countries***

A profound shift occurred in the 1980s and 1990s in the patterns and extent of the transnational corporate penetration of the Agrifood systems of developing countries. From the mid-1970s, per capita food consumption of basic staples in the developed world was reaching saturation, and overall growth suffered from the effects of the end of the baby boom. This led to a rapid process of concentration and development of oligopolies (where a few companies control a large portion of the market) as the key condition of continued growth. This slowdown in growth in food purchases in the developed countries was partially offset by a number of new initiatives. The introduction of an increasing number of unprocessed specific varieties (instead of selling undifferentiated commodities), led to a truly unbelievable proliferation of processed food products, and a segmentation of markets; a new wave of investment promoted "non-traditional exports"—particularly sea-foods, fruits, and vegetables, either off-season or exotic from developing countries to metropolitan markets. There was also renewed attention to the potential of the domestic markets of developing countries where higher demographic growth rates and rapid urbanization were creating ideal conditions for food corporations to offset the slowdown in growth in developed country markets. In earlier periods, Latin American countries were the main focus of investments directed to domestic markets within the periphery. Now, attention was being redirected to Asia where many developing countries were experiencing sustained high growth rates.

During the 1980s, biotechnology, heavily dependent on patents, was revolutionizing the genetic and agrichemical inputs sectors. Concerted lobbying by these and the pharmaceutical sectors led to the developing countries' acceptance of patents on food and as a precondition for joining the WTO. The seed, fertilizer, and chemical inputs sectors, particularly of those developing countries with an increasingly large-scale and export-oriented agriculture, as in the Southern cone countries of South America, were subject to new waves of market pressure from foreign-based transnational.

But the input sectors were not the only areas for investment. There was a rapid growth of transnational involvement in the retail food sector of the South, which had been mainly owned and organized on a domestic basis. Some European corporations had entered developing country markets as early as the 1970s. However, it was only in the 1990s that a more generalized foreign corporate penetration of the retail sector got under way, first in highly urbanized Latin America and then in key Asian countries. European retail led the way here but was then accompanied by the U.S. Wal-Mart colossus. Urbanization in developing countries also brought with it a shift in lifestyles and food habits favouring the rise of convenience foods, which, in turn, stimulated the expansion and large-scale entrance of foreign corporations into the fast-food sector.

- ***Concentration in Global Food Systems***

The changing global dynamics of demand and the acceptance of the "free market" liberal approach by developing countries led to an increasing presence of multinationals in all phases of agrifood systems. This now includes direct foreign investment in land and water resources, stimulated both by the moves to grow crops for agro-fuel feed stocks and by concerns with food security in an increasingly uncertain environment for world commodity trade. Significant concentration of control of food and agriculture had already occurred in most advanced capitalist countries. In the United States, concentration ratios for the top four or five firms have been calculated for the major upstream inputs (materials, resources, energy, fertilizers, etc.) and downstream outputs (farm products, processing, and sales markets). The main segments have ratios averaging well over the 40 per cent level—considered the threshold for a market oligopoly and often in the 70-80 per cent range. More recently, researchers have identified very high levels of concentration in the retail sectors of Europe and the United States. The major agricultural commodities that make up world trade are also subject to high levels of concentration grains and oils, coffee, cocoa, and bananas. In addition, a substantial proportion of trade is now organized and coordinated by lead firms. This is particularly the case for the so-called non-traditional exports (sea foods, fruits, vegetables, and flowers), very often under the direct control of large-scale retailers. In smaller market segments, there are even higher levels of concentration involving duopolies and even monopolies. And, although global food cartels have formed, often in oligopolistic markets, formal collusion is not necessary. Leading firms can adjust their respective behavior, creating an informal control over the market. The issue of market concentration, however, is not limited to individual markets. The major firms grow both horizontally (in all sectors) and vertically (integrating both downstream suppliers and upstream markets for a given industry)—leading to concentration and economic power that extends to broad sections of the agrifood system. It is this activity across market segments that transform market concentration into a greater position of strategic economic power. Vertical and/or horizontal integration is now being complemented by strategic alliances with firms in complementary areas. This development is particularly noticeable in the agricultural inputs and primary processing/trade sectors. Global corporate investment in the food industry was initially overwhelmingly within the leading industrialized blocs. While some firms established an international presence as early as the latter half of the nineteenth century, a more across-the-board incursion of foreign direct investment began in the 1980s. Leading agrifood transnational business is now increasingly geared to a global food commodity market.

- ***The New Position of Emerging Countries in the Global Agrifood Economy***

As mentioned earlier, two broad tendencies transformed North/South relations since the 1970s. In addition to being a source for traditional tropical exports, developing countries became increasingly important in the supply of the components of what has been called the "nutritional transition", the shift to a high animal protein diet (including sea foods) and the increasing consumption of fresh fruit and vegetables. This has provided opportunities for the expansion of domestic food companies in a few countries. Brazil and Argentina, together with Thailand, became major suppliers of animal feed and meat. Particularly in the white meats sector (poultry and pigs), this gave rise to domestic agri-business firms Sadia and Perdigão in Brazil, and the Charoen Pokphand Group in Thailand. More recently, there has been a similar surge of domestic firms in the red meat sector, with the Brazilian firm JBS/Friboi becoming the world's largest firm in that sector. The Charoen Pokphand Group similarly embarked on regional foreign direct investment.

Fresh fruit and vegetables have been piloted mainly by firms for which this previously unorganized market segment has become a key to establishing consumer loyalty. Early forays into the domestic markets of developing countries often had the character of enclave-type activities, with few or no linkages to their economies. Alternatively, they were aimed at a specific niche. Now, under the aegis of retail, the transnational objective has become corporate takeover of the domestic food systems of developing countries as a whole. In addition, this penetration now includes the large developing countries, often with strong states, with already consolidated agrifood companies, and with very distinct traditions and food habits. It also occurs in a context in which developing countries have become competitive suppliers in a number of markets, providing opportunities for the transformation of their leading domestic players into global actors.

- ***China: The New Focus for Agri-business***

The large size of China's imports, exports, and domestic urban food market has made it a focus of foreign investment, particularly of downstream activities such as processing and retail. In contrast to Brazil and many Latin American countries that readily adopted neoliberal reforms, China remained outside the WTO throughout the 1990s and was able to maintain greater control of trade and investment flows. The Chinese government has traditionally conditioned foreign direct investment on the establishment of joint ventures with local capital and agreements on technology transfer.

Although China's agriculture has responded remarkably to the new demands of an increasingly urban middle class of some 150-200 million, it is now heavily dependent on soya imports, a dependency that will likely extend to other key commodities as corn, dairy products, poultry, and red meat as land and water resources become scarcer, and as lower tariffs and a loosening of state control are put into place. China is a key exporter of seafood, fruits and vegetables, and processed food products. The main driver of its agrifood system, however, is the increased domestic market resulting from rapid urbanization in the context of sustained and high economic growth. In 2008, China became a net food importer for the first time. In only ten years, it has become not only the world's leading soya importer but also now accounts for more than 50 per cent of global imports, a percentage that is projected to increase steadily in the coming decade. China imports unprocessed grains, rather than the meal imported by European countries. Global traders have, therefore, sharply increased their investments in crushing facilities in China, taking advantage of the greater deregulation of this market following WTO membership.

A new crushing industry has emerged in China's coastal region, and some estimates put the global traders' share here at 70 per cent, led by ADM in partnership with COFCO, the largest state grain company, followed by Cargill and Bunge. Domestic soyabean production, largely situated in the North-eastern provinces, has stagnated at some 16 million tons, and the pulverized crushing industry (for soya oil production) that served this region is in crisis, although some domestic firms, like the Huanong Dalian group, are now restructuring and investing also in the coastal regions. In addition to supplying the expanding Chinese domestic market, it appears that China is becoming the principal base for soya meal exports to the rest of the Asian region and particularly to Japan, whose crushing industry is also investing there. The advance of the transnational is provoking reaction among the domestic soya sector and apparently also at the state level. Imported soya is cheaper than domestic production, creating greater margins for the international crushers and leading local firms also to source from imports at the expense of local production. Both a national and a regional soyaabean association were formed in 2007 and a call has been made for restricting foreign investment in grain storing and processing facilities.

The food price rises of 2007-2008 have sharpened criticism of the global traders, and there is evidence that China is now reviewing its policy on foreign direct investment. Chinese investments in vast agricultural projects in Asia, Africa, and Latin America, aimed at exports to is domestic market, point to the adoption of an alternative strategy for ensuring food security that may eventually challenge the hegemony of the global traders. Such a strategy, however, is not without its risks, and the hostile reactions to similar investments on the part of South Korea in Madagascar serve as an alert.

While the new dynamic of global trade has tended to reinforce Brazil's agricultural commodity export profile, China has established itself as an important exporter of "consumer oriented" and processed foods—even though, as in the case of soya, it tends to import raw materials. Global corporate investment complements this dynamic, as foreign firms are attracted both to China's domestic market and to its role as a regional exporter. Here, again, the promotion of foreign direct investment has led to the entry of a wide range of transnational and regional firms in food processing. To date, only about 5 per cent of China's supermarket products is imported, a situation that, however, may well change as global retail supply chains are put into place.

At the high-value-added end, as in the case of the chocolate industry, for which China is now the second largest market, investment by transnational has largely led to a takeover by such global players Dove, Cadbury, Hershey, Ferrero, and Barry Callebaut. In other sectors, however, the entry of foreign firms has been challenged by local and regional actors, after they copied the new competitive practices introduced by global corporations. Global players from Europe in dairy and drinks ceded ground to the leading regional players in the Chinese market Taiwan, Charoen Pokphand from Thailand, Sinar Mas from Indonesia, and Kerry from Malaysia. Domestic firms were also strengthened in this process.

Foreign investment by global corporations is well entrenched in the food service sector, which has grown at over 10 per cent annually for some fifteen years, and tends to rely on transnational food processors such as ADM for their ingredients. Yum Brands has some three thousand outlets (KFC, Pizza Hut, Pizza Hut Home Service, East Dawning Restaurants) in five hundred cities, and aims to be market leader "in every significant food service category in mainland China."

China's reputation as a processed food exporter, already tarnished by earlier scandals, has been severely damaged by the identification of melamine contamination, initially in animal feeds and later also in milk-based baby foods and soya ingredients. It is not clear what the long-term impact will be on China's food processing industry, but the Japanese food industry has seen this as an opportunity for increasing its influence, using its high food standards as a marketing advantage.

It is retail, however, that will define the dynamic of China's role in the global restructuring of the agrifood system. In the 1990s, it seemed that foreign efforts to dominate the sector had failed. However, the situation has changed dramatically in the current decade, as the combination of hypermarket and convenience stores promoted by the key global players Carrefour, Wal-Mart, Macro, Metro, and Tesco has put the leading domestic players on the defensive side. In addition, the consolidation of modern retail and the expansion of Wal-Mart may open the way for increased imports of consumer food products, a strategic goal of the U.S. food industry. At the same time, leading domestic retail chains are also internationalizing, as in the case of Lianhua, which expanded to Europe in 2003.

In the 1990s, China encouraged transnational corporate investment in partnership with domestic firms, and global players are now firmly in place in trading, food processing, and retail. The major global seed firms—Monsanto, Dupont, Syngenta, and Limagrain—are also involved in joint ventures with Chinese seed companies and research centres. While new regional actors have emerged, the historic global traders seem to have successfully repositioned themselves around the new Southern Cone-China axis. Their success, however, is beginning to provoke warning signals, particularly as China is completing its adjustment to the conditions of WTO membership. In 2008, China enacted legislation, removing fiscal incentives for foreign direct investment, a measure interpreted as part of a broader strategy to inhibit such investment and promote the international competitiveness of Chinese business. In 2008, investment by Japanese and European corporations fell 20 per cent and by the U.S. 10 per cent. These measures coincide with China's aggressive investment plans to establish agricultural supply bases in Asia, Africa, and Latin America to lessen dependence on the uncertainties of global trade.

CHAPTER 4

Secondary Economic Activities

4.1 Concept of Secondary Economic Activities

Secondary activities embrace all forms of manufacturing and processing of raw materials. Secondary production increases the value or usefulness of a previously existing item by transforming its form. Such activities include manufacturing and industrial efforts. The farmer for instance, applies seeds, fertilizers and modern technology in the form of harvesting and cultivating in the agricultural farm increased the yields of crops. Steel makers turn iron into metals in blast furnaces. Generation of power also falls under this category because it uses raw materials like coal, oil, uranium etc. to produce energy. This group is collectively known as 'blue collar' labour force.

Salient Features of Secondary Activity

- It has been indirectly related with nature in terms of man and environment relation.
- Production goods transform into more qualitative and usable goods. Food processing industries transform raw food into more suitable and tasty food.
- It has been basically done for economic as well as socio-cultural development of a region.
- Physical and simultaneously mental abilities are most important for such activities.
- Technologically efficient labour forces are required more in these economic activities.

- Mostly developed countries have been involved with secondary activities viz. countries of Europe, America and Australia.

4.2 Concept of Industrial Region

Industries are unevenly distributed in India because the factors affecting industrial location are not the same everywhere. Industries tend to concentrate in a few pockets because of certain favourable factors. The area or zones having concentration of industries are known as industrial region. Geographers and specialists in other allied fields have made several attempts to delineate industrial regions of India making use of different criteria. One of the first attempts was made by Trewartha and Brunet in 1944 using employment figures. R.L. Singh recognized ten regions based on empirical observation. They are (i) Hugli, (ii) Mumbai, (iii) Ahmedabad, (iv) The north-western extending from Ghaziabad to Amritsar, (v) Lucknow-Kanpur, (vi) Bangalore-Madras (vii) Quilon-Coimbatore, (viii) Madurai, (ix) Dalmiapuram, and (x) Digboi-Dibrugarh.

Dr. B.N. Sinha (1972) has classified industrial regions into following three categories:

(i) Major Industrial Region is identified on the basis of a minimum daily factory working force of 1.5 lakh.
(ii) Minor Industrial Region must have minimum of 25,000 working labour force.
(iii) Manufacturing District has a working labour force of less than 25,000.

A. Major Industrial Regions—India

Following are the major industrial regions of India:

1. Mumbai-Pune Industrial Region.
2. Hugli Industrial Region.
3. Bangalore-Tamil Nadu Industrial Region.
4. Gujarat Industrial Region.
5. Chotanagpur Industrial Region.

6. Vishakhapatnam-Guntur Industrial Region.
7. Gurgaon-Delhi-Meerut Industrial Region.
8. Kollam-Thiruvananthapuram Industrial Region.

B. Minor Industrial Region

1. Ambala-Amritsar in Haryana-Punjab
2. Saharanpur-Muzaffarnagar-Bijnaur in Uttar Pradesh.
3. Indore-Dewas-Ujjain in Madhya Pradesh.
4. Jaipur-Ajmer in Rajasthan.
5. Kolhapur-South Kannada in Maharashtra-Karnataka.
6. Northern Malabar in Kerala.
7. Middle Malabar in Kerala.

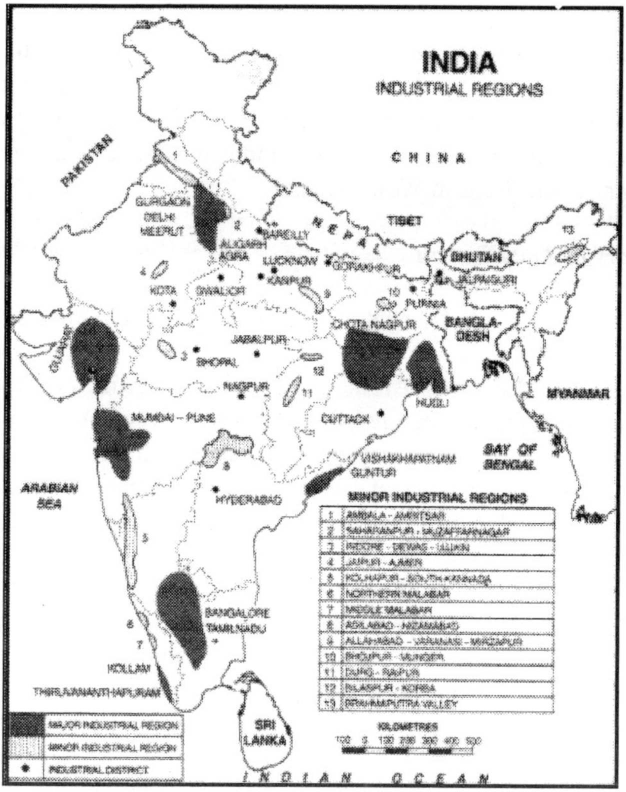

Fig. 4.1: Industrial Regions of India

8. Adilabad-Nizamabad in Andhra Pradesh.
9. Allahabad-Varanasi-Mirzapur in Uttar Pradesh.
10. Bhojpur-Munger in Bihar.
11. Durg-Raipur in Chhattisgarh.
12. Bilaspur-Korba in Chhattisgarh.
13. Brahmaputra valley in Assam.

C. Industrial Districts

1. Kanpur, 2. Hyderabad, 3. Agra, 4. Nagpur, 5. Gwalior, 6. Bhopal, 7. Lucknow, 8. Jalpaiguri, 9. Cuttack, 10. Gorakhpur, 11. Aligarh, 12. Kota, 13. Purnia, 14. Jabalpur, 15. Bareilly.

4.3 Factors of Industrial Location

Localization of industries mean concentration of most of the firms engaged in producing the same type of commodity in a particular region. For example, a large number of factories producing cotton textiles are concentrated in Mumbai and Ahmedabad. Similarly, jute industry is localized in West Bengal.

Factors of Localization

Localization of industries takes place due to the following factors:

1. Raw Materials: An industry tends to localise in the region where raw materials required for that industry are easily available. Nearness to raw materials reduces the cost of production because the costs of transporting raw materials to the factory are minimized. Sugar industry is localized in U.P and Bihar because sugarcane is easily available in these regions.

2. Market: Some industries tend to localise near the market. This helps to minimize the cost of transporting finished product from the factory to the market. Industries which export finished product and import raw materials prefer to be located near ports so as to reduce the cost of transportation. Industries were emerged near to market, when Material Index value is equal One (MI = 1), those industries are called 'foot lose industries'; like example, cotton textile industry.

In the other hand, if finishing goods are fragile and easily break during transit, those industries also localized near to market, such example, glass industries (Firozabad in Agra district of Uttar Pradesh).

3. Availability of labour: Labour is an important factor of production. Industries that require skilled labour get concentrated where such labour is easily available. Jute industry is localized in West Bengal due to availability of cheap labour from nearby regions. Due to rapid technological innovation, 'technology intensive' industries are more growing than 'labour intensive' industries.

4. Power: Industries require large quantity of power at reasonable rates. Shortage of power causes disturbance in industries. Therefore, factories like blast furnace which requires considerable amount of power prefers to be located in regions where uninterrupted power supply is available. Now a days, use of non-conventional or flow energy are also being used.

5. Transport facilities: The cost of transport plays an important role in the localization of industries. Generally, industries tend to localize in regions which have good transport facilities in the form of roadways and railways. The development of railways in India, connecting the port towns with hinterland determined the location of many industries around Kolkata, Mumbai, and Chennai etc. Communications facilities also influence localization of industries.

6. Availability of finance: Finance is the life blood of industry. Therefore, industries tend to localise in regions where financial institutions and their positive functionaries towards industrial development are available. Entrepreneur, banks, and also financial institutions pay pivotal role for industrial development. Recently, industries have been emerging with the help of PPP model (Public Private Participation).

7. Climate: In some industries, a particular type of climate is required. For example, cotton textile industry requires a moist climate, whereas watch manufacturing requires comparatively cool climate. Therefore, such industries are localized in regions having the required climate. Agro-based industries are also directly dependent on climatic conditions.

8. Taxation: Government allows tax concession to industries located in notified backward areas to remove regional imbalances in economic development. Some industrial units prefer to be localized in backward regions in order to avail of such concessions and rebates. Government subsidy also promotes industrial development.

4.4 Industrial Location: Theory of Least Cost Approach—Weber's Model

In order to explain the underlying influences on location as applied to all industries, Alfred Weber, a German economist put forward general theory of industrial location in his book "Theory of the Industrial Location" in 1909. It was translated into English in 1929 and has since become a standard reference on the subject. His overall objective was to determine the minimum cost location for a manufacturing plant. Weber tried to explain the location of industrial activity in terms of three economic factors viz. transport costs, labour costs and agglomeration economies. His explanation is based on the least-cost location for industrial production.

Plate 5: A. Weber

Assumptions and Principles

Weber made three explicit assumptions which were retained throughout his analysis:

- There is an uneven distribution of natural resources on the plain. Thus the raw materials, fuel and water needed

for industrial productions may be found only in given locations.
- The size and location of centre of consumption of the industrial products are given. The markets are thus points on the plain.
- There are several fixed location of labour where given wages rates operate labour is immobile and unlimited at these locations.

There are other assumptions which are implied in his work:

- The area has a uniform culture, race, climate and political and economic system.
- The entrepreneurs seek to minimize the total cost of production.
- Conditions of perfect competition are assumed, whereby resources and markets are unlimited at their given location and no firm may obtain a monopolistic advantage from its choice of location.
- Costs of land, building, equipment, interest and depreciation of fixed capital do not vary regionally.
- There is a uniform system of transport over a flat surface.

Several terms introduced by Weber need to be defined. Ubiquities are material available everywhere; example—water, sand, gravels etc. localized materials are available only at specific locations, i.e., coal, iron-ore, bauxites etc. Weber also made a distinction between pure materials and weight losing materials. Pure raw materials lose no weight in processing, i.e., cotton whereas weight losing materials lose weight in the finished product, i.e., iron and steel.

Weber maintains that there are three regional factors which affect the costs of production. These are the cost of raw materials and the cost of transporting raw materials and finished products, and the cost of labour, the cost of materials varies, for example, according to the nature of the deposits and the difficulty of mining them. He suggests that this variation should be reflected within the cost of transport of the materials. So, his general regional factors which affect the production are to transport costs and labour costs. He indentifies another local factor called agglomeration or de-glomeration economies. The first are the savings to the individuals' plants that result from their opening in the same location. This is possible through the common use of auxiliary industries, financial services and public utilities. In a single firm location, these processes and services have to be borne by the firm at greater cost. Agglomeration economies also include linkages between firms, where there are flows of goods between the plants, the development of a specialist labour force, and savings owing to the bulk purchasing of materials and large scale marketing of products. Weber suggests that many of these economies may be gained by the increased scale of production of one firm as well as by the clustering of several. De-glorneration economies involve the weakening of the agglomeration economies and specially, the increase in the cost of land owing to such a clustering of firms.

His analysis is divided into two major sections:

1. The identification of the point of the minimum transport costs.
2. A discussion of the circumstances under which production will be attracted away from this point owing to advantages gained from cheaper labour or agglomeration.

Transport costs: Following Weber, the cost of transportation will be considered under two simplified conditions: (A) One market and one source of material supply and (B) One market and two sources of material supply and involve Weber's classic location triangle.

(A) **One market and one source:** If the material is ubiquitous, the processing would take place at the market. If the material is pure, processing may occur at the market, the material site or any place in between. An intermediate location would entail an unnecessary additional handling cost. If the material is weight losing, the process will locate at the material sources to avoid transporting waste materials.

(B) **One market and two sources:** In the first example of the location triangle, S1 and S2 are the two material sources and M is the market location. Because distance and costs between these three points are identical, we may assign catch of the three distances a cost of, say $1.00. The processing will occur at the market; because two needed materials can be supplied three at a total unit cost of $2.00. If processing were to locate at S1, there would be cost of shipping one unit from S2 to S1 ($ 1.00), the cost of shipping that same unit, now processed, on to the market ($1.00), and the cost of shipping one unit of the material from S1, also now processed, to the market ($1.00). Thus, the total transport cost, if processing were to locate at S1 or S2 is $ 3.00 versus $2.00 per unit at the market.

The situation is different when we have two weight losing materials to be brought together in the processing centre. Let us assume that there is a 50 per cent weight loss for each of the two materials. Let the cost of transporting one unit of the weight losing material be $2. If a market location is selected, one would have to ship one of material from both S1 and S2 at total cost of $4.00. If S1 is selected for processing, the cost of obtaining the material from S2 would be $2.00. No transport cost would be changed to get the material from S1 and the cost to transport the product to market with the 50 per cent weight loss would be $2.00. The market S1 or S2 would have the same total transport cost.

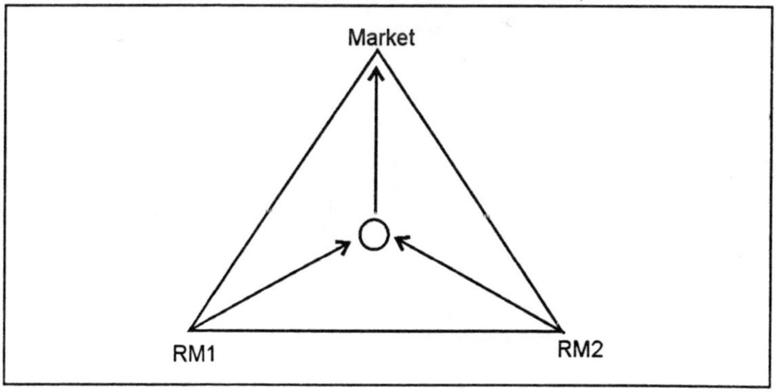

Fig. 4.2: Locational triangle (two raw materials and one market)

Weber was concerned with selecting the least-cost or optimum location. An intermediate location at P would be optimum, rather than M, S1 or S2, where the transport cost at P would be less than $ 4.00. Besides, if one material had a greater weight-loss ratio than the other, the intermediate location for processing would be pulled towards the site of the greatest weight loss.

Labour Cost: The geographic variation is the cost of labour was viewed by Weber as a distortion of the basic transport pattern. An area handicapped by high transport cost might be attractive to industry because of expensive labour. According to Weber, an industry would select the location that has the least combined cost when transport and labour are considered together.

To determine this location, Weber introduced two concepts—Isotim and Isodapane. Isotim is a line of equal transport cost for any material or product. In Fig. 4.3, the Isotim are given in $1.00 interval. The cost of shipping the finished products is shown by single line isotim. If one located processing at the material supply site (M), there would be a $4.00 transport charge to send the finished product to the market. The isotims for the material are shown by double lines. The cost of transporting the material to the market is only $2.00, with the market being the least cost location. The cost of moving the material is thus half that of shipping the finished product. So, the total transport

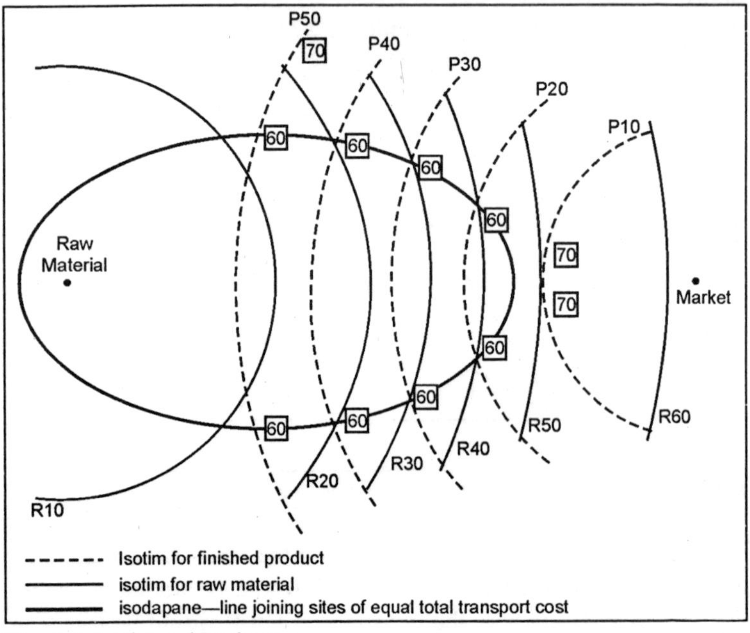

Fig. 4.3: Isotim and Isodapane

cost at location X would be $2.00 to ship the product to market plus $1.00 to obtain the material from the sources, i.e., $3.00.

The isodapane is a line of total transport cost. The isodapane is found by summing the isotims at a location. One the isodapanes are determined and one is able to identify the point of least total transport cost, then the variation in labour costs can be considered in combination with the isodapanes. The reason for using isodapanes is to introduce the labour component into Weber's location theory. In Fig. 4.4, the construction of isodapanes and the optimum location points are shown.

Agglomeration: Weber recognized that agglomeration may operate as a distinct location factor. He viewed agglomeration as the dollar savings per unit that would accrue to a plant from locating within a cluster of the other plants. Weber saw agglomeration not as producing internal-scale economies, but rather external economies including urbanization economies. Fig. 4.4 illustrates the cost of three manufacturing plants, A, B, C which have independently located at their least cost point. Around each plant is drawn a critical isodapane. If each of these three plants could locate together, the agglomeration advantages would be just matched along these lines by the higher

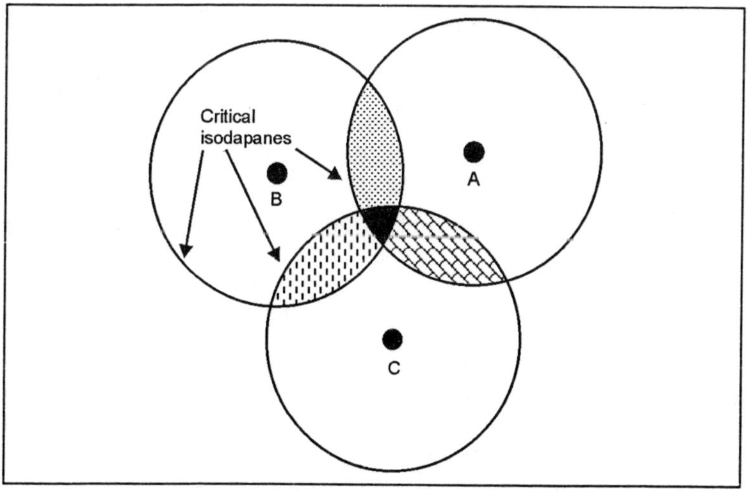

Fig. 4.4: Critical Isodapane and Urban agglomeration point (A, B, & C denote as three different urban centres, most dark point indicate point of agglomeration)

transport costs. Thus, all plants would benefit from agglomeration savings if they were to locate within the shaded triangle.

Criticism: Weber's purpose was to provide a general theory of industrial location and in this regard his contribution has proved most valuable. His work however, has a number of shortcomings that limit its application in explaining fully actual manufacturing location. His theory is a model hypothesis based on several premises which are possible only in the exceptional cases. So, the theory is an exception rather than rule. The difference between the capitalistic and socialistic economy, institutional factors and entrepreneurial decisions were not taken seriously by Weber. He did not effectively and realistically take into account geographic variation in market demand. He over-emphasized on the role of transport cost. The transport cost is not proportional to distance and weight. Moreover, the intermediate locations necessitate added terminal charges. The advantage of the "break of bulk" location was also ignored by him. Labour is normally mobile and is not always available in unlimited quantity at any location. Many manufacturing plants obtain a very large number of material inputs and produce a wide range of products for many diverse markets; Weber's theory does not apply to such circumstances. In his agglomeration concept, Weber failed to consider the space problem, energy crisis and problems of civic amenities. The assumption of perfect competition in the concept of Weber's theory is an ideal condition. In the long run, it is very difficult to sustain perfect competition in the region. Competition and price fluctuation in the economy is a natural phenomena. Weber failed to recognize that.

4.5 Theory of Profit Maximization (Market Area Analysis)—August Losch

August Losch, a German economist published his theory of profit maximization in "Economics of Location" in 1954. He noted that "in a free economy, the correct location of the individual enterprises lies where the net profit is greater". Net profit is the difference between scales receipts and minimum costs, and the entrepreneur solution is to find the location where these differences are the greatest. According to Losch, it is empirically impossible to examine all points in an area to determine cost and demand and hence "the place of greatest money profit: So, ignoring transport cost, labour cost and agglomeration cost, he emphasized more on the total production cost. To get maximum profit, Losch emphasized most on the price reduction of the commodity. Any decrease of price would stimulate the volume of consumption. This can be illustrated by Fig. 4.5. In this simple model, it is evident that when the price of the commodity drops from R to P the consumption increases from M to N.

Plate 6: A. Losch

Like Weber, Losch also considered certain assumptions for the implication of his theory. In the presence of certain optimum conditions, the maximum profit location may occur:

- The area should be an extensive homogeneous plain where raw materials are distributed evenly.
- The "transport cost" is uniform and directly proportional in all the directions.
- The people inhabiting the region have a general homogeneity either in taste, knowledge and technical skill.
- There is no economic discrimination among the people. The economic and career building opportunities are open to all individuals.
- The population distribution is very even and the area is self-sufficient in agricultural production.

To achieve homogeneity of economy within the region, the theory required some more conditions. These are as follows:

- The entire area should be equally served by the factories. No area should be exempted from the supply; therefore, no new firm would dare to venture in the area.
- There must be conformity in the range and quantum to profit. In case of abnormal profit, new firms may try to establish their own plant.

- The location must satisfy both producer and consumer. The profit of the firm and satisfaction of the consumer must be optimum through the location.
- There must be provisions for consumers to get the products from other adjacent areas.
- The number of consumers, producers and areas should be well defined and not very extensive. Only a limited number of producers within a small area will be able to overcome the complexities and satisfy completely the handful of consumers.

According to Losch, to get the desired result from the location and sustained growth of industry, these conditions are prerequisites.

Theory: The major objective of Losch's location theory is to attain equilibrium in the producing area and the product and the ability of the producer. If a single entrepreneur enters in the production process, within a vast area, the distribution cost will be very high. But when several small producers are engaged in the production process in separate regions, the distribution cost will come down and due to increasing competition, efficiency of the product and cost of production will be lower. The profit will increase substantially.

To establish his theoretical model of the theory, August Losch proposed three distinct phases of development. The phases are as follows:

(i) In the first phase Losch observed that if sufficient and symmetrical demand of a product prevails in the market, the market conditions may be explained by a demand cone. Fig. 4.5 illustrates that the effective demand of the particular product will be exactly same as the volume of the cone.
P is producer, and demand curve is lying on QF, P or price line controlled jointly by transport cost and distance. The price increases from P to F along the Y axis or PQ, demand of quantity is measured between PF and QF. When PF is taken as a measure of distance and is rotated about P, the circular market area is formed, bounded by the locus of points F, where the price becomes too high. Total scales are given by the volume of the cone produced by the rotation of PQF.

It is clear from Fig. 4.5 that, away from the centre, with increasing distance, demand of the quantity drops drastically.

(ii) In the second phase, within the vast rounded area, several factories will concentrate. The extensive market area will give a lucrative operational area, but despite the growing competition among the firms to capture larger market areas, there should be some void in the boundary zones and a certain amount of region will remain un-served or poorly served. The circular pattern of the industrial hinterland in phase-II will ultimately decide the future of the industry in that region.

(iii) In the third phase of industrial location, the intermediate space between two market areas will be narrowed. The areas fall vacant between the different market areas and become the target of new enterprises. As new firms set up within the vacuum, the hinterlands of earlier industries become reduced. The reduction of the market area results in rapid disruption of the early circular pattern. Gradually, the market areas of the industries attain a hexagonal shape. Thus, around the nucleus of a city, numerous hexagonal market areas of different commodity will grow.

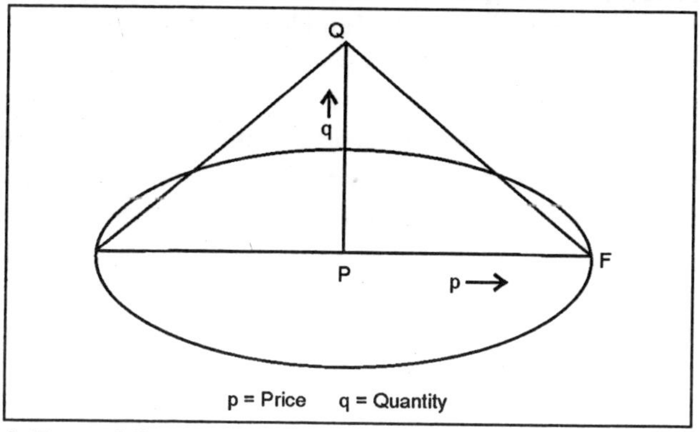

Fig. 4.5: Demand Cone

In this way, industries would concentrate within a region, each having different products. So, all types of minerals including raw materials should be available on that point. Hence, any new industry would get its raw material nearby. Obviously, the total transport cost in that place will be minimum cost. In this way, "equilibrium condition" as stated by Losch may be attained.

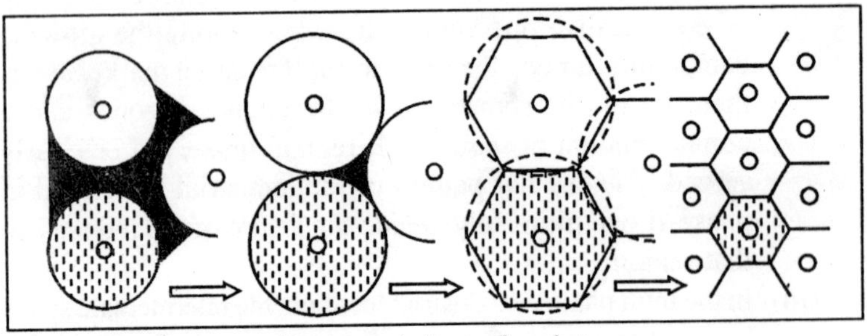

Fig. 4.6: Development of hexagonal shape of market area

Criticism: Losch was the first person to consider the influence of the magnitude of the demand on industrial location. He also emphasizes upon the rate of competition as an important determinant of location analysis. His theory has also a philosophical contribution on the motive of entrepreneur's role. His equilibrium concept is perhaps the greatest contribution among the location theories developed later on.

However, Losch's theory was not entirely flawless. His theory is essentially a simplified model of an ideal condition. In reality, only in a rare occasion, these events may occur. The assumed conditions of homogeneous plain region, equal distribution of raw materials and uniform transport rates never occur in reality. Therefore, according to some critics, this theory is nothing but an intellectual exercise. Losch even assumed the cultural homogeneity and test of people within the region and idea is quite absurd. He ignored the variation of technological development of different regions. The difference in technical know-how may offset the theoretical model. Political decisions also play an important role in the industrial location. Losch overlook this point. The variation of the cost of raw materials and labour wages rates were not given proper weightage in this theory. He categorically separated the role and effect of agriculture and industry. But this difference is somehow arbitrary in nature. The Abstract and Optimum situation demanded by the theory may be available in agriculture but not in the complex production process of modern manufacturing industries. Thus, Losch's theory is more practical in agriculture rather than in industry.

4.6 Industrial Policy in India

Industrial Policies of India Prior to Independence

It is a known fact that India was an agrarian country wherein handicrafts attained supremacy unmatched anywhere else in the world. India with abundance of natural wealth had attained excellence in handicrafts. There are very few lines of economic activity which became traditional in nature and could be included under the products produced under the factory system of 19th and 20th century. For instance silk manufacturing, utensil manufacturing, wood works, some products under pharmaceuticals etc. could be categorized as industrial activity. The evidence of India having indulged in productions of certain products like textiles can be traced from the fact that the manufactured handicrafts and textile products were traded outside the country also. During the colonial period, industrial policies and economic policies were shaped by the British Government in favour of British interests. The tariff policy pursued by British rulers in India was based on the principle of one way free trade while the Indian interest for industrialization in India remained deliberately neglected. England was principal supplier of manufactured goods and raw materials in the world. In return, England imported food stuffs and raw material for mainly its colonies. Interestingly, imports were tariff free whereas the exports were not duty free. This one sided free trade in raw material and semi and manufactured items was the established norm which very partially was industry oriented but the industrialization could not take place in India. It took place in England. It has been an established view that the British rulers in India pursued the industrial policies which were more destructive for Indian industrial base and more purposeful for England. Though the British Government established Department of Commerce and Industry in 1905 but the activities pursued through this department favoured industrial activity in England. This department was to execute the industrial policy and also act as an observer of industrial performance by the provincial governments. So the provincial governments in the country pursued the industrial activities through this department. Thereafter, the prevailing Government established Board of Scientific and Industrial Research in 1940 but not much could come out of it. India was keen to become independent and adopt industrialization as its policy. This is evident from the fact that prominent industrialists of India prepared Bombay Plan in 1944 emphasizing the importance of industrialization of the country. With the Bombay Plan, the leading Indian industrialists had sided with Jawaharlal Nehru and his preferences for planning, with emphasis on large scale industry for an extensive control over the private sector.

In 1945, the government had announced an industrial policy but this policy could never see the light. The industrial policy drafted in 1945 was referred as the Industrial Policy of 1946 also but since the said policy was drafted in haste so it could not satisfy the new leaders of independent country. Most probably this was the strong reason to frame well thought out industrial policy which could at least give a direction to the industrial sector in the country at the initial stage of free India. Therefore, Industrial Policy of 1948 was drafted on 6th April by the Government of India. All the scanty efforts made by the British Government to develop industry in the country took back seat and new revolution in industry was sought by the planners.

Industrial Policies of India after Independence up to 1990

Independent India had big challenges to face. One such challenge was to put the country on the path of economic growth for which industrialization was imperative. To industrialize the country and to achieve objectives of economic growth framing an industrial policy effective to meet the end was prime requirement. Therefore, Industrial Policy of 1948 came up to give direction to industrial movement in the county.

Industrial Policy of 1948

The Industrial Policy of 1948 broadly divided industries into four categories such as:

1. The first category enlisted (a) arms and ammunitions, (b) production and control of atomic energy, and (c) the ownership

and management of rail transport. These three were the exclusive monopoly of the Central government.

2. The second category included six basic industries and all new undertakings in these industries were reserved for the State except where, in the national interest, the State itself found it necessary to secure the co-operation of private enterprises. Such industries included: (a) Coal (the India Coalfields Committee's proposal will be generally followed), (b) Iron and Steel, (c) Aircraft manufacture, (d) Ship building, (e) Manufacture of telephone, telegraph and wireless apparatus (excluding radio sets), and (f) Mineral oils.

3. Eighteen industries under the third category were left to the private sector though their operation by the private sector was subject to Central regulation and control, which are stated below:

> (a) Salt, (b) Automobiles and tractors, (c) Prime movers, (d) Electric engineering, (e) Other heavy machinery, (f) Machine tools, (g) Heavy chemicals, fertilizers and pharmaceuticals and drugs, (h) Electro-chemical industries, (i) Non-ferrous metals, (j) Rubber manufactures, (k) Power and industrial alcohol, (l) Cotton and woolen textiles, (i) Cement, (j) Sugar, (k) Paper and Newsprint, (l) Minerals, (m) Air and Sea transport, and (n) Industries related to defense.

4. The rest of the industries were left open to the private enterprises, individual as well as co-operative. The State would intervene whenever the progress of any industry under private enterprise was found to be unsatisfactory.

In order to regulate the industry and to promote planned industrial development according to the Industrial Policy of 1948, the Industrial (Development and Regulation) Act in 1951 was passed. The principal objective of the Industries (Development and Regulation) Act, 1951 was to arm the Government with sufficient power. The important provisions of the Act were:

1. No new industrial units could be established or substantial extension to existing plants be made without a license from the Central Government, and while granting license for new

undertakings, Government could lay down conditions regarding location, minimum size, etc., if necessary;

2. Government could make investigation into certain specified industries or undertakings in industries—(a) which showed a fall in production, a deterioration in the quality of the product, a rise in the price of the product, or which showed tendencies in these directions; (b) which used resources of national importance; and (c) which were managed in a manner likely to do harm to the interests of the shareholders or consumers and issue proper directions for rectifying the drawbacks;
3. Government could takeover the management of industries which failed to carry out its instructions for improvement in management and policies;
4. The Act empowered the Government to prescribe prices, methods and the volume of production and channels of distribution;
5. The Act also empowered the Government to set up Development Councils for the individual or groups of industries; and
6. Industrial units employing less than 100 workers and having fixed assets of less than Rs. 10 lakhs were not required to obtain a license.

For the development of small scale industrial sector it was decided in the Industrial Policy of 1948 to develop this sector on co-operative lines as far as possible. Industrial Policy of 1948 also recognized the need for securing the participation of foreign capital and enterprises, particularly related to industrial technique and knowledge.

The main thrust of the 1948 Industrial Policy was to lay the foundation of a mixed economy where both the private and public enterprises were to be given importance and work together to develop economy to accelerate the pace of industrial development. The Industrial Policy of 1948, despite very effective and concrete, was not without criticism.

The first criticism was regarding the provision of the Act to retain control over private enterprises which was to be obviously held by the Government through the Industries (Development and Regulation)

Act, 1951. This has been levelled by a noted economist A.H. Hanson when he expressed that, at that time Government was more interested in the control of private enterprises than in the public-private balance. Elaborating this point The Industries (Development and Regulation) Act of 1951 empowered the government with the power to control the private sector. In the Industries (Development and Regulation) Act, 1951, it was clearly mentioned that no new industrial units could be established or substantial extension to the existing plants could be made without obtaining a license from the Central Government. The Act further stated that while granting license for new undertakings, Government could lay down conditions regarding location, size, etc., if necessary. The Act also empowered the government to prescribe prices, methods, volume of production and the channels of distribution. This clearly states that the control of the private sector was totally in the hands of government. The Industries (Development and Regulation) Act, 1951 developed a feeling of uncertainty in the minds of industrialists as it gave the government the power to investigate into any enterprise, if it had sufficient reason to believe that there had been usual decline in output or quality, or increase in price. In such a case, directions could be issued by the government to such enterprises following such investigation, and failure to follow these could result in takeover of management by the government. This was contrary to the belief that in independent India industry was to be allowed to flourish independently without stern checks. This presumption was belied by the Industries (Development and Regulation) Act of 1951.

Despite these criticisms, the Industrial Policy of 1948 determined the nature and pattern of industrial development in the country for full eight years.

Industrial Policy Resolution of 1956

The Industrial Policy Resolution of 1956 was meant to give a concrete shape to the mixed economy model and the ideology of Socialist pattern of society. The Industrial Policy Resolution of 1956 classified the entire industrial sector in three Schedules:—

Schedule A: In the first category, those industries were included whose future development was the exclusive responsibility of the

State. 17 industries were included in this category. The industries were: Arms and ammunition and allied items of defense equipment; Atomic energy; Iron and Steel; Heavy castings and forgoing of iron and steel; Heavy plant and machinery required for iron and steel production for mining, for machine tool manufacture and for such other basic industries as may be specified by the Central Government; Heavy electric plant including large hydraulic and steam turbines; Coal and lignite, gypsum, Sulphur, gold and diamond; Mining and processing of copper, lead, zinc, tin, molybdenum and wolfarm; Minerals specified in the schedule to the atomic energy (Control of Production and Use) Order 1953; Aircraft; Air transport; Railway transport; Ship-buildings; Telephones; Telephone cables; Telegraph and Wireless apparatus (excluding radio receiving sets); and Generation and distribution of electricity. Of these, four industries—arms and ammunition, atomic energy, railways and air transport were to be government monopolies. In the remaining thirteen industries, all new units were to be established by the State. However, existing units in the private sector were allowed to be subsisting and expand. The state was to render assistance to them whenever the need arises.

Schedule B: In this category those industries were included which were progressively State-owned and in which the private enterprises would be expected only to supplement the efforts of the State. In this category 12 industries were included. These were: All other minerals (except minor minerals); Aluminium and other non-ferrous metals not included in Schedule A; Machine tools; Ferro-alloys and steel tools; Basic and intermediate products required by chemicals industries such as manufacture of drugs; Antibiotics and other essential drugs; Fertilizers; Synthetic rubber; Carbonization of coal; Chemical pulp; Road transport; and Sea transport. In these industries, State would increasingly establish new units and increase its participation but would not deny the private sector opportunities to set up units or expanded existing units.

Schedule C: All industries not listed in Schedule 'A' or 'B' were included in the third category. These industries were left open to the private sector. Hence, the responsibility with regard to establishment, function and development was of private sector, though even here the state could start any industry in which it was interested. However, the main role of the state in this category was to give favourable atmosphere and facilities to private sector to develop it.

The lines of industrial activity given under all the three Schedules—A, B and C virtually became specified industrial activities for the entrepreneurs in the country, for a long time. Therefore, the Industrial Policy Resolution of 1956 became very powerful industrial Vedanta in the industrial history of the country.

To encourage small sector, in the policy resolution, various steps were proposed such as: (a) Direct subsidy was provided to small scale sector, (b) Suitable taxation relief was given to this sector, and (c) It was made objective of the State to protect small-scale sector by advancing technical assistance required for the production and improvement of competitiveness. The 1956 Industrial Policy Resolution allowed foreign capital participation in Indian economic development but the major share should belong to India. In case of already existing foreign establishments, these will be replaced by Indian technicians gradually.

Even though the policy rightly laid emphasis on building up of the basic and heavy industry in the public sector and encouragement of consumer goods production in the cottage, village and small-scale industries were visualized in the 1956 Industrial Policy Resolution as something to be patronized. But unfortunately, the Government failed to integrate these industries and their programmes with the production programmes of the large-scale sector. Moreover, the government also failed to establish suitable machinery for public sectors planning and execution.

The Industrial Policy Resolution of 1956 was based on the ideology of socialism and in order to achieve this, expansion of public sector was must. The Resolution of 1956 expanded the scope of the public sector by reserving the future development of 17 most important industries to the public sector in Schedule A. Besides these, 12 very important industries were listed in the Schedule B for the development which the public sector was to play a dominant role. But the critics pointed out that for several years even after the adoption of the Resolution, licenses were issued to private sector units in areas exclusively reserved for state ownership or where future expansion was intended to be in the public sector. These included coal, oil, fertilizers, chemicals, engineering etc.

One of the major objectives of Industrial Policy Resolution of 1956 was reduction in regional inequalities and imbalances. But contrary to this, the actual operation of this policy resulted in increased regional inequalities. This becomes evident from the report of Dutt Committee which noted that the four industrially advanced States of Maharashtra, Gujarat, West Bengal and Tamil Nadu benefited the most from the operation of this policy. In this context, the Dutt Committee report further mentioned that, in the decade 1955-65, these four industrially advanced States accounted for 59.3 per cent of the applications and 62.42 per cent of the licenses approved. On the other hand, the poor States of Bihar, Orissa, Uttar Pradesh and Madhya Pradesh received only 15.5 per cent of total licenses approved.

In spite of all above, the Policy Statement of 1956 became a Constitution of Industrial Economies for about two decades. What required after a long period of trial was another modification awaiting in 1977.

Industrial Policy of 1977

The Industrial Policy of 1977, classified the small sector into three categories:

(a) Cottage and household industries which provide self-employment on a wide scale.
(b) Tiny sector incorporating investment in industrial units in machinery and equipment up to Rs. 1 lakh and situated in towns with a population of less than 50,000.
(c) Small-scale industries comprising industrial units with an investment of Rs. 10 lakh and in case of ancillaries with an investment in fixed capital up to Rs. 15 lakh.

The purpose of the classification was to design policy measures for each category. The measures suggested for the promotion of small-scale cottage industries included the following: (a) The number of items raised from 180 enlisted in the earlier resolution to 807, (b) Special assistance to be given to tiny sector and cottage and household industries in the form of margin money assistance, (c) Setting up of District Industries Centre (DIC) in each district as an agency to serve as the focal point of development for small-scale and cottage industries. This agency would provide under a single roof all the services and support required by small and rural entrepreneurs, (d) Revamping the Khadi and Village Industries Commission. It was found that the promotional work of 22 village industries which came under the control of Khadi and Village Industries Commission has been haphazard, and the pace of the progress is also very slow. Hence, the government decided to work out detailed plans for the development of these village industries by adopting modern management techniques.

The Industrial Policy of 1977 attempted to define the role of large-scale sector by declaring them: (a) Basic industries for providing infrastructural items like cement, non-ferrous, steel, oil etc. to small industries and others; (b) Capital goods industries required by small-scale industries; (c) High technology industries widely required by small-scale and agriculture sector producing items such as fertilizers, pesticides and petro-chemicals; and (d) Other industries not enlisted as reserved items for small-scale but essential for the development of economy. For the promotion of technological self-reliance, the Policy had place for indigenous technology. It was envisaged that all possible efforts be made in the direction of development of indigenous technology, which should ensure efficient production, continued inflow of technology in sophisticated and high priority areas where Indian skills and technology are not adequately developed.

The Industrial Policy of 1977 specified that the public sector would not only be the producer of important and strategic goods of basic nature, but it would also be used effectively as a stabilizing force for maintaining essential supplies for the consumer. The strategy of Industrial Policy of 1977 depended on the enforcement of Foreign Exchange Regulations Act (FERA). Accordingly, foreign investment would be encouraged only for those industries in the national interest decided by the Government. This clearly meant that in areas where the foreign collaboration was not required, such case would not be reviewed. Yet, the Industrial Policy of 1977 came under the attack of critics. For encouraging small-scale industries, the 1977 policy suggested measures to reserve exclusive production of certain articles for the small-scale industrial sector only, thereby, limiting the productive capacity of large-scale industries. To achieve this, 1977

Industrial Policy had increased the number of goods to be produced by small-scale industrial sector from 180 to 807. But though this number was increased, the critics point out that most of these articles were continued to be produced by large-scale sector contrary to the provision of Industrial Policy of 1977. Reference of the cases where Government failed to effectively shift their production to the small-scale sector was given by Alak Ghosh. He stated that articles like footwear, bread and biscuits, brushes etc. continued to be produced by large-scale industries and multinational companies. The critics also pointed out that the lengthened list of 807 items which the Industrial Policy of 1977 reserved for small-scale sector was deceptive as these were more repetitive rather new lines of small units. As pointed out by Nirmal K. Gupta that the Policy had created confusion by bringing 807 items on the list of small-scale sector, many of these items were repetition.

The Industrial Policy of 1977 was shortlived to pave way for another policy of 1980.

Industrial Policy of 1980

The industrial policy regularized 34 industries producing items not reserved for small-scale sector and which had installed capacity in excess of licensed capacity. These industries were not under the MRTP Act, 1989 or FERA, 1973. The Industrial Policy of 1980 decided that while regularizing installed capacities in excess of the 'licensed capacities', Foreign Exchange Regulation Act (FERA) and Monopolies and Restrictive Trade Practices Act (MRTP) Companies would be considered on a selective basis, (and that) this facility would not be given in respect of items reserved for the small sector. Besides the 19 industries, the Industrial Policy Statement of February 2, 1973, the following industries would also be benefitted from the regularization of excess capacity: Oil drilling accessories; Power transmission accessories; Railway safety equipment and signaling equipment; Special alloy castings and stainless castings; Pumps and compressors; High tensile steel nuts and bolts; Electric generators; Engineering production aids; Two-wheelers and three-wheelers; Refrigerators up to 167 liters; Electric ceiling fans; Dry cell batteries; GLS lamps and fluorescent tubes; Bicycles; and Drugs and pharmaceuticals.

In order to fasten the pace of growth of small-scale industrial sector, investment limits were raised for definition purpose as under—for small-scale units from Rs. 10 lakhs to Rs. 20 lakhs; for tiny units from Rs. 1 lakh to Rs. 2 lakhs; and for ancillaries from Rs. 15 lakhs to Rs. 25 lakhs. In order to promote village industries, the 1980 Industrial Policy decided to promote industrialization in the country in such a way as it can generate economic viability in the villages. Promotion of handlooms, handicrafts, khadi and other village industries would receive greater attention to achieve a faster rate of growth in the villages.

With the objective of creating a more favourable balance of trade, the Industrial Policy of 1980 decided to sympathetically consider requests for setting up of 100 per cent export oriented units and for expansion of existing units exclusively for purpose of export. The Industrial Policy of 1980 made provision to facilitate the transfer of technology from efficient operating units to new units. Those companies which have well established Research and Development (R&D) organization and have demonstrated their ability to absorb, adapt and spread modern technology would be permitted to import such technology as they were supposed to increase the efficiency and cost-effectiveness of new units.

The Industrial Policy Statement of 1980 made provision for the development of industry in backward areas and attain economic federalism through restructuring the locational policy, introducing technological changes, providing infrastructural facilities to industrial sector, introduce special incentives for both small and cottage industries at times. In the light of energy crisis by India, the Industrial Policy of 1980 proposed search for other forms of energy. These included solar insulation, biogas, tidal and sea-power energy etc. The Industrial Policy of 1980 also proposed advanced technology and transfer of technology at national and international level to improve industrial competitiveness.

Though industrial policy of 1980 aimed at removing constraints to industrial production by revising the definition of small industries, regularization of installed capacity beyond the licensed capacity, a scheme of automatic expansion of capacity and evolution of monitoring system yet it was also not free from criticism.

The policy approach of regularization of installed productive capacity in excess of licensed capacity came under the attack of critics. In this context, Nirmal K.Gupta observed that there were also more chances of not genuine cases availing benefits.

In order to fasten the pace of growth of small-scale industries, the Industrial Policy of 1980 decided to give priority to this sector in allocation of raw material. But in actual practice this sector was given a residuary treatment. The Seventh Plan expressed its dissatisfaction in this regard in the following words, "While various measures have been taken for supply of raw materials to the small-scale units through State Small Industries Development Corporations, import quota etc., in actual practice the sector gets more or less a 'residuary' treatment in raw material distribution/allocation." (Planning Commission, Seventh Five Year Plan (1985-90), Vol. II, p. 9). Despite the policy of encouraging dispersal of industries in industrially backward areas adopted by the Industrial Policy of 1980, in actual practice it has been observed that still these units remained concentrated in developed States like Maharashtra, Tamil Nadu, West Bengal and Gujarat. The States like Bihar, Madhya Pradesh and Orissa still lagged behind. Not only had this but within developed States also the industrial units remained concentrated only in developed areas. The Industrial Policy of 1980, in short, focused attention on the need for promoting competition in the domestic market, technological upgradation and modernization. The policy laid the foundation of an increasingly competitive export base and for encouraging foreign investments in high-technology areas.

Industrial Policy of 1991 and thereafter Policies

The year 1991 witnessed a drastic change in the industrial policy governing industrial development in the country since decades. This landmark change which in the economic history of India in the form of Industrial Policy of 1991 actually was entirely a new chapter which was to enforce totally open economic system as compared to the earlier mixed system. The country decided to follow the lines of capitalism.

Features of the New Industrial Policy

Industrial licensing policy: In a major move to liberalize the economy, the new industrial policy abolished all industrial licensing, irrespective of the level of investment, except for a short list of 18 industries related to the security and strategic concerns, social reasons, hazardous chemicals and overriding environmental reasons and items of elitist consumption. However, of these 18 industries, three industries (motor cars, white goods and raw hides and skins and leather) were delicensed in April 1993. In 1996, another industry was delicensed namely entertainment and electronic industry. Further, in July 1997, five other industries were delicensed (animal fats and oils, tanned or dressed fur skins, chamois leather, asbestos and asbestos-based products, plywood and other wood and paper and newsprint). In continuation with the process of delicensing, three other industries were included in this category in 1998-99 namely coal and lignite, petroleum products and sugar. Later on drugs and pharmaceuticals industries were also exempted from licensing. Thus, at present only 5 items of health, strategic and security considerations remain under the purview of industrial licensing—alcohol, cigarettes, hazardous chemicals, electronic, aerospace and all types of defense equipment. The exemption from licensing will apply to all substantial expansion of existing units. The projects where imported capital goods are required, automatic clearance will be given. In cases where foreign exchange availability is ensured through foreign equity; or if the CIF value of imported capital goods required is less than 25 per cent of total value of plant and equipment, up to a maximum value of Rs. 2 crore. In view of the current difficult foreign exchange situation, this scheme came into force from April, 1992. In other cases, imports of capital goods will require clearance from the Secretariat of Industrial Approvals (SIA) in the Department of Industrial Development according to availability of foreign exchange resources. In respect of locations other than cities of more than 1 million populations, the industrialists will not be required to obtain industrial approval from the Centre, except for industries subject to compulsory licensing. In the cities with population greater than 1 million, industries other than those of non-polluting nature such as electronics, computer software and printing will be allowed outside 25 km of the periphery, except in prior designated industrial areas. Major amendments were made in the industrial location policy during 1997-98. The requirement of obtaining industrial approvals from the Central Government (except for the industries under compulsory licensing) for establishing units at locations not falling within 25 kms the periphery of cities having a population of more than 1 million was dispensed with. However, notified industries of a non-polluting nature such as electronics, computer software and printing, may be located within 25 kms of the periphery of cities with more than 1 million populations. Other industries are permitted only if they are located in designated industrial area set up prior to July 25, 1991. Zoning and land use Regulations as well as Environment Legislation continues to regulate industrial locations.

Policy on Public Sector

The 1956 Resolution had reserved 17 industries for the public sector. The 1991 industrial policy reduced this number to 8 naming—Arms and ammunition; Atomic energy; Coal and lignite; Mineral oils; Mining of iron ore, manganese ore, chrome ore, gypsum, sulphur, gold and diamond; Mining of copper, lead, zinc, tin, molybdenum and wolfarm; Minerals specified in the schedule to the atomic energy (Control of Production and Use Order), 1953; and Rail transport.

But later on five during these reserved industries under public sector were also dereserved. On May 9, 2001, the government opened up arms and ammunition sector also to the private sector. Now there were only three industries left reserved exclusively for the public sector. The policy also suggested that those public enterprises which are chronically sick and which are unlikely to be turned around will, for the formation of revival/rehabilitation schemes, be referred to the Board for Industrial and Financial Reconstruction (BIFR), or other similar high level institutions created for the purpose, in order to protect the interests of workers likely to be affected by such rehabilitation package a social security mechanism will be created. The government has announced its intention to offer a part of government shareholding in the public sector enterprises to mutual funds, financial institutions, the general public and the workers. A beginning in this direction was made in 1991-92 themselves by diverting part of the equities of selected public sector enterprises.

Monopolistic and Restrictive Trade Practice Limit

Under the Monopolistic and Restrictive Trade Practice Act, all firms with assets above a certain size (Rs. 100 crore since 1985) were classified as MRTP firms. Such firms were permitted to enter selected industries only and this also on a case by case approval basis. In addition to control through industrial licensing, separate approvals were required by such large firms for any investment proposals. The New Industrial Policy therefore removes the threshold limit in assets in respect of MRTP companies and dominant undertakings. This eliminates the requirements of prior approval of the Central Government in respect of the activities concerning expansion, new undertakings etc. The MRTP Act has been accordingly amended. In the now amended Act, emphasis has shifted to taking appropriate action against monopolistic, restrictive and unfair trade practices on the part of monopolies. These dominant undertakings or monopolies have now been identified as those who control over 25 per cent share of the market. The New Industrial Policy has widened and strengthened the provisions of the MRTP Act, and their implementation through the Monopoly Commission.

Policy on Foreign Investment and Technology Agreements

In the case of both foreign technology agreements sought by the Indian firms as well as foreign investment, it was necessary to obtain specific prior approval from the government for each project. It was argued that this caused undue delays and government interference and also hampered business decision making. The New Industrial Policy, therefore, prepared a specified list of high technology and high investment priority industries, wherein automatic permission was to be made available for direct foreign investment up to 51 per cent foreign equity. The industries in which automatic approval was granted included a wide range of industrial activities in the capital goods and metallurgical industries, entertainment electronic, food processing and the services sectors having significant export potential. Besides, these included a number of other industries which were important for the rapid growth of the economy.

In January 1997, the government also announced the first ever guidelines for foreign direct investment for expeditious approval of foreign investment in areas not covered under automatic approval. Priority areas for foreign direct investment proposals as mentioned in the guidelines included infrastructure, export potential, large-scale employment potential particularly for rural areas, items with linkages with the farm sector, social sector projects like hospitals, health care and medicines, and proposals that led to induction of technology and infusion of capital.

The list of industries eligible for foreign direct equity investment under the automatic approval route by Reserve Bank was further expanded in 1997-98 and 1998-99. In 1997-98, equity investment up to 100 per cent by NRIs/OCBs (Overseas Corporate Bodies) was permitted in high priority industries. These included 9 high priority industries in metallurgical and infrastructure sectors and 13 other priority industries, hitherto eligible for 74 per cent and 51 per cent equity investment respectively. Foreign equity investment in mining (3 categories of industries) was also allowed up to 100 per cent for NRIs/OBCs. During 1998-99, the scope of foreign direct equity investment under the automatic approval route of Reserve Bank was enhanced. In a major drive to simplify foreign direct investment procedures, Indian companies were permitted to accept investment under automatic approval route without obtaining prior permission from Reserve Bank of India. Foreign equity up to 100 per cent has been permitted in electricity generation, transmission and distribution (excluding atomic reactor power plants) and in construction and maintenance of roads, highways, vehicular bridges, toll roads, vehicular tunnels, parts and harbours. However, foreign equity in projects of these industries under the automatic approval route was not to exceed Rs. 1,500 crore. During 1991-2000, the government decided to pull all items under the automatic route for foreign direct investment/ NRI & OCB investment except for a small negative list, which includes all proposals requiring industrial license under the Industries (Development and Regulation) Act, 1951; cases having foreign investment more than 24 per cent in the equity capital of units manufacturing items reserved for the small-scale sector; and for all its requiring industrial license in terms of the location policy notified under the New Industrial Policy, 1991.

In order to licensed foreign direct investment policy further, the government took some important decisions such as: 100 per cent foreign direct investment allowed in Special Economic Zones (SEZs) for all manufacturing activities; 100 per cent foreign direct investment permitted for Business to Business commerce; Removal of cap on investment in the power sector; 100 per cent foreign direct investment permitted in oil refining; 100 per cent foreign direct investment allowed in telecom sector for certain activities with some conditions; Off-shore Venture Capital Funds/Companies allowed to invest in domestic venture capital undertakings as well as other companies through the automatic route, subject to only SEBI (Securities and Exchange Board of India) regulations and sector specific caps on foreign direct investment; Existing companies with foreign direct investment are eligible for automatic route to undertake additional activities covered under automatic route; Foreign direct investment up to 26 per cent is eligible under automatic route in the Insurance sector, as prescribed in the Insurance Act, 1991, subject to obtaining a license from the Insurance Regulatory and Development Authority (IRDA); and Automatic route is available to proposals in the Information Technology sector, even when the applicant company has a previous joint venture or technology transfer agreement in the same field, etc.

On May 9, 2001, the government announced a number of concessions and incentives to Foreign Direct Investment (FDI). The main incentives given by the government are as follows:

In the pharmaceutical sector, 100 per cent Foreign Direct Investment has been allowed through the automatic route (earlier on, the limit was 74%); 100 per cent Foreign Direct Investment has been allowed in airports against the prevailing 74 per cent; For the hotels and tourism industry the Foreign Direct Investment limit has been raised to 100 per cent through the automatic route from the prevailing 51 per cent; 100 per cent Foreign Direct Investment has also been allowed in two fresh areas—Courier services and Mass Rapid Transport System (MRTS); 100 per cent Foreign Direct Investment has been allowed in township development; In the telecom sector, Foreign Direct Investment limit has been raised to 74 per cent from the existing 49 per cent for Internal Service Providers (ISPs). Subject to Reserve Bank guidelines, the foreign investment limit in the banking sector has been hiked from 20 per cent to 49 per cent; and

Foreign Direct Investment up to 267 per cent has been allowed in defense production.

•

Abolition of Phased Manufacturing Programmes for New Projects

In order to force the pace of indigenization in manufacturing sector, Phased Manufacturing Programmes have been in force in a number of engineering and electronic industries. The new policy abolished such programmes for future.

Removal of Mandatory Convertible Clause

Since large part of industrial investment in India is finance by loans from banks and financial institutions, these institutions followed a mandatory practice of including a convertibility clause in their lending operations for new projects which provide them adoption of converting part of their loans into equity of felt necessary by their management. This has been interpreted as an unwarranted threat to the private firms to be taken over by the financial institutions. Hence, the new industrial policy provided that financial institutions will not impose this mandatory convertible clause.

From the above discussion, it can be concluded that prior to independence during the colonial period, both the industrial policies as well as economic policies were completely shaped by the British Government in favour of British interests. Immediately after independence, India came up with Industrial Policy of 1948 which adopted mixed economic system approach, wherein public and private sectors were to operate together but the ground practicalities insisted to frame another Industrial Policy within short period of time. The 1956 Industrial Policy Resolution gave effective space to the centrally controlled industries, State controlled industries and Joint ventures for industrial development. The Policy Resolution introduced the proposals to liberalize the Industrial Policy by relaxations to MRTP and FERA Acts, re-defining the investment limits, de-licensing and exemption to same categories of industrial sector, incentives for export promotion, broadbanding of industries, introduction of cottage industries and several other financial concessions. After 1956 Industrial Policy Resolution, came Industrial Policy of 1973, 1977, 1980, 1982-

83 and 1990, with very minor changes. The Industrial Policy approach turned full circle with the advent of the Narsimha Rao government in 1991 in the form of New Industrial Policy of 1991. The country decided to follow the lines of capitalism. The watchword for the New Industrial Policy thus became liberalization, globalization and privatization and towards this end, the Government introduced three sets of reforms: **first:** deregulation, delicensing, decontrol and de-bureaucratization of industrial licensing system; **two:** liberalization of foreign trade and currency transactions and **third:** institute several measures to facilitate foreign direct investment inflows. All these measures were launched in the year 1991 and since then, further liberalizations have been introduced every year with each new budget.

4.7 Trend of Modern Economy

4.7.1 Liberalization

By the end of the 1970s, India had acquired a reputation as one of the most protected and heavily regulated economies in the world. Starting in the mid-1970s and then later on in the 1980s, a few tentative steps were taken to liberalize the regulatory regime. In 1991, more extensive reforms followed. Since then there have been further policy changes in diverse sectors all aimed at opening up the economy to greater private sector entrepreneurship as well as to foreign trade and investment.

These two decades (1980-2000) have been quite special in the course of Indian economic development. The growth rate of GDP that had stayed around 3.5 per cent per annum for 20 years prior to 1980, shot up to about 5 per cent in the eighties (1980 to 1989) and increased further in the nineties (1990 to 1999) to 6 per cent. Over the last few years, it has reached as high as 9 per cent. Moreover, the growth in the post-reform period has also been stable. In the decade of the 1970s, the variance in GDP growth rate was 15.8. It came down to 4.6 in the 1980s (i.e., 1981-82 to 1990-91) and further down to 1.5 in the 1990s (1992-2002). Most importantly, GDP growth has been accompanied by a poverty decline. The proportion of the population below the poverty line (at $1.08 a day in 1993 PPP USD) declined from about 44.5 per cent in 1983-84 to 27.5 per cent in

2004-05. The fast and stable growth accompanied by a decline in poverty has also raised many questions: What triggered growth in India? What is the Indian model? Is it replicable in other developing countries? Is it sustainable? How does it compare with the East Asian model in its growth as well as distributional consequences? How does the growth process impinge on India's central problem—its mass poverty? Indian economic growth during 1980-2004, seems to have little in common with the so-called 'Asian Model'. Its savings rate has improved over time but has not reached the East Asian level. Its growth so far has not been driven by manufactured exports. Nor has it attracted massive inflows of foreign investment. There is no industrial policy targeted towards developing specific industries. On the contrary, it is the service sector that has led the charge in the Indian growth experience. Another aspect of the Indian experience that makes it very different from that of other Asian countries is that despite a fast growing non-agricultural part of the economy, the share of agriculture in the total labour force has declined very slowly. In fact, the agricultural labour force in absolute number has increased since 1980s, dampening the process of poverty decline.

Why do We Expect Economic Liberalization to Produce Growth?

Import liberalization provides domestic firms access to capital equipment embodied with new technologies, better intermediate inputs and expands their choice set to act. A freedom to invest and enter the market increases the extent of competition and puts pressure on the incumbents to upgrade their technologies often through imported machinery. With the entry of new firms in a more competitive market, the process of creative destruction goes to work. Efficient firms drive out inefficient firms, factors gets reallocated to more productive use increasing the overall productivity of factors in the economy. Due to technology transfer, productivity in industry and service sectors grows rapidly attracting labour from agriculture. The re-allocation of labour from agriculture to more productive sectors contributes further to growth. This process also makes the workers left behind in agriculture better off because the real wage rises as labour markets tighten in agriculture.

What is Distinct about India's Experience?

It is clear from the earlier sections that the growth episode in India since the 1980s is not another instance of State driven growth in Asia. Instead, it is the co-incidence of the ready availability of new technologies and having the skilled manpower that would be necessary to take advantage of these new technologies. Technology transfers in the 1980s and early 1990s took place mostly through easier and cheaper access to imported machinery that was made possible by trade liberalization. Improved communications (especially cell phones) and the diffusion of internet were other technologies that played a big role in driving growth from the mid-1990s on. It is inconceivable that without the break-up of government monopolies and the advent of competition in the communication sector, there would have been a revolution in communication technology in India. And, without such a revolution, the fastest growing sectors (e.g., business services) would not have taken off in India. The sustained growth that we have seen since the mid-1990s would clearly not have been possible without the liberalizing reforms of 1991. The importance of liberalization measures can be appreciated by imagining the counterfactual that India had stayed in its pre-reform state of constraints on entrepreneurial freedoms to invest and import. New technologies would not have diffused at such a speed and growth would have been much slower. At the same time, as stressed by Kochhar, *et al.* (2006), it should be acknowledged that some aspects of the earlier economic regime played a positive role in the pattern of development later. For example: the creation of a diverse set of skills through import substitution, an emphasis on tertiary education creating a pool of university graduates for sophisticated service sector jobs and a government induced expansion of banking network that helped in mobilizing savings. The initial conditions and their interaction with the fortuitous arrival of new technologies created a distinctive pattern of growth that would have been hard to predict at the time of liberalization.

Another distinctive feature of the Indian growth experience is the dominance of the service sector. In East and South-east Asia, it was the manufacturing sector. One could look at this in several different ways. If we compare China with India, it is indeed the manufacturing sector that grew fastest in China and *vice versa* in India. However, both sectors grew faster in both countries than in the rest of the world and both sectors grew faster in China than in India. Yes, even services grew faster in China than in India. The main distinction is in terms of what comprised their exports. Here it is service for India and manufacturing for China. Indeed, it is the software exports to the developed countries that spread over the world that India was unique as a developing country to have developed a comparative advantage in high-end services. In a curious way, this was the reason for it being accepted as a development success story despite the fact that it continues to house more of the world's poor than any other country. What are the implications of the fast growing component of the exports being high-end services as opposed to manufacturing? For one thing, manufacturing uses unskilled labour more intensively. In the Indian context, this is especially true of unorganized manufacturing and it is conceivable that manufacturing exports would have generated a great deal of sub-contracting to the unorganized sector. This, in turn, would have drawn labour out of agriculture to a greater extent. Indeed, one major feature of India's development pattern is that the share of agriculture in employment has not come down rapidly. In fact, the absolute amount of labour in agriculture has risen continuously in India while it fell in all countries now developed during their comparable development phases. An important component of growth—moving labour from low to high productivity activities—has been conspicuous by its absence in India. Also, as the labour to land ratio grows, it becomes that much more difficult to increase agricultural wages and reduce poverty. There has been much discussion in the literature as to why the manufacturing sector has not grown faster in India. Inadequate infrastructure, restrictive labour laws and small-scale reservation policy have been identified as the main reasons. It is very possible that these factors reduced the possibility of India emerging as an exporter of labour intensive manufacturers—a possibility that would have hastened the decline in poverty. Finding export markets in high-income countries makes the choice set of production activities independent of domestic demand composition. The growth in domestic demand will depend on the composition of income growth. In other words, if the growth in income is skewed in favour of high skilled and therefore high-income groups, it will be the kind of goods and services catered to by the rich that will be found lucrative by investors. Few of them will be unskilled labour intensive. As a result, the trickle down to the unskilled (and hence the poor) will be weak. One possible bottleneck for the Indian pattern of growth is 'educated workforce'. Given that the educational statuses have been rising rapidly, it does seem like a real possibility. Most of the fast growing sectors are completely dependent on skilled manpower. If they run into a serious bottleneck, growth may get choked. A related question is that of quality. According to a report by the McKinsey Global Institute (2005), "India's vast supply of graduates is smaller than it seems once their suitability for employment by multinational companies is considered." The report stresses that the government must "adjust the country's educational policy to ward off the looming squeeze on talent". McKinsey estimates that India has 14 million young university graduates (those with seven years or less of work experience). This pool is 1.5 times the size of China's and almost twice that of the United States. Every year 2.5 million new graduates are added to this pool. However, according to thc report, while the numbers seem encouraging at first glance, a closer look reveals that India is likely to face a talent crunch in the coming years. The problem might get further exacerbated with the current state of primary schooling in India. ASER (Annual Status of Education Report) (2010), a unique survey of learning in rural India, estimates that about 47 per cent of rural Indian children in class 5 cannot read a simple class 2 level text. Even, in class 8, about 17 per cent children cannot read a class 2 level text. Many of these children may never reach university, but those who do not go to university will join the labour force and ASER's results are indicative of the future quality of the labour force. The Right of Children to Free and Compulsory Education Act, which was passed by the Parliament in April 2010, makes sure that no child will be held back till the age of 14 (approximately class 8), regardless of how they perform. This will mean that children could easily pass middle school (class 7/8) without being tested on any learning indicators. Even if they drop out after class 8, they would enter the skilled labour force (by our definition) and could be potentially unemployable. Therefore, it is quite possible that the so-called demographic dividend may disappear if the quality of the labour force is not improved, even if the non-farm sector creates sufficient jobs to absorb the increase in labour force. A larger point is that India's economic growth is not accompanied by an equally fast improvement in the functioning of India's institutions such as the legal system, the governance and the educational system (Subramanian, 2007). Indeed, it is easier and faster to transfer technology and bring about productivity improvements. But it is harder and slower to bring about institutional improvements for sustaining and stabilizing the growth process. One important lesson from the Indian experience and especially from its comparison with other Asian countries is that a country can neglect agriculture at its own peril. The growth process in India was accompanied by a reduction in poverty at the lower level (Rs. 356 per capita per month or approximately $1.08 per day). If we consider double the poverty level ($2.16 per day), a staggering 80 per cent of India's population was poor in 1983 and the number is about the same in 2004. This is a startling fact and indicates that there are two Indians: one of educated managers and engineers who have been able to take advantage of the opportunities made available through globalization and the other—a huge mass of undereducated mass of people who are making a living in low productivity jobs in the informal sector—the largest of which is still 'agriculture'. The most direct impact on the second India could only come about through improvements in agricultural productivity. But unfortunately, agriculture is dependent on well functioning rural institutions. In general, the productivity improvements in the informal sector depend crucially on access to credit, know-how and skills and therefore on the quality of institutions. India's future will depend a great deal on how these institutional improvements shape up.

More so than other developing countries, India has experienced the fastest economic growth. Despite being considered a poor country after its independence in 1947, India has bounced back to become one of the most powerful emerging economies in the entire world. How has India been able to achieve this incredible goal? What are the lessons that other South Asian countries can take from India's success? Various policies were implemented after 1991 that were key to India's economic success. First, India followed the Solow growth model theory on its way to success. According to the Solow model, long-term growth is a direct result of the Solow residuals. This paper argues that international trade and openness of the economy increased the overall level of output leading to a faster economic growth. The initial hypothesis proved to be correct as International trade was the difference between a poor India and an emerging India. Between 1950s-1980s, protectionism swept the shores of India. Politicians favoured policies that restricted movement of goods and services from other countries. India was destined to become independent of the world markets. However, India could not sustain this phenomenon forever. It realized that restriction of trade had a negative effect on the economic growth of India. Also, policy-makers realized that in order for India to prosper like other South East Asian countries like Singapore, Taiwan and South Korea, it had to open its borders. This notion proved to be true as India's growth rate between 1988-2006 was 6 per cent annually compared with 4.8 per cent annually during 1981-1988, right before reformation. The economy grew even faster during the period from 2003-2004 to 2005-2007, when India's GDP at factor cost grew at an impressive rate of 8.6 per cent annually. Opening the economy to the world market has been the reason for India's impressive success. This openness increased the rate of investment at home, which in turn led to a high economic growth just like Solow had predicted. There are multiple lessons that other South Asian countries can learn from the case of India. One of the keys to economic success depends on the country's political structure. In other words, the more interest there is politically to economically advance, the higher the chances of achieving that particular goal. In the case of other South Asian countries, that has been the main problem, political incentives have overlooked the potential economic growth. These countries need to realize that India, by changing its political ideologies helped itself to grow tremendously. Other countries also need to learn that India had to sacrifice deep cultural beliefs that prevented effective policies to be put into effect before the 1980s. These sacrifices may be hard to make but in the end, the benefits of liberalization outweigh these sacrifices as has been seen in the case of India. Overall, the experience of liberalization in India has been better compared to other developing countries. For India, the future is very bright if it continues to follow the same path since the late 1980s. India needs to carry the liberalization forward. India has the possibility to achieve long-term growth just like the East Asian tigers in the 1960s and 1970s, if policies are passed that favour more integration with the world markets. India already has a booming informational technology sector that has played a vital role in its economic growth. Now, India needs to focus on opening its borders even more to encourage further foreign investment. This will provide further investment opportunities internally and help the country to achieve an unprecedented economic success.

4.7.2 Privatization

Privatization is a managerial approach that has attracted the interest of many categories of people—academicians, politicians, government employees, players of the private sector, and public on the whole. As per the opinion by the subject experts, privatization can be advantageous in terms of the higher flexibility and scope of innovation it offers along with cost savings, many a times. However, other specialists defiantly debate that privatization has an adverse impact on the employee morale and generate fear of dislocation or termination. More likely it also adds on to the apprehensions pertaining to accountability and quality. Experts both advocate and criticize privatization making it more or less a provocative decision that calls for a diligent scrutiny by the decision makers in assessment of pros and cons attached to the concerned policy. In India, privatization has been accepted with a lot of resistance and has been dormant initially during the inception period of economic liberalization in the country. Here intends to analyze the present status of privatization in India and summarize its advantages and disadvantages in context with the Indian Economy.

Primary Features of Privatization

Market principles by public policy-makers have evolved as one of the prominent characteristics of the contemporary public enterprise management which encompasses privatization as a primary facet. Privatization of State owned enterprises have developed as a critical tool for economic policies pertaining to progress and development of developing countries. One of the prominent feature of privatization is the enhanced competitive characteristics it provides to the enterprises which prove to be fruitful.

Lobbying and bribery are the common issues tarnishing the practical applicability of privatization. Privatization loses the mission with which the enterprise was established and profit maximization agenda encourages malpractices like production of lower quality products, elevating the hidden indirect costs, price escalation etc. Privatization results in high employee turnover and a lot of investment are required to train the lesser-qualified staff. There can be a conflict of interest amongst stakeholders and the management of the buyer private company and initial resistance to change can hamper the performance of the enterprise. Privatization escalates price inflation in general as privatized enterprises do not enjoy government subsidies after the deal and the burden of this inflation affects the common man.

Privatization contracts are greatly influenced by merger variables and even global issues and are structured on the basis of manipulation of the government and the private players along with the administering jurisdiction. Perotti and Guney (1993) cited in Al-Zuhair, have supported privatization as a vital source to enhance economic enticements, magnetize better managerial skills of the private sector, extend the share ownership, lower the public borrowings in order to sustain sustainable services. Shirley (1988) cited in Al-Zuhair, view privatization as an attempt to enhance market potencies. Privatization is an essentially effective tool for restructuring and reforming the public sector enterprises running without significant aim and mission as private sector is perceived to be fundamentally more self-motivated, prolific and reliable for superior quality of products and services. Privatization can be of three prominent types:

1. **Delegation:** Government keeps hold of responsibility and private enterprise handles fully or partly the delivery of product and services.
2. **Divestment:** Government surrenders the responsibility.
3. **Displacement:** The private enterprise expands and gradually displaces the government entity.

Privatization in India: An Overview

Privatization in India is still at a minimum level. Privatization by way of sale of public sector enterprises is almost negligible while divestment is also existent by way of selling of a portion of shares of the 31 public sector enterprises. Privatization got tremendous boost by the introduction of new economic policy in 1991 that allowed delicensing, relaxing entry restrictions and equity funding. This heightened the competition in the industries that were monopolized by the public sector earlier. State owned enterprises were lacking the finesse that private enterprises employed as the competitive edge. Deregulation in India was facilitated by laws like the Industries (Development & Regulation) Act, 1951 (IDRA), Monopolies and Restrictive Trade Practices Act, 1969, (MRTPA), Foreign Exchange Regulation Act, 1973 (FERA), Capital Issues Control and technical scrutiny by the Directorate General of Technical Development (DGTD). Post-independence, the Indian government adopted socialistic economic strategies. It was in 1980s, that Rajiv Gandhi initiated economic restructuring. With the help of IMF, Indian government commenced a sequential economic reorganization. P.V. Narasimha Rao brought in the revolutionary economic developments with the help of Dr. Manmohan Singh. The results of these reforms can be assessed statistically by comparing the total overseas investment in terms of portfolio investment, FDI and investments from foreign equity capital markets. In 1995-1996, it was $ 5.3 billion as compared to $ 132 million in 1991-1992. The highlights of the reforms including eradicating license raj for all except 18 critical sectors for licensing; tempering the control on industries; Foreign Technology Agreements; FDI & FII; amendment of MRTP Act, 1969; Deregulation; Regulation of Inflation; Tax restructuring; encouraging overseas business relations. Few examples of privatization in India are Lagan Jute Machinery Company Limited, Modern Food Industries Limited, BALCO, Hotel Corporation of India Limited, Hindustan Zinc Limited, Paradeep Phosphates Limited, BSNL etc.

Advantages of Privatization

Privatization indeed is beneficial for the growth and sustainability of the state-owned enterprises. The advantages of privatization can be perceived from both micro-economic and macro-economic impacts that privatization exerts.

A. Micro-economic Advantages

State owned enterprises usually are outdone by the private enterprises competitively. When compared the latter show better results in terms of revenues and efficiency and productivity. Hence, privatization can provide the necessary impetus to the underperforming PSUs. Privatization brings about radical structural changes providing momentum in the competitive sectors. Privatization leads to adoption of the global best practices along with management and motivation of the best human talent to foster sustainable competitive advantage and improvised management of resources.

B. Macro-economic Advantages

Privatization has a positive impact on the financial health of the sector which was previously state dominated by way of reducing the deficits and debts. The net transfer to the State-owned Enterprises is lowered through privatization. Helps in escalating the performance benchmarks of the industry in general can initially have an undesirable impact on the employees but gradually in the long-term, shall prove beneficial for the growth and prosperity of the employees. Privatized enterprises provide better and prompt services to the customers and help in improving the overall infrastructure of the country.

Disadvantages of Privatization

Privatization in spite of the numerous benefits it provides to the state-owned enterprises, there is the other side to it as well. Here are the prominent disadvantages of privatization: Private sector focuses more on profit maximization and less on social objectives unlike public sector that initiates socially viable adjustments in case of emergencies and criticalities. There is lack of transparency in private sector and stakeholders do not get the complete information about the functionality of the enterprise. Privatization has provided the unnecessary support to the corruption and illegitimate ways of accomplishments of licenses and business deals.

Future Prospects for India

Indian economy is a dynamic one that is showing tremendous potential of growth. Globalization, liberalization and privatization are the key strategic mandates for economic policies. Market oriented reforms are sustainable and are gaining acceptance with resistance to privatization going down due to the benefits like enhanced efficiency through target oriented management and disposition of public funds into social and physical infrastructure of the country. Privatization has shown great outcomes in the development of sectors like banking, insurance, telecom, power, civil aviation etc. However, the lobbying in domestic circuits was enfeebled by the surprising reversal of the Indian economy in present time. Indian economy registered an average growth of 8.5 per cent in the past four years and it is evident enough to highlight the potential of privatization and its need and likelihoods of privatization. However, it is disheartening to acknowledge that India is not a very alluring destination for foreign investors. Bureaucracy, red tapes, political hiccups, corruption are also prominent hindrances in the development of India that offers ample of skilled and cheap labour and inadequate capital. In spite of all the hurdles, it is a viable to expect higher rate of returns as compared to capital intensive industrialized countries. Complete privatization is still a far-fetched dream. In most of the liberalized sectors, government control is still evident and there is more of delegation or joint ventures between public and private sector (PPP).

4.7.3 Globalization

Most people would agree that globalization brings opportunities and benefits. But few would agree that those opportunities and benefits are fairly distributed. Globalization is widely seen as unbalanced and unequal, a process that benefits only a minority of people and of countries, leaves many excluded and brings real disadvantage to some. Of course, most of today's critical social problems—poverty and exclusion, disease and illiteracy, insecurity and unemployment, lack of voice and lack of respect for basic rights predated the present phase of globalization, and have other immediate causes, so at worst globalization has exacerbated them. But globalization, precisely because it creates new opportunities, has the potential to be part of the solution. The persistence of these problems in a globalized world is a fundamental failing of the present pattern of globalization. This paper explores some of the ways in which globalization might better serve social goals, drawing on the work of the World Commission on the Social Dimension of Globalization (2004). As its name implies, the World Commission argued that it is essential to pay more attention to the social dimension of globalization. The word "social" covers a lot of ground. Education and health are social domains, as are political rights and collective organization. The social dimension of globalization includes issues of social inclusion and exclusion, inequality and discrimination, culture and identity, rights and responsibilities. These, as much as economic goals, are everyday concerns of people and priorities of the societies in which they live. Many aspects of globalization have both economic and social dimensions. That is particularly true of work. Work is about production and income. But it is also about identity and social integration. This gives work and employment a critical position in any effort to simultaneously achieve economic and social goals. If globalization is to provide benefits for all, it must be the source of a sufficient volume of productive employment. At the same time, that work must meet people's aspirations for security and voice, for rights and representation, for identity and dignity. That challenge is hard to meet at national level. In the global economy it is harder still.

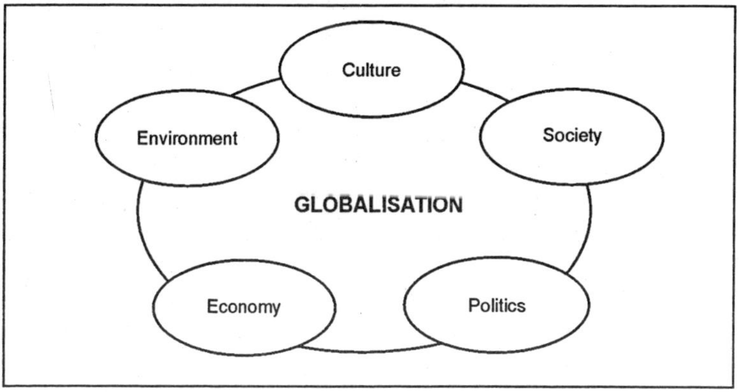

Fig. 4.7: Dimension of globalization

The Process of Globalization

Globalization is widely conceived as a process which is essentially driven by economic and technological forces increasingly global markets for goods and capital, new communication technologies which reduce the natural barriers of time and space. As such it is often seen as the motor of economic growth. It is therefore striking that globalization, at least as a phenomenon of recent decades, has not been associated with higher growth of the global economy. As the World Commission's report points out, the impact of globalization on growth and development has at best been ambiguous. World GDP growth has been declining as globalization has accelerated. One cannot demonstrate that growth would not have declined further in the absence of globalization, but as the World Commission report points out "at the very least this outcome is at variance with the more optimistic predictions on the growth-enhancing impact of globalization". This is all the more notable since positive growth impacts are widely expected both from the liberalization of international trade and capital markets and from the surge of new developments in information technology which underpin the present pattern of globalization. Nor has globalization led to convergence between countries in incomes and factor remunerations, contrary to simplistic models of the international economy. In reality, the gap between richest and poorest countries has widened. The ratio between the 20 richest and 20 poorest countries in GDP per capita rose from 53 in 1960-62 to 121 in 2000-02 (World Commission report). On the whole, the dynamics of international integration reward those economies where there is already a concentration of capital and skills, strengthened by their capacity to invest in education, and in research and development, which increases their comparative advantage further. So there is a built-in tendency to polarization, reinforced by highly concentrated flows of FDI in global production systems. The result is vast differences between countries in opportunities and in the ability to take advantage of those opportunities. It is true that some countries have succeeded in traversing, to a greater or lesser degree, the gap between developing and developed. Higher rates of economic growth and poverty reduction in East Asia, notably in China, and to a lesser extent in India and a few countries in other parts of the world, cannot only be attributed to globalization, for many other factors were involved, but successful exploitation of global economic opportunities played an important role. At the same time, these countries have used a variety of devices to protect themselves from competitive forces in the global market, while they increased national capacity. Opening up to the global economy without that capacity is a recipe for de-industrialization, as uncompetitive enterprises fail. Meanwhile, in other parts of the world, notably but not exclusively in Africa, growth has been low and poverty increasing. But it is hard to generalize from these patterns. There are always exceptions to any trend, suggesting that national and regional structures, institutions, capabilities and policies have a major effect. As in all walks of life, the new opportunities are disproportionately captured by those with the capabilities, the determination, the resources and the power to do so. Globalization may well be a positive sum game, but that does not mean that all benefit. The impact of globalization on work and employment illustrates this well. Successful integration in the global economy can lead to increased employment and rising wages. This was the experience of several East and South-east Asian countries for extended period's up to the financial crisis of the late 1990s. Chile, Ireland and a number of other small, open economies have likewise experienced periods of sustained employment creation. At the same time, there are a number of ways in which different aspects of globalization can have adverse effects on the labour market.

First, increased economic and financial volatility, associated with the liberalization of international financial markets, has led to more frequent economic crises, with significant consequences for unemployment. A ratchet effect can often be observed, in which unemployment does not fall to pre-crisis levels in the recovery (World Commission report). Thus in Latin America, open unemployment ratcheted up during the crises of the 1980s and 1990s to reach historic highs of around 10 per cent for the continent as a whole in 2003 (ILO, 2003).

Second, increased competitive pressures in global markets are widely observed to result in erosion of labour protection or informalization of employment relationships. There are frequent reports of restrictions on trade union rights in export processing zones, for example. Workers who are essentially organized at the national level find their bargaining power limited by the ability of enterprises to readily shift production to lower cost countries.

Third, increased tax competition results in lower taxation of high personal incomes and of corporate profits (KPMG, Corporate Tax Rate Survey, 2003, quoted in the World Commission Report), and the liberalization of trade reduces government revenues from tariffs—all of which is likely to reduce the resources available for government social expenditure, and to put pressure on public sector employment.

Fourth, globalization leads to increased restructuring of production, involving relocation and outsourcing, substantial job loss in some countries and gains in others, and labour market instability. While the adverse impact in industrialized countries is given most coverage by the global media, developing countries are not always beneficiaries. For instance, changes in the rules of the international trading system for textiles and garments are likely to lead to substantial job losses in Bangladesh and some other low and medium income countries, to China's advantage. There is an important gender dimension, since women's jobs seem more vulnerable to these swings. More generally, the drive for productivity growth in global production systems seems to result in relatively low levels of formal employment creation, intensifying the parallel growth of a large informal economy.

Fifth, as noted above, the capability of countries to take advantage of global market opportunities is highly polarized, so that in many countries there is little opportunity for employment creation though participation in global markets. On the contrary, low productivity national industries in developing countries may collapse when exposed to international competition, enterprises close and jobs are lost. On the other hand, some countries have been able to take advantage of a reservoir of skills and entrepreneurial capabilities to generate substantial employment growth—the software industry in India is a good example. All this implies that globalization can and often does increase deficits in both the quantity and quality of employment. This is not inevitable. There are countries which have successfully used the space for national policy and taken advantage of global opportunities. But insofar as globalization is identified with increasingly liberalized global markets, there is a tendency to polarization rather than convergence, and the simultaneous creation of large groups of both winners and losers, both within and between countries.

The Wider Context

Globalization is not only about increased international trade and capital flows. These macro-economic changes are themselves associated with changes in the organization of production at the global level. Global production systems, involving chains of interdependent enterprises contributing to different stages of the production process, are not new, but improved technology, better communications and the liberalization of markets have boosted them enormously. A relatively small number of multinational firms manage these processes, in some cases all the way from the production of raw materials to the final consumer. A substantial fraction of international trade in manufactures now takes place within firms, and in many sectors the success or failure of individual countries to take advantage of global opportunities depends on their ability to integrate global supply chains. Initially confined to certain manufacturing sectors (electronics, auto manufacture, garments), this trend is now extending to some services too. So globalization is more than the growth of efficient global markets. New institutions are developing, economic firms, brands and markets—and social, in the sense of cross border organization and interaction. There are many possible patterns, depending on the underlying forces and interests and the institutions and regulatory frameworks which are put in place. The shape and impact of globalization is not predefined. This is particularly obvious once we step beyond the economic domain. The present model of globalization leads to greater flows of information and exchanges between cultures and a greater global sharing of both goods and bad. It includes cultural changes which range from the penetration of Bollywood and Hollywood to global sporting events or world music. The availability of new consumer goods—the mobile phone, for example leads to changes in social patterns. Dress codes change. Cheap communications mean that every country's diaspora is in touch with what happens at home, and also acts as a channel for ideas and behaviours. What is happening might reasonably be seen as the first stage in the constitution of a global society. That might result from the spread of similar technologies, both in production and in daily life. Or it might reflect an increasingly common pattern of consumption or social habits, especially among transnational elite. It could also come from an increasing consciousness of people that they belong to a single world, as communications improve. It might be fostered by the global presence of particular powerful actors' nations, corporations. International organizations, both intergovernmental and private, can also play an important role. Whatever the starting point, with increased interconnection we can plausibly argue that the reach of global society will extend further; but only fragments of a global society can be observed today. The majority of people rarely if ever leave the country where they were born. Large numbers of countries are on the margins of the global market, too small to interest the important players. For them, globalization is more a source of disruption and of dispossession than of opportunity. In most countries, the main focus of human interest and of government policy remains national. Throughout the world, the middle classes and the rich are vastly more globalized than the poor, the young more globalized than the old. The benefits of globalization reach only a part of each country's population and in the poorest countries only a small fraction. Nevertheless, as education levels rise, markets are liberalized, and telecommunications spread, the level of penetration of globalization is rising, and the process looks set to continue.

Many of these national mechanisms have no real counterpart at the global level. Whereas the public interest is in principle represented by the State at the national level, at the global level it will for the foreseeable future be represented by a community of independent sovereign States. What is more, the power of those States and their willingness to accept collective responsibility is unevenly distributed, their democratic credentials vary greatly, and their interests often do not coincide. The absence of global central authority, both now and in the foreseeable future, drastically restricts the range of instruments that might be applied, and so the policies that are pursued within States are not necessarily a guide to what may be possible at the global level, because the instruments for their replication are not available at that level. Nevertheless, many of the key questions are the same. The issue is how coordinated action in the interests of all can be achieved and the approaches and instruments which may promote this. Globalization also poses questions that lie beyond the normal purview of the nation State. Questions of global peace and security, of climate change, of the global commons, of access to scientific knowledge and technology, of the volatility of the global economy all are international by nature. Such global public goods call for global policy interventions that are qualitatively different from those applied at the national level. Multilateral institutions already exist, essentially in the United Nations system, to pursue these issues, but their capacity to act remains limited. In the absence of an overall public policy framework for pursuing the common interest at the global level, we must consider the objectives and roles of all the different actors who influence economic and social outcomes at this level. Any attempt to manage globalization must first understand the forces behind it. It can be argued that in previous globalizations, notably the imperial expansions of the sixteenth and nineteenth centuries, there was a plan, an active and coordinated policy to achieve a particular goal of global power. Is that true today? Many argue that the driving force behind the present pattern of globalization is the neo-liberal economic model, with its accompanying domination of production and markets by a small number of States and large corporations. This is certainly the basis for the critique of globalization by many civil society movements. Nevertheless, even if this is part of the story, there are many other factors involved. Communications technology plays a role in its own right, as do increasingly outward looking political systems in many parts of the world, involving a greater willingness by States to accept interdependence. There are opportunities in global markets for both producers and consumers, and many factors engaged in taking advantage of them. So the current process of globalization reflects the multiple objectives of many factors. Within it, as in any human activity, there are centres of power and influence. There is a political economy of globalization that it would never ignore. But there is also much space for intervention. It is not utopian to try to design a framework for the governance of globalization, and the report of the World Commission addresses precisely this issue.

CHAPTER 5
Service Activities

5.1 Concept, Classification and Salient Feature of Service Activities

In simply manner, service means to do for others. Service activities have been classified into three category, i.e., privately organized service activities (tertiary sector), institutional service activities (quaternary sector) and high thinking and upper level management activities by 'think tanker' (Quinary Sector).

Tertiary activities include all the services other than primary and secondary activities. Tertiary production involves the service sector rather than tangible goods. This work refers to a range of personal and business services involving a rapidly growing share of the labour force in highly developed countries. Rental clerks, barbers, beauticians and secretaries all fall into the personal and business service categories as a group and they have been described as *'pink-collar'* workers.

Quaternary services represent a special type of service work, focusing on professional and administrative services including financial and health service work, information processing, teaching and government service and entertainment activity. Specialized technical, communication and motivation and leadership skills provide the common thread linking these activities. Practically quaternary activity occurs in office building environment or specialized environment provided by schools, theaters, hotels and hospitals. This group has been termed as the *'white-collar'* work force.

Quinary activities, the upper most one in hierarchy, remain more restricted in size compared to other groups of activities. The most visible persons in this group include chief executive officers and other top-management executive in both government and private service. Research scientist, legal authorities, financial advisers and professional consultants who provide strategic planning and problem-solving services belong to this group. Most of these high order analytical and managerial activities occur in larger urban centres or in close proximity to large university/medical or research centres. An appropriate level for this group is the *'gold-collar'* workers. Quinary activities view from two broad aspects:

(a) High-level managerial and executive administrative positions (public and private),
(b) Scientific research and development services.

Salient Features of Service Sector

Services can be paraphrased in terms of their key characteristics, sometimes called the "Five I's of Services".

1. Intangibility: Services are intangible and insubstantial, they cannot be touched, gripped, handled, looked at, smelled, and tasted. Thus, there is neither potential nor need for transport, storage or stocking of services. Furthermore, a service can be (re)sold or owned by somebody, but it cannot be turned over from the service provider to the service consumer. Solely, the service delivery can be commissioned to a service provider who must generate and render the service at the distinct request of an authorized service consumer.

2. Inventory (Perishability): Services have little or no tangible components and therefore cannot be stored for a future use. Services are produced and consumed during the same period of time.

Services are perishable in two regards:

- The service relevant resources, processes and systems are assigned for service delivery during a definite period in time. If the designated or scheduled service consumer does not request and consume the service during this period, the service cannot be performed for him. From the perspective of the service provider, this is a lost business opportunity as he cannot charge any service delivery; potentially, he can assign the resources, processes and systems to another service consumer who requests a service. Examples: The hair dresser serves another client when the scheduled starting time or time slot is over. An empty seat on a plane never can be utilized and charged after departure.

- When the service has been completely rendered to the requesting service consumer, this particular service irreversibly vanishes as it has been consumed by the service consumer. Example: the passenger has been transported to the destination and cannot be transported again to this location at this point in time.

3. Inseparability: The service provider is indispensable for service delivery as he must promptly generate and render the service to the requesting service consumer. In many cases, the service delivery is executed automatically but the service provider must preparatory assign resources and systems and actively keeps up appropriate service delivery readiness and capabilities. Additionally, the service consumer is inseparable from service delivery because he is involved in it from requesting it up to consuming the rendered benefits. Examples: The service consumer must sit in the hair dresser's shop and chair or in the plane and seat; correspondingly, the hair dresser or the pilot must be in the same shop or plane, respectively, for delivering the service.

4. Inconsistency (Variability): Each service is unique. It is one-time generated, rendered and consumed and can never be exactly repeated as the point in time, location, circumstances, conditions, current configurations and/or assigned resources are different for the next delivery, even if the same service consumer requests the same service. Many services are regarded as heterogeneous or lacking homogeneity and are typically modified for each service consumer or each new situation.

5. Involvement: One of the most important characteristics of services is the participation of the client/customer in the service delivery process. A client/customer has the opportunity to get the services modified according to specific requirement.

Each of these characteristics is retractable and their inevitable coincidence complicates the consistent service conception and makes service delivery a challenge in each and every case. Proper service marketing requires creative visualization to effectively evoke a concrete image in the service consumer's mind. From the service consumer's point of view, these characteristics make it difficult, or even impossible, to evaluate or compare services prior to experiencing the service delivery.

Mass generation and delivery of services is very difficult. This can be seen as a problem of inconsistent service quality. Both inputs and outputs to the processes involved providing services are highly variable, as are the relationships between these processes, making it difficult to maintain consistent service quality. For many services there is labour intensity as services usually involve considerable human activity, rather than a precisely determined process; exceptions include utilities. Human resource management is important. The human factor is often the key success factor in service economies. It is difficult to achieve economies of scale or gain dominant market share. There are demand fluctuations and it can be difficult to forecast demand. Demand can vary by season, time of day, business cycle, etc. There is consumer involvement as most service provision requires a high degree of interaction between service consumer and service provider. There is a customer-based relationship for creating long-term business relationships. Accountants, attorneys, and financial advisers maintain long-term relationships with their clients for decades. These repeat consumers refer friends and family, helping to create a client-based relationship.

5.2 Transportation

5.2.1 Modes of Transport

Transportation is the movement of goods and people from place to place communication, the movement of ideas from place to place, is also a type of transportation

From the standpoint of value, there are two types of transportation. The first is economic transportation by which goods and people are carried for the purpose of economic profit. Such transportation is a change in place utility—the value of commodity is worth more after it has been transported from region of production to that of consumption. Transportation accounts for increase in value by moving commodities to location of demand. Non-transportation includes all movements which are carried on for some purpose other than economic profit. Recreational travel and military logistics are two examples.

The significance of transportation in economic geography cannot be overemphasizing. In its own right transportation is an important geographic element—a spatial variable by which regions can be delimited and their characteristics studied and in terms of which relationships can be analyzed, such as relationship among route location, traffic flow and other phenomena. In addition, organized transportation is a geographic factor—an influence on the location of other economic activities. Without means of transport there would be no commercial coal mining, no commercial surplus production and no commercial lumbering or fishing. In fact, without commercial transportation, the world's economy would remain at subsistence level and regional specialization yielding exchangeable surpluses would be impossible.

Transportation involves two aspects: (a) a vehicle or unit of conveyance, and (b) a medium upon which to move. The form of one transport mode differs from that of another because of technological difference between them. The necessary requirements of any mode of transport are: (1) route, (2) vehicle, (3) motive power, and (4) terminal.

Route: All modes of transport require some of route, the way, course or tract on which to operate. Both roads and railways, the basic forms of land transport cannot take place without the construction of suitable routes ways. Rail transport requires a more specific route in the form of special tract and other operational infrastructure like signaling equipments etc. Sea and air transport are free from construction of route ways and can be operated in a natural environment. The inland water transport requires the construction of canals. The construction of pipelines involves heavy initial investment and maintenance.

Vehicle: There is requirement for the conveyance of persons or goods by any means of transport. As a result of man's increased technological knowledge and expertise and his demand for increased speed and improved carrying capacity, there is an ever-increasing complexity in the character of vehicles. The animal driven vehicles are still popular, so is the bicycle. The auto vehicle has now become an internal part of our transport system. The railway locomotive, ships and aero-planes are the principal vehicles serving the entire world community. There is a variation in the carrying capacity of different vehicles.

Motive power: Motive power is necessary to drive the vehicle. There are two main sources of power for transport: coal and oil. The invention of steam engine and harnessing of stream power affect the forms of transport to a great extent. With this development transport became available on a mass basis. The air transport is exclusively based on oil products for their source of power. The use of electric driven engines in railways has enhanced the speed. The cost of motive power is a determining factor for the user. Air transport is the most expensive of all forms of transport.

Terminal: The terminal provides access to the transport route or network. It is also a point to which motion ends. In rail transport, the terminus is the station at the end of the line. For bus, the bus stop is the terminal. The terminals are designed according to the mode of transport, their location, capacity and importance in relation to overall transport network. The sea terminals are very complex. There are ports with their docks, wharves, warehouse, customs offices etc. For air terminals, there are arrangements for the take off and landing of aircraft.

Means and modes of transport: Modes and means are interrelated and integral part of any transport system. Transportation can be classified on the basis of power, route and vehicle. On the basis of power, the significant categories are (i) man and animal power used as a force in transportation, (ii) mechanical power in the form of force driving automobiles, trains, ships, aeroplanes etc., and (iii) physical power like wind or running water facilitating movement of goods. The classification on the basis of nature of routes are (i) the land routes including transportation by path or tract, road, rail and pipeline, (ii) water routes including inland and oceanic routes, and (iii) air routes. Similarly, according to mode of transport, it can be classified into (i) man and animal, (ii) wheeled vehicles driven either by man or animal, (iii) automobiles, (iv) railways, and (v) ship or plane.

Roads: A road is a symbol of motion. In the reconstruction of a region, roads play a positive role. Roads are the veins and arteries of a country through which every improvement circulates. No other form of transport is able to provide such a comprehensive door-to-door or origin to-destination services nor does any other mode have such an extensive route network. Road transport also provides a feeder or connection with other modes. Road transport is important for its flexibility. Motor vehicle can supply services over public highways on even or uneven terrain or on poor roads. Traffic in "small" can be sent daily and easily by road service, for example milk, eggs, vegetables etc. Now every country of the world is having a dense network of roads. The efficiency of a road depends on maintaining a surface on which wheels will run without obstruction. The relative cost of road as compared with rail transport depends on: (i) the length of the haul, (ii) possibility of obtaining return loads, (iii) the liability of the goods carried to damage or pilferage, (iv) the case of commodity to be transported, (v) the volume of traffic offering, and (vi) the service rendered. In the present state of economy, roads are most suitable means of transport.

Railways: Railways are a product of the industrial revolution and afterwards become a predominant mode of inland transport. Railways solved two important needs: (i) the economic carriage by land of materials in bulk and bulky commodities, and (ii) the relatively

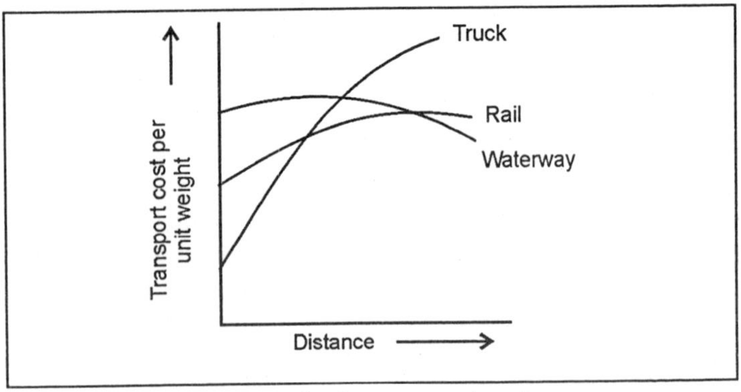

Fig. 5.1: Transport cost curves for three transport modes

rapid movement of large numbers of people and goods. The rails always revolve around its fixed tract. This provides guidance for the wheels and also enables very heavy loads to be carried. There are national and international railways. Some intercontinental railways are also in function. The trains are powered either by diesel oil or electricity. In recent years, in order to achieve increased speeds, a continuous welded tract has replaced the traditional rails. The design of carriage units has promoted a better ride for passengers. The main advantage of rail is the movement heavy, bulky goods, mineral ores etc. Because of heavy capital investment, the railway must be used up to capacity. Capacity depends on a combination of train load, average speed and the frequency of the service.

Ocean Transport: The Sea offers a ready-made carriage way for ships which requires no maintenance. Ships can travel within a limited number of constraints, because of floatability and reduced friction; ocean vessels are capable of carrying far greater loads and weights than can be handled by train. Ships try to keep certain lanes because of (i) physical conditions and (ii) economic considerations. The Suez and Panama canals have revolutionized the pattern of sea trade. The Red-Suez-Mediterranean route has become the most important in the world. Ocean shipping has now become a landmark in heavy load transportation between all parts of the world.

Inland Waterways: Inland movement by water is undertaken by either natural waterways (river) or artificial waterways (canals). Such movement is governed by depth, width and direction of waterways and by such physical impediments as rapids, waterfalls, swiftness of flow and seasonal freezing. The principal disadvantages of inland waterways are: (i) rivers may involve devious journeys and may flow in the wrong direction; (ii) navigable rivers may be interrupted by falls or rapids; (iii) change in river levels and winter freezing may cause discontinued services; and (iv) canal construction involves heavy capital investment and regular maintenance. Six major navigable systems of inland waterways are—the rivers of the western and Central Europe, the Volga-Don system, the North American rivers, the Amazon system, the Panama-Paraguay system and Chinese waterways.

Airways: Air communication belongs to the twentieth century. Air routes are theoretical and aircrafts are not tied to the surface. All transport is controlled by terminals and prevailing weather conditions. Air routes are determined by: (i) adequate ground facilities for operation; and (ii) availability of traffic for economic working. Air transport is still very costly and this limits its use. It is best suited for the carriage of commodities which are low in bulk but high in value. Air services are of two main kinds: (i) short-distance services operating within a country, called domestic service; (ii) long-distance services like trans-continental and trans-oceanic flights, called international services. There is a worldwide network of air routes providing very good and speedy transport services.

Pipelines: A pipeline is a line or conduit of pipe of variable diameter and length and traditionally used for carrying liquid or gas from a point of supply to a point of consumption. The first successful pipeline made of cate iron was laid down in Pennsylvania (USA) in 1865. Total nearly half a million kilometers of oil pipeline exist in the world together with a small distance of natural gas pipeline. Pipelines require maintenance against external rusting and internal corrosion. Pipeline are used for transporting—(i) liquids and gases; (ii) solids in suspension; (iii) solids by pneumatic pressure; and (iv) materials enclosed in capsules.

4.2.2 Transport Cost

In dealing with transport costs distinction must be made between private costs and social costs. Private costs are the costs incurred by the individual or transport operator in providing a particular service. Social costs are the costs imposed on society as a whole through an individual making a trip or transport operator providing a service. These costs are not paid for by the user—social costs are incurred as a result of external effects of the transport activity.

Private transport costs are made up of three elements:

(i) **Track Costs** – of providing and maintaining a surface cover which transport services can operate.

(ii) **Running Costs** – the cost of purchasing, maintaining and operating a vehicle to run on the track surface.

(iii) **Interchange Costs** – the cost of providing facilities at the beginning and completion of a journey.

Categories of Transport Cost

Fixed costs: These cost which are incurred before any traffic at all passes. They include the costs (i) of providing the infrastructure (i.e. the road, the port, or the railway line); (ii) of providing, equipping and staffing the terminal facilities (i.e. bus depots, railway stations or airport); (iii) of providing marginal, administrative and maintenance staff and their offices and workshops. These costs are inescapable because they cannot be avoided except by abandoning the whole operation. They also do not vary with the level of traffic, but remain independent of it. A railway signal-box must be manned (and thus incurs wage costs) whether there is one train or six trains per hour over the line.

Variable costs: These are costs incurred by the actual movement of traffic and they vary with the level of the traffic passing. They include the costs of fuel, crew wages and the maintenance of vehicles, for example, routine inspection of an aircraft after a flight. They are called escapable because they may be avoided or escaped by not running a particular train, suspending a particular flight or a private motorist leaving his car in the garage and walking to the officc/shops.

Terminal cost: Terminal costs are those associated with loading and unloading the commodities and the accompanying paperwork. The terminal costs are both fixed and variable. The proportion of terminal costs in the total costs varies between modes. In road haulage, the terminal costs can be negligible. On the other hand, to send goods by rail may entail conveying them by lorry or truck from factory to goods depot, loading them into wagons and receiving the process at the other end.

Marginal and Average Costs: Marginal cost is the additional cost incurred in order to produce one more unit of output. Marginal cost may be incurred by carrying an extra passenger on a bus with seats to spare or another ton of goods on a half empty lorry or of a wagon on a freight train. It may be even mean allow 25 trains in a day instead of 20. Marginal costs are therefore time linked and it may be of short run or long run nature. It does not represent constant additional total costs. Up to the capacity of the transport unit transport mode (bus, aircraft, train, ship), any further increase in traffic incurs negligible marginal costs. Then there is sharp increase at the point, where a second unit becomes necessary. Marginal costs do vary between modes of transport.

Average costs are obtained by dividing the total costs of the operation by the work done, expressed in terms of passenger-km, ton-km or transport-unit-km. Average costs will of course vary with output, for greater the product the more the fixed costs can be spread.

5.2.3 Comparative Cost Advantage

Two factors influence the rate difference for alternative transport modes—terminal costs and line haul (or over-the-road) costs. These costs of course vary with the type of commodity being moved. But it is also possible to generalize about the level of terminal costs by mode of transportation. Over a short distance, truck transportation of commodities is cheap, and this is reflected in the prices offered to the customer. For longer distance, however, railway transportation comes into its own. In a sense, therefore this cost structure preserves a certain complementarities among the different media, with the trucking companies feeding goods over short distances to railheads where they will be transferred over longer distances for possible oceanic shipment overseas or to another point in the nation.

Line-haul costs, in contrast to terminal cost, vary with distance; but, because of the tapering effect already discussed, they are not linearly related to mileage. Water movement is invariably the least expensive whereas over-the-road operating costs are highest for truck. Once again, rail transport falls in between. Looking at the distance at which each of the three modes are most competitive, it is seen that truck transportation, owing to low terminal costs, is the lowest cost mode at short distances. Beyond certain distances, water is the most economical form of transport and it is, of course, the dominant mode in world trade.

The freight rate is only one factor a shipper must consider in choosing among alternative transport modes. Another equally important factor is service. Transportation service implies a great many things, including speed of delivery, scheduling convenience, avoidance of damage and reliability. The figure below illustrates how four modes, with air cargo now added, stack up, on the average, with respect to speed of service, probably the most important service consideration. Loading time is indicated where the respective meet the vertical axis. The line themselves show total delivery time as it increases over distance. Loading times is highest for ocean shipping, followed by rail, air and truck. Movement time as opposed to loading time, naturally favours air by a sizable margin. Water and rail again are slow in moving freight whereas truck services, by contrast, fast.

5.2.4 Concept of Connectivity and Its Measurement Procedure

"The connectivity of a network may be defined as the degree of completeness of the links between nodes" (Robinson and Bamford, 1978). It is indicative of the complexity of the spatial order that imposes on the region it serves. The greater the degree of connectivity, the more efficient is the network system.

K.J. Kansky (1963) has studied the structure of transportation networks, developed several descriptive indices for measuring the connectivity of networks, i.e., Alpha, Beta, Gamma indices and Cyclomatic Number.

Alpha Index (α) = (Actual Circuits/Maximum Circuits) or

$$\alpha = (e - v + 1)/(2v - 5)$$

[e = number of nodes and v = maximum number of linkage]

Beta Index (β) = (Arcs/Nodes) or $\beta = (e/v)$

Gamma Index (γ) = $e/(3\ (v - 2))$

Cyclomatic Number (μ) = $e - v + p$

where

e = number of edges or arcs,

v = number of vertices or nodes,

p = Number of non-connected sub graphs (see Fig. 5.2).

5.2.5 Accessibility

One of the most important attributes of a transportation network is accessibility, and the geographers are particularly concerned with accessibility as a locational feature. Accessibility is the case of movement among the nodes or points on the network. Several methods have been used to measure or to represent the accessibility. The traditional method is to measure the distance along the routes or from centres. Thus, an area adjoining to a routes or centres is more accessible or inaccessibility increases with the distance from the routes or centres. Within a network, accessibility can be measured in three ways—(i) by shortest path matrix; (ii) by the associated number; and (iii) by the Shimbel Index.

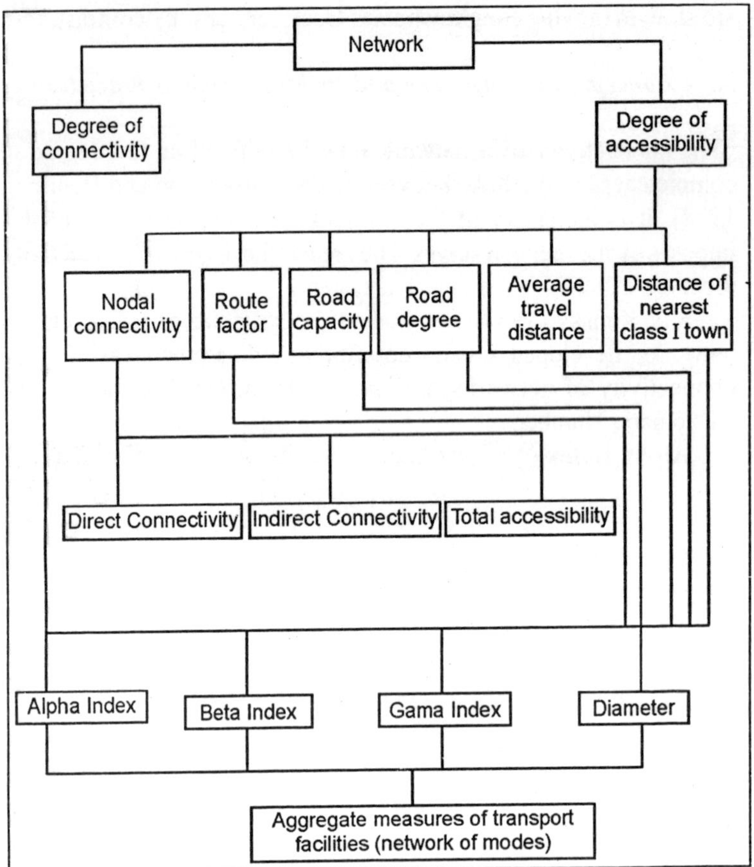

Fig. 5.2: Network graph

5.3 Market-Network Linkage

5.3.1 Concept of Market and Market Centre

Marketing is the process of communicating the value of a product or service to customers, for the purpose of selling that product or service.

Marketing techniques include choosing target markets through market analysis and market segmentation, as well as understanding consumer behaviour and advertising a product's value to the customer. From a societal point of view, marketing is the link between a society's material requirements and its economic patterns of response. Marketing satisfies these needs and wants through exchange processes and building long term relationships. Marketing blends art and applied science (such as behavioural sciences) and makes use of information technology.

Plate 7: Market Square in USA

After World War II, the variety of products increased and hard selling no longer could be relied upon to generate sales. With increased discretionary income, customers could afford to be selective and buy only those products that precisely met their changing needs, and these needs were not immediately obvious. The key questions became:

- What do customers want?
- Can we develop it while they still want it?
- How can we keep our customers satisfied?

In response to these discerning customers, firms began to adopt the marketing concept, which involves:

- Focusing on customer needs before developing the product.

- Aligning all functions of the company to focus on those needs.
- Realizing a profit by successfully satisfying customer needs over the long-term.

When firms first began to adopt the marketing concept, it was space from where commodity communication would be done; they typically set up separate marketing departments whose objective was to satisfy customer needs. Often these departments were sales departments with expanded responsibilities. While this expanded sales department structure can be found in some companies today, many firms have structured themselves into marketing organizations having a company-wide customer focus. Since the entire organization exists to satisfy customer needs, nobody can neglect a customer issue by declaring it a "marketing problem" everybody must be concerned with customer satisfaction. The marketing concept relies upon marketing research to define market segments, their size, and their needs.

Recent approaches in marketing include relationship marketing with focus on the customer, business marketing or industrial marketing with focus on an organization or institution and social marketing with focus on benefits to society. New forms of marketing also use the internet and are therefore called internet marketing or more generally e-marketing, online marketing, "digital marketing", search engine marketing, or desktop advertising. It attempts to perfect the segmentation strategy used in traditional marketing. It targets its audience more precisely, and is sometimes called personalized marketing or one-to-one marketing. Internet marketing is sometimes considered to be broad in scope, because it not only refers to marketing on the Internet, but also includes marketing done via e-mail, wireless media as well as driving audience from traditional marketing methods like radio and billboard to internet properties or landing page.

Now the concept of market centre has been changing; from space reality to it has arrived virtual world. One man can easily marketing through online via different agencies viz. amazon.com, snapdeal.com

5.3.2 Periodic-Daily Marketing

Periodic marketing concept coming from rural area marketing namely as 'Hat'; still so many underdeveloped areas in rural India it should be noticed. Due to increasing of population, daily goods demand is also increasing; gradually daily market centres ('Bazar' as called in rural area), has developed. Not only increasing population; annual income, and improved road network also help to emerging daily market centres.

Plate 8: Rural daily market

5.3.3 Retailing

Retailing is a distribution channel function where one organization buys products from supplying firms or manufacturers product themselves, and then sells these directly to consumers. There are many ways. Retailers can be categorized depending on the characteristics of evaluatation. For our purposes we will separate retailers based on six factors directly related to major marketing decisions:

- Target Markets Served
- Product Offerings
- Pricing Structure
- Promotional Emphasis
- Distribution Method
- Service Level

and one operational factor:

- Ownership Structure

However, these groups are not meant to be mutually exclusive. In fact, as we will see in some way all retailers can be placed into each category.

Plate 9: A Retailer

Retail Categories

Target Based Served: The first classification looks at the type of markets a retailer intends to target. These categories are identical to the classification scheme we saw in the Distribution Decisions tutorial when we discussed the levels of distribution coverage.

- **Mass Market:** Mass market retailers appeal to the largest market possible by selling products of interest to nearly all consumers. With such a large market from which to draw customers, the competition among these retailers is often fierce.
- **Speciality Market:** Retailers categorized as servicing the speciality market are likely to target buyers looking for products having certain features that go beyond mass marketed products, such as customers who require more advanced product options or higher level of customer service. While not as large as the mass market, the target market serviced by speciality retailers can be sizable.

- **Exclusive Market:** Appealing to this market means appealing to discriminating customers who are often willing to pay a premium for features found in very few products and for highly personalized services. Since this target market is small, the number of retailers addressing this market within a given geographic area may also be small.

Product Offerings: Under this classification retailers are divided based on the width (i.e., number of different product lines) and depth (i.e., number of different products within a product line) of the products they carry.

- **General Merchandisers:** These retailers carry a wide range of product categories (i.e., broad width) though the number of different items within a particular product line is generally limited (i.e., shallow depth).
- **Multiple Lines Speciality Merchandisers:** Retailers classified in this category stock a limited number of product lines (i.e., narrow width) but within the categories they handle they often offer a greater selection (i.e., extended depth) than are offered by general merchandisers. For example, a consumer electronics retailer would fall into this category.
- **Single Line Merchandisers:** Some retailers limit their offerings to just one product line (i.e., very narrow width), and sometimes only one product (i.e., very shallow depth). This can be seen online where a relatively small website may sell a single product such as computer gaming software. Another example may be a small jewelry store that only handles watches.

Pricing Strategy: Retailers can be classified based on their general pricing strategy. Retailers must decide whether their approach is to use price as a competitive advantage or to seek competitive advantage in non-price ways.

- **Discount Pricing:** Discount retailers are best known for selling low priced products that have a low profit margin (i.e., price minus cost). To make profits these retailers look to sell in high volume. Typically discount retailers operate with low overhead costs by vigorously controlling operational spending on such things as real estate, design issues (e.g., store layout, website presentation), and by offering fewer services to their customers.

- **Competitive Pricing:** The objective of some retailers is not to compete on price but alternatively not to be seen as charging the highest price. These retailers, who often operate in speciality markets, aggressively monitor the market to insure their pricing is competitive but they do not desire to get into price wars with discount retailers. Thus, other elements of the marketing mix (e.g., higher quality products, nicer store setting) are used to create higher value for which the customer will pay more.
- **Full Price Pricing:** Retailers targeting exclusive markets find such markets which are far less price sensitive than mass or speciality markets. In these cases, the additional value added through increased operational spending (e.g., expensive locations, more attractive design, more services) justify higher retail prices. While these retailers are likely to sell in lower volume than discount or competitive pricing retailers, the profit margins for each product are much higher.

Promotional Focus: Retailers generate customer interest using a variety of promotional technique, yet some retailers rely on certain methods more than others as their principle promotional approach.

- **Advertising:** Many retailers find traditional mass promotional methods of advertising, such as through newspapers or television, continue to be their best means for creating customer interest. Retailers selling online rely mostly on Internet advertising as their promotional method of choice.
- **Direct Mail:** A particular form of advertising that many retailers use for the bulk of their promotion is direct mail advertising through postal mail. Using direct mail for promotion is the primary way catalog retailers distribute their materials and is often utilized by smaller local companies who promote using postcard mailings.

- **Personal Selling:** Retailers selling expensive or high-end products find a considerable amount of their promotional effort is spent in person-to-person contact with customers. While many of these retailers use other promotional methods, in particular advertising, the consumer-salesperson relationship is key to persuading consumers to make purchase decisions.

Distribution Method: Retailers sell in many different formats with some requiring consumers visit a physical location while others sell to customers in a virtual space. It should be noted that many retailers are not tied to a single distribution method but operate using multiple methods.

- **Store-Based Sellers:** By far the predominant method consumers use to obtain products is to acquire these by physically visiting retail outlets. Store outlets can be further divided into several categories. One key characteristic that distinguishes categories is whether retail outlets are physically connected to one or more other stores:
  - **Stand-Alone:** These are retail outlets that do not have other retail outlets connected.
  - **Strip-Shopping Centre:** A retail arrangement with two or more outlets physically connected or that share physical resources (e.g., share parking lot).
  - **Shopping Area:** A local centre of retail operations containing many retail outlets that may or may not be physically connected but are in close proximity to each other such as a city shopping district.
  - **Regional Shopping Mall:** Consists of a large self-contained shopping area with many connected outlets.
- **Non-Store Sellers:** A fast growing method used by retailers to sell products is through methods that do not have customers physically visiting a retail outlet. In fact, in many cases customers make their purchase from within their own homes.
  - **Online Sellers:** The fastest growing retail distribution method allows consumer to purchase products via the Internet. In most cases delivery is then handled by a third party shipping service.

- **Direct Marketers:** Retailers that are principally selling via direct methods may have a primary location that receives orders but does not host shopping visits. Rather, orders are received via mail or phone.
- **Vending:** While purchasing through vending machines does require the consumer to physically visit a location, this type of retailing is considered as non-store retailing as the vending operations are not located at the vending company's place of business.

Service Level: Retailers attract customers not only with desirable products and affordable prices, but also by offering services that enhance the purchase experience. There are at least three levels of retail service:

- **Self-Service:** This service level allows consumers to perform most or all of the services associated with retail purchasing. For some consumers self-service is considered a benefit while others may view it as an inconvenience. Self-service can be seen with: (1) self-selection services, such as online purchasing and vending machine purchases, and (2) self-checkout services where the consumer may get help selecting the product but they use self-checkout stations to process the purchase including scanning and payment.
- **Assorted-Service:** The majority of retailers offer some level of service to consumers. Service includes handling the point-of-purchase transaction, product selection assistance; arrange payment plans, offer delivery and many more.
- **Full-Service:** The full-service retailer attempts to handle nearly all aspects of the purchase to the point where all the consumer does is to select the item they wish to purchase. Retailers that follow a full-price strategy often follow the full-service approach as a way of adding value to a customer's purchase.

Ownership Structure: Finally, we can categorize retailers based on the ownership structure of the business:

- **Individually Owned and Operated:** Under this ownership structure an individual or corporate entity owns and operates one or a very small number of outlets. Single ownership of retail outlets most frequently occurs with small retail stores, though there are some cases, for instance in the automotive or furniture industries, where single ownership involves very large outlets.
- **Corporate Chain:** A retail chain consists of multiple retail outlets owned and operated by a single entity all performing similar retail activities. While the number of retail outlets required to be classified as a chain has never been specified, we will assume that anyone owning more than five retail locations would be considered a chain.
- **Corporate Structure:** This classification covers large retailers predominantly operating in the non-store retail arena such as online, catalogue and vending.
- **Contractually Licensed and Individually Operated:** The contractual channel arrangement discussed in the distribution decisions tutorial has lead to a retail ownership structure in which operators of the retail outlet are not the out-right owners of the business. Instead, the arrangement often involves a legal agreement in which the owner of the retail concept allows the operator to run the owner's business concept in exchange for financial considerations such as a percentage of revenue. This structure is most often seen in retail franchising.

5.3.4 Wholesale Marketing

The consumption and production of marketed food are spatially separated. Production is primarily in rural areas while consumption is in urban areas. Agricultural marketing is the process that overcomes this separation, allowing produce to be moved from an area of surplus to one of need. Food reaches the consumer by a complex network, involving production, assembly, sorting, packing, reassembly, distribution and retail stages. In developing countries, the linkage between the producer and the retailer is still usually provided by assembly and wholesale markets, where wholesale marketing takes place using a variety of transaction methods. The growth of supermarkets in many regions has seen the development of direct marketing and a reduced role for wholesale systems.

Secondary wholesale markets are generally found only in developing countries these days. They are located in district or regional cities and take the bulk of their produce from rural assembly markets located in production areas, where the transactions are small scale and usually take place between farmers and traders. The distinction between rural assembly markets and secondary wholesale markets is that secondary wholesale markets are in permanent operation (rather than being seasonal in nature or dealing in specialized produce), larger volumes of produce are traded than at the rural assembly markets and specialized functions may be present, such as commission agents and brokers. Wholesaling include all the activity involved in selling goods and services to those buying for resale or business use. Firms engaged primarily in wholesaling are called wholesalers.

Types of wholesalers:

1. Merchant wholesalers
2. Agents
3. Brokers

1. Merchant wholesalers are the largest single group of wholesalers, accounting for roughly 50 per cent of all wholesaling. Merchant wholesalers include two broad types: full-service wholesalers and limited-service wholesalers.
2. Brokers and agents differ from merchant wholesalers in two ways: They do not take title to goods and they perform few functions like merchant wholesalers, they generally specialize by product line or customer type. A broker brings buyers and sellers together and assists in negotiation. Agents represent buyers or sellers on a more permanent basis.

Terminal wholesale markets are located in major metropolitan areas, where produce is finally channeled to consumers through trade between wholesalers and retailers, caterers, etc. Produce may also be assembled for export. In some countries, such as India and China, terminal markets also supply other parts of the country. For example,

New Delhi serves as a distribution centre to the south of India for apples grown in the Himalayan foothills. The problems of terminal wholesale markets are usually ones of congestion caused by an unsuitable location or by an inappropriate mixture of wholesale and retail functions. Traditionally, wholesale markets were built adjacent to city centres, located at a focal point of the inter-city transport facilities and close to the main retailing areas. Population growth, changes in urban land-use patterns and the development of modern transport systems have all influenced the suitability and functionality of existing sites.

Wholesaling facilitates the economic function of buying and selling (usually termed as "price formation") by allowing the forces of supply and demand to converge to establish a single price for a commodity. The wholesaler may also perform storage and warehousing functions, as well as allowing economies of scale to be obtained in the transportation of produce from farm to market. The people involved in wholesaling can act simply as merchants, buying and selling produce, can be brokers dealing in orders rather than goods, or can be commission agents. Prices are normally established by negotiation but some wholesale markets use the auction system. The auction is compulsory in all wholesale markets in big cities in Japan. A comparison of the Japanese system with that in Brisbane, Australia, found that prices moved more frequently and with a greater degree of volatility in Japan than those at Brisbane.

Development of Wholesale Market: Wholesale markets develop in a number of stages. They start as general markets, and then become more specialized by trading in specific types of product. A later stage is to transact only graded and well packaged product. A recent trend in Western Europe and the USA is for large retailers to by-pass the wholesale market system. Direct links are created between producers and supermarket chains, often by means of contract farming arrangements or through the use of preferred suppliers. Following the collapse of the iron curtain, a large number of markets were developed in Eastern and Central Europe in the 1990s and early 2000s. Examples include markets in Warsaw, Gdansk, Budapest, and Bucharest. In other parts of the world, new markets have been built in Amman, Cairo and Mumbai, among many recent developments. Very few new wholesale markets have been built in western countries in the last decades, although old markets have been relocated to new sites (e.g. the new Covent Garden Market relocated to Nine Elms in London and Rome's new wholesale market, relocated from the centre to the east of the city). Those that already exist have tended to also attract warehouses for integrated food distribution, changing their role to "food centres" (in the USA) and including other non-fresh food products. Wholesale markets still have a role in the marketing of horticultural produce but the traditional fresh meat and fish wholesale markets, particularly those dealing with wholesale live produce, are generally being closed down in major urban centres. In developing countries, changes in work patterns, particularly the employment of women, and the impact of technological innovations in post-harvest handling, food processing and storage, including the use of domestic refrigerators, tends to encourage the development of one-stop shopping at supermarkets, often on a once-a-week basis. The challenge for wholesale markets in such a trading environment is to retain turnover, both by providing new services to supermarkets and by developing services to the non-supermarket trade and the growing hotel and catering sectors.

Plate 10: Wholesale market—Rural and Urban

5.3.5 Labour Market Mobility

Links between geographic and labour market mobility can be very complex, both on the level of the individual and society at large. From an economic point of view, geographic mobility is frequently put forward as a precondition for successful labour market integration of individuals. Possible advantages of geographic mobility are: enhancement of employment opportunities, higher economic well-being, or last but not least the prevention of unemployment. However, not everybody can make use of these options and some people, particularly families, may be more inclined to have combined trajectories of labour market and geographic mobility than others. From a social point of view, a geographic move can be a precondition for a better job and consequently lead to a higher motivation and job satisfaction on the level of the individual. Also, it can prevent social exclusion caused by unemployment. Possible negative effects are the loss of social networks, which may lead to the necessity to purchase certain services, such as care for elderly relatives, or own children on the market. This in turn will increase organization costs for buying such services on the market, which were previously organized within the wider family or social network. Difficulties to coordinate employment careers of spouses may imply a negative impact on the work life balance of all household members. On the level of society at large the optimal matching between job openings and accordingly qualified people searching for a job is an important element of sustainable growth. But the combination of geographic and labour market mobility can also lead to selective migration of youth and brain drain (meritorious people permanently move towards abroad for education or better opportunity for job). A necessary precondition for the optimal matching between vacancies and labour force, however, is people's willingness to be mobile between jobs and between regions, within a country or national borders of member states. Job mobility and even broader labour market mobility belong to the major ways to overcome gender segregation. Concerning the gender issue regional context and restricted job search processes due to regional immobility are crucial to derive. Several forms of selectivity occur in the decision-making process for or against labour market and geographic mobility, e.g., selectivity by age or birth cohorts, selectivity according to the level of education, as well as marital and/or labour market status. However, the interrelation between geographic and labour market mobility has so far received little attention as a special focus.

The Willingness to Move in Case of Unemployment

Most economic theories of labour market processes assume that people are ready to move to where the jobs are. The low skilled and/ or lower income groups of society, a lack of resources may inhibit an otherwise gainful move to re-enter employment. These persons are at risk of becoming 'locked in' in an immobile situation respectively a region. In structurally weak regions with high unemployment rates people tend to substitute a lack of mobile resources, such as capital, with immobile resources such as the provision of resources within informal networks. Home ownership also strongly ties persons to a location, if real estate prices are very low and the rent in a different area is not affordable. Frequent job hoppers are also likely to move to new places more often. Imperfect capital markets, as in the case of inflexible transfer possibilities of mortgages work as an impediment to geographic mobility. Hence, inflexible capital markets may contribute to the polarization of society into two groups. The highly mobile persons in all forms of mobility on the one side, as opposed to the 'bounded rational' movers, who find it difficult to organize one or the other type of mobility on the other side. In this sense, the term interregional geographic mobility can imply either a residential move or an increase in the commuting time. By selecting at least another region as the minimum distance of the previous job, a considerable change in geographic mobility. Labour market mobility implies a mutually reinforcing effect, which can lead to the accumulation of inequality over the life course for persons, who do not have the initial resources or (language) skills to be more mobile. The probability to have experienced a geographic move at the last job change is higher for men and increases with both educational level as well as education abroad. Job security and housing security as well as flexibilities in both areas seem to be linked to each other. In a wider sense living and working conditions are closely linked to job and geographic mobility and studying one without due recognition of the processes in the other field might yield suboptimal outcomes.

5.4 Trade—An Engine to Growth

The positive impact of national and international trade on economic growth has been widely documented from both a theoretical and empirical point of view. To this respect, it has been argued that openness is important for growth because it generates channels for technology diffusion, which makes possible for less developed countries to import productivity gains from overseas. The literature on trade and growth has paid special attention to technological spillovers as channels of diffusion. Developing countries learn from imported technology and also from technological progress embodied in imported goods. This learning increases domestic stock of knowledge and, hence, domestic productivity and growth. Thus, one could argue that the greater the trade volume (imports and exports) is, the more knowledge can be potentially accumulated. However, the access to lower prices may also constitute a way of importing foreign productivity gains. Technological progress makes possible to produce goods of increasing quality at each time lower costs. Thus, there is also a trade benefit from having access to more productive intermediate and capital goods at a lower cost than their opportunity cost. Therefore, international trade can potentially play a crucial role in fueling economic growth of less developed countries. In other words, it can become one of the engines of growth for a country. But, going a step further might a stagnant economy import sustained growth by trading? An affirmative answer would be an argument in favour of views on trade as a way to escape from poverty. If this is the case, what are the mechanisms through which trade could transmit sustained growth? The above discussion seems to suggest that trade could operate via trade volume and/or via prices, even in absence of diminishing returns in production and technological spillovers, trade leads to a stable world income distribution. This is because countries that accumulate capital faster than the world average undergo declining terms of trade, which restrains incentives for further accumulation. At long-run, the terms of trade become constant and countries grow at the same rate. Though they were not directly interested with the transmission of sustained growth through trade, their model also has the implication that trade can emerge as an engine of growth for stagnant economies. Diewert and Morrison (1986) aimed at developing an empirical method for properly measuring the contribution of factor inputs to output growth of open economies. They proved, with an empirical model based on index numbers. As indicated at the beginning of this section, the casuality going from trade to growth is a well-established empirical result. Ekholm and Södersten (2002) emphasized the importance of considering income-terms of trade when analyzing the relationship between trade and growth. Regarding the second mechanism of transmission, the growth regressions by Barro (1991) showed that the economic growth is significantly positively related to the terms of trade.

5.5 Economies of Global Trade

5.5.1 Balance of Payment (BoP)

The International Monetary Fund (IMF) use a particular set of definitions for the BoP accounts, which is also used by the Organisation for Economic Co-operation and Development (OECD), and the United Nations System of National Accounts (SNA). The main difference in the IMF's terminology is that it uses the term "financial account" to capture transactions that would under alternative definitions be recorded in the capital account. The IMF uses the term capital account to designate a subset of transactions that, according to other usage, form a small part of the overall capital account. The IMF separates these transactions out to form an additional top level division of the BoP accounts. Expressed with the IMF definition, the BoP identity can be written:

The IMF uses the term current account with the same meaning as that used by other organizations, although it has its own names for its three leading sub-divisions, which are:

- The goods and services account (the overall trade balance).
- The primary income account (factor income such as from loans and investments).
- The secondary income account (transfer payments).

On general viewpoint, the balance of payments (BoP or BOP) of a country is the record of all economic transactions between the residents of a country and the rest of the world in a particular period (over a quarter of a year or more commonly over a year). These transactions are made by individuals, firms and government bodies. Thus the balance of payments includes all external visible and non-visible transactions of a country during a given period, usually a year.

It represents a summation of country's current demand and supply of the claims on foreign currencies and of foreign claims on its currency.

Balance of payments accounts are an accounting record of all monetary transactions between a country and the rest of the world. These transactions include payments for the country's exports and imports of goods, services, financial capital, and financial transfers. The BOP accounts summarize international transactions for a specific period, usually a year, and are prepared in a single currency, typically the domestic currency for the country concerned. Sources of funds for a nation, such as exports or the receipts of loans and investments, are recorded as positive or surplus items. Uses of funds, such as for imports or to invest in foreign countries, are recorded as negative or deficit items. When all components of the BoP accounts are included they must sum to zero with no overall surplus or deficit. For example, if a country is importing more than it exports, its trade balance will be in deficit, but the shortfall will have to be counterbalanced in other ways such as by funds earned from its foreign investments, by running down central bank reserves or by receiving loans from other countries.

While the overall BoP accounts will always balance when all types of payments are included, imbalances are possible on individual elements of the BoP, such as the current account, the capital account excluding the central bank's reserve account, or the sum of the two. Imbalances in the latter sum can result in surplus countries accumulating wealth, while deficit nations become increasingly indebted. The term balance of payments often refers to this sum: a country's balance of payments is said to be in surplus (equivalently, the balance of payments is positive) by a specific amount if sources of funds (such as export goods sold and bonds sold) exceed uses of funds (such as paying for imported goods and paying for foreign bonds purchased) by that amount. There is said to be a balance of payments deficit (the balance of payments is said to be negative) if the former are less than the latter. A BoP surplus (or deficit) is accompanied by an accumulation (or de-accumulation) of foreign exchange reserves by the central bank.

Under a fixed exchange rate system, the central bank accommodates those flows by buying up any net inflow of funds into the country or by providing foreign currency funds to the foreign exchange market to match any international outflow of funds, thus preventing the funds flows from affecting the exchange rate between the country's currency and other currencies. Then the net change per year in the central bank's foreign exchange reserves is sometimes called the balance of payments surplus or deficit. Alternatives to a fixed exchange rate system include a managed float where some changes of exchange rates are allowed, or at the other extreme a purely floating exchange rate (also known as a purely flexible exchange rate). With a pure float the central bank does not intervene at all to protect or devalue its currency, allowing the rate to be set by the market, and the central bank's foreign exchange reserves do not change, and the balance of payments is always zero.

Components of BoP: The current account shows the net amount a country is earning if it is in surplus, or spending if it is in deficit. It is the sum of the balance of trade (net earnings on exports minus payments for imports), factor income (earnings on foreign investments minus payments made to foreign investors) and cash transfers. It is called the current account as it covers transactions in the "here and now"—those that don't give rise to future claims.

The Capital Account records the net change in ownership of foreign assets. It includes the reserve account (the foreign exchange market operations of a nation's central bank), along with loans and investments between the country and the rest of world (but not the future regular repayments/dividends that the loans and investments yield; those are earnings and will be recorded in the current account). The term "capital account" is also used in the narrower sense that excludes central bank foreign exchange market operations: Sometimes the reserve account is classified as "below the line" and so not reported as part of the capital account.

Expressed with the broader meaning for the capital account, the BOP identity states that any current account surplus will be balanced by a capital account deficit of equal size or alternatively a current account deficit will be balanced by a corresponding capital account surplus.

The balancing item, which may be positive or negative, is simply an amount that accounts for any statistical errors and assures that the current and capital accounts sum to zero. By the principles of double entry accounting, an entry in the current account gives rise to an entry in the capital account, and in aggregate the two accounts automatically balance. A balance isn't always reflected in reported figures for the current and capital accounts, which might, for example, report a surplus for both accounts, but when this happens it always means something has been missed most commonly, the operations of the country's central bank and what has been missed is recorded in the statistical discrepancy term (the balancing item).

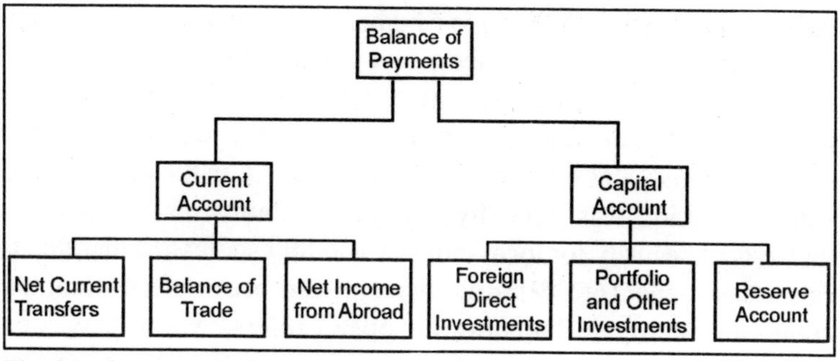

Fig. 5.3: Components of Balance of Payment

An actual balance sheet will typically have numerous sub-headings under the principal divisions. For example, entries under Current account might include:

- Trade–buying and selling of goods and services
  - Exports – a credit entry
  - Imports – a debit entry
    - Trade balance – the sum of Exports and Imports
- Factor income – repayments and dividends from loans and investments
  - Factor earnings – a credit entry
  - Factor payments – a debit entry
    - Factor income balance – the sum of earnings and payments.

Especially in older balance sheets, a common division was between visible and invisible entries. Visible trade recorded imports and exports of physical goods (entries for trade in physical goods excluding services is now often called the merchandise balance). Invisible trade would record international buying and selling of services, and sometimes would be grouped with transfer and factor income as invisible earnings.

History of Balance of Payments Issues

Historically, accurate balance of payments figures were not generally available. However, this did not prevent a number of switches in opinion on questions relating to whether or not a nation's government should use policy to encourage a favourable balance.

Pre-1820: Mercantilism: Until the early 19th century, international trade was generally very small in comparison with national output, and was often heavily regulated. In the middle Ages, European trade was typically regulated at municipal level in the interests of security for local industry and for established merchants. From about the 16th century, mercantilism became the dominant economic theory influencing European rulers, which saw local regulation replaced by national rules aiming to harness the countries' economic output. Measures to promote a trade surplus such as tariffs were generally favoured. Power was associated with wealth, and with low levels of growth, nations were best able to accumulate funds either by running trade surpluses or by forcefully confiscating the wealth of others. Rulers sometimes strove to have their countries outsell competitors and so build up a "war chest" of gold.

This era saw low levels of economic growth; average global per capita income is not considered to have significantly risen in the whole 800 years leading up to 1820, and is estimated to have increased on average by less than 0.1 per cent per year between 1700 and 1820. With very low levels of financial integration between nations and with international trade generally making up a low proportion of individual nations' GDP, BOP crises were very rare.

1820–1914: Free Trade: Gold was the primary reserve asset during the gold standard era. From the late 18th century, mercantilism was challenged by the ideas of Adam Smith and other economic thinkers favouring free trade. After victory in the Napoleonic wars Great Britain began promoting free trade, unilaterally reducing her trade tariffs. Hoarding of gold was no longer encouraged, and in fact Britain exported more capital as a percentage of her national income than any other creditor nation has since. Great Britain's capital exports further helped to correct global imbalances as they tended to be counter-cyclical, rising when Britain's economy went into recession, thus compensating other states for income lost from export of goods.

According to historian Carroll Quigley, Great Britain could afford to act benevolently in the 19th century due to the advantages of her geographical location, its naval power and economic ascendancy as the first nation to enjoy an industrial revolution. A view advanced by economists such as Barry Eichengreen is that the first age of Globalization began with the laying of transatlantic cables in the 1860s, which facilitated a rapid increase in the already growing trade between Britain and America.

Though Current Account controls were still widely used (in fact all industrial nations apart from Great Britain and the Netherlands actually increased their tariffs and quotas in the decades leading up to 1914, though this was motivated more by a desire to protect "infant industries" than to encourage a trade surplus, capital controls were largely absent, and people were generally free to cross international borders without requiring passports.

A gold standard enjoyed wide international participation especially from 1870, further contributing to close economic integration between nations. The period saw substantial global growth, in particular for the volume of international trade which grew tenfold between 1820 and 1870 and then by about 4 per cent annually from 1870 to 1914. BOP crises began to occur, though less frequently than was to be the case for the remainder of the 20th century. From 1880 to 1914, there were approximately 8 BOP crises and 8 twin crises—a twin crises being a BOP crises that coincides with a banking crises.

1914–1945: De-globalization: The favourable economic conditions that had prevailed up until 1914 were shattered by the First World War, and efforts to re-establish them in the 1920s were not successful. Several countries rejoined the gold standard around 1925. But surplus countries didn't "play by the rules", sterilising gold inflows to a much greater degree than had been the case in the pre-war period. Deficit nations such as Great Britain found it harder to adjust by deflation as workers were more enfranchised and unions in particular were able to resist downwards pressure on wages. During the Great Depression most countries abandoned the gold standard, but imbalances remained an issue and international trade declined sharply. There was a return to mercantilist type "beggar thy neighbour" policies, with countries competitively devaluing their exchange rates, thus effectively competing to export unemployment. There were approximately 16 BOP crises and 15 twin crises (and a comparatively very high level of banking crises.)

1945–1971: Bretton Woods: Following World War II, the Bretton Woods institutions (the International Monetary Fund and World Bank) were set up to support an international monetary system designed to encourage free trade while also offering states options to correct imbalances without having to deflate their economies. Fixed but flexible exchange rates were established, with the system anchored by the dollar which alone remained convertible into gold. The Bretton Woods system ushered in a period of high global growth, known as the Golden Age of Capitalism, however it came under pressure due to the inability or unwillingness of governments to maintain effective capital controls and due to instabilities related to the central role of the dollar.

Imbalances caused gold to flow out of the US and a loss of confidence in the United States ability to supply gold for all future claims by dollar holders resulted in escalating demands to convert dollars, ultimately causing the US to end the convertibility of the dollar into gold, thus ending the Bretton Woods system. The 1945-71 era saw approximately 24 BOP crises and no twin crises for advanced economies, with emerging economies seeing 16 BOP crises and just one twin crises.

1971–2009: Transition, Washington Consensus, Bretton Woods II: Manmohan Singh, Former PM of India, showed that the challenges caused by imbalances can be an opportunity when he led his country's successful economic reform programme after the 1991 crisis. The Bretton Woods system came to an end between 1971 and 1973. There were attempts to repair the system of fixed exchange rates over the next few years, but these were soon abandoned, as were determined efforts for the U.S. to avoid BOP imbalances. Part of the reason was displacement of the previous dominant economic paradigm 'Keynesianism' by the Washington Consensus, with economists and economics writers such as Murray Rothbard and Milton Friedman arguing that there was no great need to be concerned about BOP issues.

In the immediate aftermath of the Bretton Woods collapse, countries generally tried to retain some control over their exchange rate by independently managing it, or by intervening in the foreign exchange market as part of a regional bloc. From the mid-1970s however, and especially in the 1980s and early 1990s, many other countries followed the US in liberalizing controls on both their capital and current accounts, in adopting a somewhat relaxed attitude to their balance of payments and in allowing the value of their currency to float relatively freely with exchange rates determined mostly by the market. Developing countries who chose to allow the market to determine their exchange rates would often develop sizeable current account deficits, financed by capital account inflows such as loans and investments, though this often ended in crises when investors lost confidence. The frequency of crises was especially high for developing economies in this era—from 1973 to 1997 emerging economies suffered 57 BOP crises and 21 twin crises. Typically but not always, the panic among foreign creditors and investors that preceded the crises in this period was usually triggered by concerns over excess borrowing by the private sector, rather than by a government deficit. For advanced economies, there were 30 BOP crises and 6 banking crises.

A turning point was the 1997 Asian BOP Crisis, where unsympathetic responses by western powers caused policy-makers in emerging economies to re-assess the wisdom of relying on the free market; by 1999 the developing world as a whole stopped running current account deficits while the U.S. current account deficit began to rise sharply. This new form of imbalance began to develop in part due to the increasing practice of emerging economies, principally China, in pegging their currency against the dollar, rather than allowing the value to freely float. The resulting state of affairs has been referred to as Bretton Woods II. According to Alaistair Chan, "At the heart of the imbalance is China's desire to keep the value of the Yuan stable against the dollar. Usually, a rising trade surplus leads to a rising value of the currency. A rising currency would make exports more expensive, imports less so, and push the trade surplus towards balance. China circumvents the process by intervening in exchange markets and keeping the value of the Yuan depressed." According to economics writer Martin Wolf, in the eight years leading up to 2007, "three-quarters of the foreign currency reserves accumulated since the beginning of time have been piled up". In contrast to the changed approach within the emerging economies, US policy-makers and economists remained relatively unconcerned about BOP imbalances. During mid-1990s, many free market economists and policy-makers such as U.S. Treasury Secretary Paul O'Neill and Fed Chairman Alan Greenspan went on record suggesting the growing US deficit was not a major concern. While several emerging economies had intervening to boost their reserves and assist their exporters from the late 1980s, they only began running a net current account surplus after 1999. This was mirrored in the faster growth for the US current account deficit from the same year, with surpluses, deficits and the associated build-up of reserves by the surplus countries reaching record levels by the early 2000s and growing year by year. Some economists such as Kenneth Rogoff and Maurice Obstfeld began warning that the record imbalances would soon need to be addressed from as early as 2001, joined by Nouriel Roubini in 2004, but it was not until about 2007 that their concerns began to be accepted by the majority of economists.

2009 and later: post-Washington Consensus: Speaking after the 2009 G-20 London summit, Gordon Brown announced "the Washington Consensus is over". There is now broad agreement that large imbalances between different countries do matter; for example mainstream U.S. economist C. Fred Bergsten has argued the U.S. deficit and the associated large inbound capital flows into the U.S. was one of the causes of the financial crisis of 2007–2010. Since the crisis, government intervention in BOP areas such as the imposition of capital controls or foreign exchange market intervention has become more common and in general attracts less disapproval from economists, international institutions like the IMF and other governments.

In 2007, when the crises began, the global total of yearly BOP imbalances was $ 1680 billion. On the credit side, the biggest current account surplus was China with approx. $ 362 billion, followed by Japan at $ 213 billion and Germany at £ 185 billion, with oil producing countries such as Saudi Arabia also having large surpluses. On the debit side, the US had the biggest current account deficit at over $ 1100 billion, with the UK, Spain and Australia together accounting for close to a further $ 300 billion.

While there have been warnings of future cuts in public spending, deficit countries on the whole did not make these in 2009, in fact the opposite happened with increased public spending contributing to recovery as part of global efforts to increase demand. The emphasis has instead been on the surplus countries, with the IMF, EU and nations such as the U.S., Brazil and Russia asking them to assist with the adjustments to correct the imbalances.

Economists such as Gregor Irwin and Philip R. Lane have suggested that increased use of pooled reserves could help emerging economies not to require such large reserves and thus have less need for current account surpluses. Writing for the FT in January 2009, Gillian Tett says she expects to see policy-makers becoming increasingly concerned about exchange rates over the coming year. In June 2009, Olivier Blanchard, the chief economist of the IMF wrote that rebalancing the world economy by reducing both sizeable surpluses and deficits will be a requirement for sustained recovery.

In 2008 and 2009, there was some reduction in imbalances, but early indications towards the end of 2009 were that major imbalances such as the U.S. current account deficit are set to begin increasing again.

Japan had allowed her currency to appreciate through 2009, but has only limited scope to contribute to the rebalancing efforts thanks in part to her aging population. The Euro used by Germany is allowed to float fairly freely in value, however further appreciation would be problematic for other members of the currency union such as Spain, Greece and Ireland who run large deficits. Therefore, Germany has instead been asked to contribute by further promoting internal demand, but this hasn't been welcomed by German officials.

5.5.2 Regional Blocs in International Trade

A trade bloc is a large free trade zone or near-free trade zone formed by one or more tax, tariff and trade agreements." (Trade Bloc, 2008). International trade closely related with globalization. Globalization describes the changes in societies and the world economy that result from dramatically increased international trade and cultural exchange. It describes the increase of trade and investing due to the falling of barriers and the interdependence of countries. In specifically economic contexts, the term refers almost exclusively to the effects of trade, particularly trade liberalization or "free trade". From their definitions, there seems no difference in their natures. Both of them pursue "free trade" between countries while the main difference lies in their scopes. To be more precise, the former one is regional and the latter is global. Virtually, as what is discussed above, "free trade" is much more practiced in regional trading blocs than on the global level, e.g., the EU as the most famous regional trading bloc has not only formed a market in which essential factors of production can be traded freely, but also launched a common currency called Euro, which is of great significance to regionalization. But the WTO has only reduced tariffs and restricted some non-tariff barriers. Obviously, the global free trade is not as developed as the regional free trade. However, it cannot be deduced that trading blocs are a barrier to globalization from the above facts. Because the trading blocs which first appeared as early as fifty years ago did not stop or even slow the process of globalization. The multilateral talks of the WTO and its predecessor, the GATT, constantly reached many agreements. Though there were difficulties and contradictions in these talks, the results proved to be good. The world free trade has been achieved well than ever in many fields. Since 1990s, the world market which based upon market mechanism has been formed as well as a global financial market. Generally, when the relationship between trading blocs and globalization is discussed, countries are the very basic members and factors of international trade organizations and are of great importance. No matter what a country does, should it be joining regional trading blocs or multilateral talks, its ultimate purpose is to get as much economic interest as possible from it. This purpose is beyond all others, e.g., the so-called regional economic interest and global economic interest.

A country joins a regional trading bloc not because of the abstract supranational "regional interest", but because it wants to reach its economic, political and other purposes with the power of the bloc. It cannot be denied that in order to compete with the EU and Japan, the U.S. formed the NAFTA with Canada and Mexico. Under the pressure brought by the EU and the NAFTA, Japan also strongly promotes the economic cooperation among the East Asian countries. Another good example is the ASEAN, which consists of smaller countries, because each of them does not have sufficient strength to compete with big countries, they hope that they will have it by getting together. On the contrary, if the regional trading blocs cannot give what their member countries want, there would most probably be problems that will slow the process of regionalization. For instance, the reason why Germany and France compete for the regional economic leadership and the UK is out of the Euro system, is that the above three countries' interests conflict with the whole region's interest. Many countries join regional trading blocs with the hope that the power of the blocs would help them to speak louder in multilateral talks. They want the blocs to be their "speakers". To achieve this, all the member states in one trading bloc have to speak in "one voice", which represents their common economic interest. And if one of the member countries' interests is out of the whole, it will surely speak in a different voice. And what the country would do next is probably to seek other cooperation, such as bilateral and other multilateral talks, which could help them with their economic development. Again a good example of this is the formation of NATFA. Why does the U.S. need NAFTA? One of the important reasons is that it found the GATT was unable to eliminate the competitive advantage that Japan's industrial structure and distribution system and the EC's agricultural and high-technology subsidies provided. In other words, no matter what means a country uses, it is always oriented by its interest, especially the economic interest.

The Motivation to Establish Regional Trading Blocs: Competing with the Outside World

Looking through the world since the 1960s, we can see that an important motivation of the formation and development of regional trading blocs is to compete with the outside world. After the World War II, the Western European countries had once been very dependent on the United States (the U.S.), which charged something else from them. Therefore, since their economy recovery after the 1960s, they began to search for economic and political independence. Another important fact that stimulated the process of their cooperation is Japan's fast economic development. In order to compete with the U.S. and Japan and some other developed countries, the Western European countries started to search for ways of cooperation in many fields in the early 1960s. Since the 1980s, there have been plenty of changes of the strengths of the main economically strong countries. These changes, especially Japan's fast development, made some other developed countries search for the protection of regional trading blocs, which could preserve their economic interest and prevent the loss of their competitive edge. At the same time, more and more developing countries also had to do the same thing out of their dissatisfaction with the unfair and unbalanced economic situation.

On 12 April 1989, "The Delors Committee presented the report on the economic and monetary union." (The History of the European Union, 2008) On 2 October 1997, "The Ministers for Foreign Affairs of the Member States of the European Union signed the Treaty of Amsterdam" (The History of the European Union, 2008), which cleared away the last obstacle to the Euro and provided it with a legal guarantee. The fast development of the European Union (EU) and Japan reminded the U.S. of its relative falling position in the world economy. According to Mason and Turay, "business and political leaders saw that the USA was becoming less and less competitive with Japan and the EC. In the 1970s and 1980s US manufacturers lost their strong market positions in several key sectors, including consumer electronics, commercial aircraft, apparel, machine tools, semi-conductors and automobiles." General Agreement on Tariffs and Trade (the GATT) less important than before, the U.S. began to think about Canada and Mexico, two of its closest countries. At the same time, Canada and Mexico also hoped that their products could enter the American market and that they could attract more of the American investment. "Both Canada and Mexico have had difficult economic and political relations with the USA, but each wants NAFTA more than the USA itself." Therefore, in 1992, the three countries formed the North American Free Trade Agreement (the NAFTA). This was the first time a regional trading bloc made up of countries with a considerable disparity between them came into being. On 8 August, 1967, Thailand, Indonesia, Malaysia, Singapore and the Philippines formed an organization called the Association of South-East Asian Nations (the ASEAN). Later, other states Brunei, Vietnam, Laos, Myanmar and Cambodia joined. Being faced with the keen competition among the U.S., Japan, China and some other big countries, these relative small countries found that the only way to ensure their security and competitiveness is to unite and cooperate.

Regional Trading Blocs' Effect on Globalization

In recent years, regionalization has been more and more popular and common in the world. For America, the NAFTA has achieved a positive result. For Europe, "one in eight numbers of the United Nations (UN) is the member of the EU." Europe is an equal partner to the United States in trade negotiations. The launching of Euro has an epoch-making significance to the world economy. For Asia-Pacific region, the Asia-Pacific Economic cooperation has become one of the most influential forums. In South-east Asia, the ASEAN member countries have obviously strengthened their cooperation in economic fields. The formation of the NAFTA, the EU, the Asia-Pacific Economic Cooperation (the APEC), the ASEAN and other regional trading blocs have to some extent changed the pattern of world economy and trade. There is no doubt that the increase of the dependence of the member countries on the regional trade blocs and their negotiating abilities towards the outside world will bring keener competition to the world, which proves to be harmful to globalization.

5.6 Trade Strategies: Import Substitution and Export Promotion

Government intervention in foreign trade is often associated with the concepts "Import Substitution" (IS) and "Export Promotion" (EP). The former entails higher intervention, the latter less intervention. It is difficult to have a precise definition for the concepts IS and EP. Two basic approaches measuring the intensity of intervention may be distinguished. One was a single-criterion based on the underlying incentive structure; the other is multiple-criteria using choice of trade policy variables.

Greenaway and Num (1988) adopted a multiple criteria approach. They argued that a single criterion approach is not appropriate for a number of reasons. First, classification into import and export sectors is difficult as industries produce a range of products. Second, the actual and intended effects of policies may be entirely different in developing countries. Third, the evidence suggests that only a few economies persistently pursue a strategy through time. The authors noticed that the initial stages of industrialization are characterized by import substitution and that it is only after some 'take off' point that resources need to be mobilized into higher value added activities through export promotion. Michaely, Papageorgiou and Choksi (1991) adopted multiple criteria and introduced liberalization indices for each country in a study of nineteen countries and twenty-nine episodes. The liberalization indices were constructed for each episode annually during the period studied and were assigned a value ranging from 1 (for the highest possible degree of trade intervention) to 20 (for complete trade liberalization). For each episode intensity was derived based on strength and speed and their sustainability. Various quantitative and qualitative factors were taken into account. The difficulties in defining trade strategies are reflected in the vast variation in approaches to measurement. Between the two extremes, stringent import control and export-orientation policy exist various degrees of combinations. In brief, trade strategy can be defined in terms of changes to incentive structure using a single criterion and changes in the choice of trade policy instrument using multiple criteria. However, the single criterion definition is used in most of the literature.

Import Substituting Industries: Development economists justify import substituting industrial policies on a number of grounds. Given the low productivity and low income elasticity of demand for the primary goods mainly produced by developing nations known as periphery underwent long-term deterioration of prices and short-term export revenue instability (Prebisch, 1984). Given the high productivity and high income elasticity of demand for the manufacturing goods produced by rich countries known as centre received continuously higher prices for their products. If a secular decline of terms of trade of periphery is true forecast for future trends, long-lasting expansion of traditional exports cannot be relied upon for sustained long-run growth. It was felt that switching into import-substitution industrialization was the only option for periphery to grow with the given export pessimism case. Switching into import substituting industries was also perceived as a means of reducing the income elasticity of demand in the periphery for its manufacturing imports from the centre.

The classical economists and later structuralists brand the manufacturing sector as an engine of growth. This sector relatively generates increasing returns in the long-run not only within the sector itself but also in the other major sectors, which are raising productivity as output expands. Manufacturing sector has the potential of interrelated branches of activities and generates greater linkages and externalities. Agricultural and service sectors do generate linkages. However, the expansion of these sectors does not offer specialization and division of labour within the sectors as like manufacturing sector. Productivity gains and technical change arising in manufacturing sector pass on to these sectors through purchase of capital and intermediate goods. Switching into domestic production satisfying domestic demand replaces the imports. The government interventions in foreign trade and the price distortions arise due to that is to protect the import substituting manufacturing industries. Price distortions are expected to shelter the higher-cost local producers by allowing the domestic production more profitable. The above process can be an important strategy in raising manufacturing sector through foreign exchange savings and the generation of externalities and learning effects. The danger is that this strategy targets the internal demand and neglects the external demand from export sector. Weiss (1988) has noted developing countries failed to lower their imports, while reducing the exports below its long-run potential for many cases. One can look at various explanations for this. First the composition of imports may change but not overall imports that include capital and intermediate goods. Second the growing income inequalities can lead to shifts in consumer demand towards import-intensive commodities. Finally, there is also a tendency that import substitution policy creates biases in the incentive structure, lower the growth of potential exports. It is inevitable to call for an export-oriented policy at this stage which demands removal of biases in the incentive structure.

Interventions in Export: Export interventions are export quotas, export tax and export subsidy. Export quotas are rarer, but tend to be more severe, than import quotas. For example to avoid national famines governments used to control exports in the past. In the extreme they can take the form of an export ban or export embargo, both refers to complete bans or economic sanctions. For example United States impose export bans and quotas more often than other industrial nations. Export tax is common, which has effects that are symmetrical to those of an import tax. An export tax, in the face of a fixed world price, discourages exports and directs supplies back onto the home market, pushing down the domestic price. Exports are often subsidized. For example, governments use taxpayers' money to give low-interest loans to exporters, engage in advertising and export promotion on behalf of exporters and give tax relief based on the value of goods or services each firm exports. Lower prices of exports due to subsidy likely to benefit consumers and harm producers of importing countries; the governments of importing countries have a good reason to protect their producers from unfair competition. They do retaliate by imposing a tariff against exporters which is widely known as countervailing duties. Higher domestic prices of importing countries as a result of countervailing duties suppose to protect the domestic producers. GATT/WTO does proscribe export subsidies as "unfair competition" and allow importing countries to retaliate with protectionist countervailing duties. The net effect of the subsidy plus countervailing duty together determines the world welfare. Advocates of strategic trade policy support granting subsidies to strategic industries/firms. This form of subsidy is different from the infant industry argument for protection. Countries may predominate in the export of certain products because they had firms that were foremost in technology and able to attain first-mover advantages in industries that would support only a few firms because of substantial economies of scale. Government should use subsidies to support promising firms in emerging industries and should provide this support until the domestic firms establish first-mover advantage in the world market. Both home market protection and export subsidies are advocated. For example, the United States of America supports Boeing and a number of European countries support Airbus.

Export Orientation: Trade Liberalization

The concept 'trade liberalization' does not mean complete free trade, but fewer trade barriers or a neutral trade regime. The process of removal of quota and tariff may continue until a neutral trade regime appears. A neutral trade regime may be defined as a situation with equal incentives to domestic sales and exports. Trade protection instruments such as tariffs and non-tariff barriers tend to discriminate between domestic and border prices. Trade reforms in this respect are likely to reduce the gap between domestic and border prices and tend to narrow the market prices with opportunity costs.

As a result of liberalization, some activities may contract while others may expand. As resources in the contracting activities are likely to be affected, this would involve some political implications. Macroeconomic imbalances such as higher inflation and severe balance of payments problems are likely with liberalization. To avoid uncertainties Michaely (1986) suggested an optimal path to trade liberalization. Michaely recommended a multi-stage implementation, as being superior to a one-stage implementation on the grounds that one-stage implementation is not feasible politically or socially, as this would lead to greater unemployment and larger changes in income distribution. Michaely further argues that the desirable first step is to eliminate all forms of quantitative restrictions. Further he suggested a uniform treatment of activities as far as tariff reductions are concerned. Three alternative "uniform" paths can be looked into. First, equi-proportional (across-the-board) reduction of protection of various activities; this would lead to a gradual reduction of the protection system. Second, equally large absolute reductions between various activities; the third method is named the 'concertina method'. In the initial stage of the policy, all protection rates above a certain ceiling are lowered to that ceiling, with no changes in other rates. The next step is that all rates are again brought to the lower ceiling and so on. This would allow consistency in the lowering of the variance in the protection system. This tends now to be the approach used as bringing highest net benefit. It is recognized within the neoclassical literature that effective trade liberalization requires the effective operation of all interrelated and interdependent markets, such as those for foreign exchange, financc, labour and capital market. In the absence of free movements in related markets, the benefits that accrue from liberalization may be significantly reduced. Macroeconomic policies appear to be important in determining the survivability of trade liberalization. Trade liberalization may not be effective in countries with growing fiscal deficits, worsening external balance and rising inflation. For example, with the liberalization, inflationary pressures lead to appreciation in the real exchange rate and worsen the current account deficit. High real lending and excessive debt-burden rate due to inflationary pressures lead to lower investment. Adjustment assistance is the policy of compensating those jobs and investments that are displaced by import competition. Greater import competition entails displacement costs, in terms of worker, capital and other resources. Job losses need to be addressed in order to avoid the social and political unrest. Who pays this cost? One can argue that as long as the free-trade policy brings net gains to the nation, the gainers can compensate the injured while still retain the net gains from the free trade. The Government can play the mediator role between gainers and losers. This is referred to as adjustment assistance. This assistance can be used to relocate and retrain workers (and firms) for re-employment in sectors where employment is expanding.

Import-substituting industrialization can be an important strategy for raising earnings and savings of foreign exchange, generating externalities and learning effects. In general, misallocation of resources and consumer welfare loss due to misalignment of domestic and world prices and rent-seeking activities are costs associated with protectionism. Import-substituting strategy creates biases in the incentive structure and likely to reduce the potential exports. Focus is also on limited domestic market where industry unlikely to reap the benefits of economies-of-scale. The expectation of the trade reforms is to generate trade efficiency in the short-run by eliminating allocative and technical inefficiency that possibly arises from trade protection. Long-run productivity growth is ambiguous one as there is vast range of changes in technical conditions and prices both internationally and domestically. It is possible to capture the short-run effects of trade reforms by using static and dynamic measures.

5.7.1 An Analytical Study on Theory of Free International Trade—David Ricardo

Plate 11: David Ricardo

David Ricardo was born in London in 1772. His parents were Sephardic Jews who had immigrated to England. His father, Abraham, was a successful stockbroker. Ricardo's business career started when he began working for his father at age 14, but at 21 he married a Quaker, which created a family rift that sent Ricardo into the world completely on his own. He nonetheless prospered as a stockbroker and left a vast estate at his death. Having no money problems, Ricardo could afford to spend a great deal of time in intellectual pursuits, and he became interested in many subjects.

Besides political economy, which he took up after reading Adam Smith's 'Wealth of Nations' in 1799, he also studied mathematics, mineralogy, chemistry and geology. His career as an active political economist lasted but 14 years. Ricardo's first major work in the field of economics, *The High Price of Bullion, a Proof of the Depreciation of Bank Notes* was published in 1810. This pamphlet became very influential, making Ricardo's name familiar to those in government who sought economic advice. A parliamentary inquiry into the high bullion price may have been the direct result of the pamphlet's publication, but that's speculative. In any case, the government report's conclusion that the inflation then occurring in England was the result of too many paper banknotes being created and was Ricardo's own claim in his pamphlet. This helped to cement in the public's mind the idea that Ricardo was an economist of some standing. That status brought him into contact with other famous political economists of his time, notably James Mill and Thomas Robert Malthus. Mill became Ricardo's mentor, coaching him and inspiring him to write more in their shared field. In 1814, Ricardo retired from business life and bought an estate in Gloucestershire. A year later, he published his next major work in economics, *Essay on the Influence of a Low Price of Corn on the Profits of Stock.* In that work, Ricardo lay out what was to become a key idea in neo-classical economics: the so-called law of diminishing returns as it applied to labour and capital. Generally, as it applies to cultivation of crops, this law states that increasing the quantities of inputs will increase total production up to a point, but then output must decline, given that the land used is fixed in size. Although increasing production is possible, and perhaps common at first, at some point the marginal returns to additional inputs must decline, followed by their average returns and, thus, total output must decline as well. Ricardo's purpose in exploring the issue of land rents was British legislation called the 'Corn Laws'. Passed in 1815, these laws forbade the importation into England of food grown elsewhere and sought to maintain the rising prices for British agricultural products that had occurred during the Napoleonic wars, when the French navy had embargoed British ports. Facing the loss of food imports, Britain had to use more of its own land to feed its population. This caused crop prices, and hence, land rents to rise at rapid rates during the war period. The protectionist Corn Laws was an attempt to maintain the agricultural status after Napoleon's defeat and a return to peaceful conditions. Ricardo, himself a landowner who was profiting from the rising rents, nevertheless argued that the Corn Laws should not be enacted and after they were continued to argue strenuously for their repeal. Beyond that, the observed rent increases suggested to Ricardo a general theory of land rent. The reason rent exists, he argued, was that as more and more land of diminishing fertility was applied to growing food, the better lands commanded a premium. This was an argument for rent on the *extensive margin*, that is, as more land was cultivated. But Ricardo also argued for rent on the *intensive margin*, that is, where similar lands experienced different diminishing returns to capital and labour. In Ricardo's view, the Corn Laws generated rents both extensively and intensively. His analysis of the effects of the Corn Laws produced the famous Ricardian theory of rent. In 1817, he expanded his pamphlet on rent and re-titled it *On the Principles of Political Economy and Taxation*. By 1819, he had been elected to the House of Commons, where he continued to be an active participant in the policy discussions of his time. Ricardo died suddenly of an ear infection in 1823, leaving an estate estimated at $126 million (current dollars). As Mark Blaug comments: "Ricardo may or may not have been the greatest economist that ever lived, but he was certainly the richest."

Ricardo's Contributions and System: Ricardo's approach to economics differed markedly from that of Adam Smith. Ricardo was a pure theoretician, an architect of a simple, highly abstract model from which he drew policy conclusions. His most important assumption was that economic growth must decline and end due to the scarcity of land and its falling marginal productivity. In this, we see the origin of John Stuart Mill's later contention that economic stagnation would flow from the working out of the capitalist productive process. It also is very suggestive of later arguments by John Maynard Keynes of the continuing potential macro stagnation that, according to Keynes and many of his followers, flows from a chronic insufficiency of aggregate demand in any relatively closed-market economy. Ricardo's foremost contemporary critic was Malthus, author of the famous pamphlet *An Essay on the Principle of Population.* It was from Malthus that Ricardo took the argument of an ever-growing population that pressed against all economic expansions, an assumption that lay at the heart of Ricardo's model. His central consideration in his *Principles* was to show how distributional changes between wages, rent, interest and profit affected the prospects for long-run capital accumulation and economic growth, because his model produced a falling rate of profit and an ever-rising price for corn (grains), Ricardo favoured an end to the Corn Laws, arguing that Britain ought to import corn from countries better equipped to produce it at lower cost. He hated the rising rents he attributed to the laws, since they came, in his view, at the expense of the driving force of the economy. Twenty-three years after his death, the laws were repealed and Ricardo's international free trade agenda became one with British public policy. Ricardo had provided an answer to Britain's long-term growth problems, and Britain became the "workshop of the world", importing most of its food and "outsourcing" most of its agricultural employment. Ricardo's ideas became "the fountainhead of all nineteenth-century free trade doctrine!"One of the ideas for which Ricardo is most remembered is the theory of comparative advantage. Ricardo demonstrated that for two nations without input factor mobility, specialization and trade could result in increased total output and lower costs than if each nation tried to produce in isolation. Since Ricardo's exposition, the distinction between absolute and comparative advantage has been taught as one of the field's most brilliant insights. Nations will export not only what they have an absolute advantage in producing, but also what they have a *comparative cost edge in producing*. Some historians of economic thought have sought to show that others, specifically James Mill and Robert Torrens, stated the idea, or something close to it, prior to Ricardo. Such writers tend to discount Ricardo's version of the theory as very short and possibly even incorrect. Other economic historians defend Ricardo and argue the contrary. Regardless of ongoing academic disputes, it is unlikely that historians of economic thought will reverse their position on Ricardo's original authorship of this idea. Another major contribution Ricardo made to economics was the doctrine of fiscal equivalence, or, as it has come to be known today, Ricardian equivalence. His argument is as follows: It doesn't matter whether government finances itself through taxes or debt. They are equivalent and have no appreciable effect on household consumption or capital formation. This is because either the public sector will save or run a deficit, or households will do likewise and at the same rate. Further, expectantly, taxpayers view a deficit as a future tax increase and will save to pay for it, while a surplus is viewed as a future tax cut with an opposite result. Households will arrange their private affairs to frustrate the long-run effects of either finance approach, as judged from a macroeconomic policy perspective. (To be sure, Ricardo did not want government to issue debt rather than raise tax revenue, regardless of the truth of his equivalence insight.) Other concerns that Ricardo devoted himself to were monetary reform, the distribution of national income and the determination of an invariant measure of value. Ricardo favoured redemption of paper money in gold bullion, argued for decoupling the Bank of England from that nation's money supply creation and contended that labour costs were the best long run invariant measure of the value of goods and services—a labour cost theory of value not unlike what Smith had also proposed in *Wealth of Nations*. Ricardo was a believer in the strict quantity theory of money, whereby the price level is directly proportional to the quantity of money circulating and changes in that quantity of money change prices instead of real factors.

Ricardo's theory of rent was tied directly to the marginal productivity of land; his theory of value was tied directly to labour costs, and his theory of distribution concepts, with Malthusian economic stagnation as a major assumption. Ricardo was not as naive as to attempt to explain all market prices by labour costs. He recognized the importance of "non reproducible" commodities whose value was solely determined by their rarity in the market. He allowed a role for capital in determining value and argued that an increase in fixed (more permanent) capital as opposed to circulating (perishable) capital would increase value. By allowing value to be influenced by capital, Ricardo indirectly suggested that time played a major role in value, a discovery later generally attributed to other economists. Ricardo's model, abstract and highly deductive, became the means by which he advocated public policy. A free trade enthusiast, he also was not a fan of public expenditure, believing most such spending to be at worst wasteful or at best incapable of changing aggregate well-being and output. His influence should not be underestimated, especially in Great Britain, for as Keynes wrote, "Ricardo conquered England as completely as the Holy Inquisition conquered Spain."

5.7.2 GATT and WTO

The World Trade Organization (WTO) and its predecessor, the General Agreement on Tariffs and Trade GATT) have been enormously successful over the last 50 years at reducing tariff and other trade barriers among an ever-increasing number of countries. The predecessor to the WTO began in 1947 with only 23 members; today it has 146 members, comprising approximately 97 per cent of world trade. Although the WTO, established in 1995, is relatively young for an international institution, it has its origins in the Bretton Woods Conference at the end of World War II. At this conference, finance ministers from the Allied nations gathered to discuss the failings of World War I's Versailles Treaty and the creation of a new international monetary system that would support post-war reconstruction, economic stability, and peace. The Bretton Woods Conference produced two of the most important international economic institutions of the post-war period: the International Monetary Fund (IMF) and the International Bank for Reconstruction and Development (the World Bank). Recognizing that the 'beggar-thy-neighbor' tariff policies of the 1930s had contributed to the environment that led to war, ministers discussed the need for a third post-war institution, the International Trade Organization (ITO), but left the problem of designing it to their colleagues in government ministries with responsibility for trade. By the late 1940s, representatives of the American government had met several times with representatives of other major nations to design a post-war international trading system that would parallel the international monetary system. These meetings had two objectives: (1) to draft a charter for the ITO and (2) to negotiate the substance of an ITO agreement, specifically, rules governing international trade and reductions in tariffs. Although a charter was drafted, the ITO never came into being. By 1948, support for yet another international organization had waned in the U.S. Congress. Without American participation, the institution would have been greatly weakened and, in the event, the effort to create an organization to manage problems relating to international trade was abandoned.

However, although the U.S. Congress would not support another international institution, in 1945 it had given the U.S. president the authority to negotiate a treaty governing international trade by extending the 1934 Reciprocal Trade Agreements Act. This led to the establishment of the General Agreement on Tariffs and Trade (GATT) in 1948 a treaty whereby 23 member countries agreed to a set of rules to govern trade with one another and maintained reduced import tariffs for other members. The GATT treaty did not provide for a formal institution, but a small GATT Secretariat, with a limited institutional apparatus, was eventually headquartered in Geneva to administer various problems and complaints that might arise among members. Over the next 40 years, GATT grew in membership and in its success at reducing barriers to trade. GATT members regularly met in what came to be known as negotiating rounds. These rounds were primarily focused on negotiating further reductions in the maximum tariffs that countries could impose on imports from other GATT members. Several problems had surfaced with the GATT apparatus. Firstly, the dispute resolution mechanism of GATT was not functioning as effectively as had been hoped. Countries with long standing disagreements were unable to reach any sort of resolution on a number of issues, ranging from government subsidies for exports to regulations regarding foreign direct investment. Secondly, a number of commodities, most importantly, agricultural products and textiles, were widely exempt from GATT disciplines. Thirdly, it was widely believed that certain forms of administered trade protection anti-dumping duties, voluntary export restraints, and countervailing duties were restricting trade and distorting trade patterns in many important sectors. Fourthly, trade in services was expanding rapidly and GATT had no rules regarding trade in services. Fifthly, countries that produced intellectual property movies, computer programs, patented pharmaceuticals were becoming increasingly frustrated by the lack of intellectual property protection in many developing nations. Lastly, the rules regarding trade-related investment measures for example, domestic purchase requirements for plants built from foreign direct investment were hotly disputed. To address these problems, a new round of trade negotiations—the Uruguay Round was launched in

1986. The goals of the Uruguay Round were far more ambitious than in previous rounds. It sought to introduce major reforms into how the world trading system would function. The treaty negotiated during the Uruguay Round, the GATT treaty of 1994, established the WTO—the international institution to govern trade that was first visualized by the attendees of the Bretton Woods Conference 50 years earlier. The new GATT treaty provided for an entirely new and different dispute resolution mechanism to eliminate the gridlock of the old system. Furthermore, the Uruguay Round expanded GATT's authority to new areas agreements regarding trade in textiles, agriculture, services, and intellectual property were major achievements. Finally, new sets of rules regarding administered protection came into effect with the creation of the WTO in 1995.

- ***Role of WTO in Globalization***

1. WTO plays an important role in the principle of trade without discrimination in the free market trade. Most-favoured-nation (MFN) treating other people equally. Under the WTO agreements, countries cannot normally discriminate between their trading partners. Grant someone a special favour (such as a lower customs duty rate for one of their products) and you have to do the same for all other WTO members.

2. *National treatment*: Treating foreigners and locals equally. Imported and locally-produced goods should be treated equally, at least after the foreign goods have entered the market.

3. *Freer trade—gradually, through negotiation*: Lowering trade barriers is one of the most obvious means of encouraging trade. The barriers concerned include customs duties (or tariffs) and measures such as import bans or quotas that restrict quantities selectively.

4. *Predictability—through binding and transparency*: With stability and predictability, investment is encouraged, jobs are created and consumers can fully enjoy the benefits of competition choice and lower prices. The multilateral trading system is an attempt by governments to make the business environment stable and predictable.

5. *Promoting fair competition*: The WTO is sometimes described as a "free trade" institution, but that is not entirely accurate. The system does allow tariffs and, in limited circumstances, other forms

of protection. More accurately, it is a system of rules dedicated to open, fair and undistorted competition.

6. *Encouraging development and economic reform*: The WTO system contributes to development. On the other hand, developing countries need flexibility in the time they take to implement the system's agreements.

Table 5.1: GATT & WTO at a Glance

Year	
1944	At the Bretton Woods Conference, which created the World Bank and International Monetary Fund (IMF), there is talk of a third organization, the International Trade Organization (ITO).
1947	As support for another international organization wanes in the U.S. Congress, the General Agreement on Tariffs and Trade (GATT) is created. The GATT treaty creates a set of rules to govern trade among 23 member countries rather than a formal institution.
1950	Formal U.S. withdrawal from the ITO concept as the U.S. administration abandons efforts to seek congressional ratification of the ITO.
1951-86	Periodic negotiating rounds occur, with occasional discussions of reforms of GATT. In the 1980s, serious problems with dispute resolutions arise.
1986-94	The Uruguay Round, a new round of trade negotiations, is launched. This culminates in a 1994 Treaty that establishes the World Trade Organization (WTO).
1995	The WTO is created at the end of the Uruguay Round, replacing GATT.
2003	The WTO consists of 146 members, accounting for approximately 97 per cent of world trade.

• *TRIPs*

The **Agreement on Trade-Related Aspects of Intellectual Property Rights (TRIPs)** is an international agreement administered by the World Trade Organization (WTO) that sets down minimum standards for many forms of Intellectual Property (IP) regulation as applied to nationals of other WTO Members. It was negotiated at the end of the Uruguay Round of the General Agreement on Tariffs and Trade (GATT) in 1994.

The TRIPs agreement introduced intellectual property law into the international trading system for the first time and remains the most comprehensive international agreement on intellectual property to date. In 2001, developed countries were insisting on an overly narrow reading of TRIPs, initiated a round of talks that resulted in the Doha Declaration. The Doha Declaration is a WTO statement that clarifies the scope of TRIPs, stating for example that TRIPs can and should be interpreted in light of the goal "to promote access to medicines for all."

Specifically, TRIPs requires WTO members to provide copyright rights, covering content producers including performers, producers of sound recordings and broadcasting organizations; geographical indications, including appellations of origin; industrial designs; integrated circuit layout-designs; patents; new plant varieties; trademarks; trade dress; and undisclosed or confidential information. TRIPs also specify enforcement procedures, remedies, and dispute resolution procedures. Protection and enforcement of all intellectual property rights shall meet the objectives to contribute to the promotion of technological innovation and to the transfer and dissemination of technology, to the mutual advantage of producers and users of technological knowledge and in a manner conducive to social and economic welfare, and to a balance of rights and obligations.

TRIPs were negotiated at the end of the Uruguay Round of the General Agreement on Tariffs and Trade (GATT) in 1994. Its inclusion was the culmination of a programme of intense lobbying by the United States, supported by the European Union, Japan and other developed nations. Campaigns of unilateral economic encouragement under the Generalized System of Preferences and coercion under Section 301 of the Trade Act played an important role in defeating competing policy positions that were favoured by developing countries, most notably Korea and Brazil, but also including Thailand, India and Caribbean Basin states. In turn, the United States strategy of linking trade policy to intellectual property standards can be traced back to the entrepreneurship of senior management at Pfizer in the early 1980s, who mobilized corporations in the United States and made maximizing intellectual property privileges the number one priority of trade policy in the United States.

After the Uruguay round, the GATT became the basis for the establishment of the World Trade Organization. Because ratification of TRIPs is a compulsory requirement of World Trade Organization membership, any country seeking to obtain easy access to the numerous international markets opened by the World Trade Organization must enact the strict intellectual property laws mandated by TRIPs. For this reason, TRIPs is the most important multilateral instrument for the globalization of intellectual property laws. States like Russia and China that were very unlikely to join the Berne Convention have found the prospect of WTO membership a powerful enticement.

Furthermore, unlike other agreements on intellectual property, TRIPs has a powerful enforcement mechanism. States can be disciplined through the WTO's dispute settlement mechanism.

The requirements of TRIPs: TRIPs require member states to provide strong protection for intellectual property rights. For example, under TRIPs:

- Copyright terms must extend at least 20 years, unless based on the life of the author. (Art. 12 and 14)
- Copyright must be granted automatically, and not based upon any "formality", such as registrations, as specified in the Berne Convention. (Art. 9)
- Computer programs must be regarded as "literary works" under copyright law and receive the same terms of protection.
- National exceptions to copyright (such as "fair use" in the United States) are constrained by the Berne three-step test.
- Patents must be granted for "inventions" in all "fields of technology" provided they meet all other patentability requirements (although exceptions for certain public interests are allowed (Art. 27.2 and 27.3) and must be enforceable for at least 20 years (Art. 33).
- Exceptions to exclusive rights must be limited, provided that a normal exploitation of the work (Art. 13) and normal exploitation of the patent (Art. 30) is not in conflict.
- No unreasonable prejudice to the legitimate interests of the right holders of computer programs and patents is allowed.
- Legitimate interests of third parties have to be taken into account by patent rights (Art. 30).
- In each state, intellectual property laws may not offer any benefits to local citizens which are not available to citizens of other TRIPs signatories under the principle of national treatment (with certain limited exceptions, Art. 3 and 5). TRIPs also have a most favoured nation clause.

Trade Related Investment Measures (TRIMs)

The Agreement on Trade Related Investment Measures (TRIMs) is rules that apply to the domestic regulations a country applies to foreign investors, often as part of an industrial policy. The agreement was agreed upon by all members of the World Trade Organization. The agreement was concluded in 1994 and came into force in 1995. The WTO wasn't established at that time, it was its predecessor, the GATT (General Agreement on Trade and Tariffs. The WTO came about in 1994-1995.)

Policies such as local content requirements and trade balancing rules that have traditionally been used to both promote the interests of domestic industries and combat restrictive business practices are now banned.

Trade Related Investment Measures is the name of one of the four principal legal agreements of the WTO trade treaty. TRIMs are rules that restrict preference of domestic firms and thereby enable international firms to operate more easily within foreign markets.

In the late 1980s, there was a significant increase in foreign direct investment throughout the world. However, some of the countries receiving foreign investment imposed numerous restrictions on that investment designed to protect and foster domestic industries, and to prevent the outflow of foreign exchange reserves. Examples of these restrictions include local content requirements (which require that locally-produced goods be purchased or used), manufacturing requirements (which require the domestic manufacturing of certain components), trade balancing requirements, domestic sales requirements, technology transfer requirements, export performance requirements (which require the export of a specified percentage of production volume), local equity restrictions, foreign exchange restrictions, remittance restrictions, licensing requirements, and employment restrictions. These measures can also be used in connection with fiscal incentives as opposed to requirement. Some of these investment measures distort trade in violation of GATT (Article III and XI), and are therefore prohibited. Until the completion of the Uruguay Round negotiations, which produced a well-rounded Agreement on Trade-Related Investment Measures (hereinafter the "TRIMs Agreement"), the few international agreements providing disciplines for measures restricting foreign investment provided only limited guidance in terms of content and country coverage. In addition, there are other international treaties, bilateral and multilateral, under which signatories extend most-favoured-nation treatment to direct investment. Only a few such treaties, however, provide national treatment for direct investment. Moreover, although the APEC Investment Principles adopted in November 1994 provide rules for investment as a whole, including non-discrimination and national treatment, they have no binding force. GATT 1947 prohibited investment measures that violated the principles of national treatment and the general elimination of quantitative restrictions, but the extent of the prohibitions was never clear. The TRIMs Agreement, however, contains statements prohibiting any TRIMs that are inconsistent with the provisions of Article III or XI of GATT 1994. In addition, it provides an illustrative list that explicitly prohibits local content requirements, trade balancing requirements, foreign exchange restrictions and export restrictions (domestic sales requirements) that would violate Article III:4 or XI:1 of GATT 1994. TRIMs prohibited by the Agreement include those that are mandatory or enforceable under domestic law or administrative rulings, or those with which compliance is necessary to obtain an advantage.

5.8.1 Export Processing Zone (EPZ)

The prevailing development strategy places emphasis upon the 'outward orientation' of countries, with particular emphasis on exports. Export promotion is now seen as an important policy for economic growth in developing countries. Various measures are being adapted to promote export competitiveness by governments in these countries. In this scenario, Export Processing Zones (EPZs) have become rather popular trade policy instruments due to their catalytic role in imparting outward orientation to the economies. There were 176 zones across 47 countries in 1986. In 2003, the number of zones increased to over 3000 across 116 countries.

In India, the first zone was set up in Kandla as early as 1965. It was followed by the Santacruz Export Processing Zone which came into operation in 1973. The government set up five more zones during the late 1980s. These were at Noida (Uttar Pradesh), Falta (West

Bengal), Cochin (Kerala), Chennai (Tamil Nadu) and Visakhapatnam (Andhra Pradesh). Surat EPZ became operational in 1998. The EXIM Policy, 2000 launched a new scheme of Special Economic Zones (SEZs). Under this scheme, EPZs at Kandla, Santacruz, Cochin and Surat were converted into SEZs. In 2003, other existing EPZs namely, Noida, Falta, Chennai, Vizag were also converted into SEZs. In addition, approval has been given for the setting up of 26 SEZs in various parts of the country. Apparently, India is now promoting the EPZ programme much more vigorously than in the initial phases of their evolution. Huge amounts of public resources are being invested in the zones. This warrants an in-depth analysis of the performance of EPZs and their contribution to the country's export performance. Though there have been studies on Indian EPZs (Kumar 1989, Kundra 2000) any comprehensive and over time analysis with a focus on the export performance of Indian EPZs is virtually non-existent.

The basic objective of setting up EPZs in India is to promote exports and foreign exchange earnings. Though the objectives of EPZs were not clearly spelt out in India until the late 1980s, in actual practice the predominant condition in selecting EPZ units had been the expected value addition component of exports (Kumar 1989). This indicator was also used to assess the performance of the units. In 1989, a report of the 'Comptroller and Auditor General of India' (CAG) clarified that EPZs were meant for earning foreign exchange, develop export oriented industries, stimulate investment and generate employment opportunities besides creating an internationally competitive environment for export production at low cost. Subsequent policy documents have however, reiterated that EPZs are meant to provide an internationally competitive environment for export production at low cost. The 'Draft SEZ Bill 2004' also considers 'promotion of foreign trade in goods and services' the most important objective of SEZs. The present study therefore focuses on the export and foreign exchange performance of EPZs/SEZs in India. First, it discusses the economic rationale of better export performance by EPZs/SEZs. Then, it reviews the evolution of the EPZ policy through different phases of growth and examines trends and patterns of EPZ exports. Analysis of the EPZ/SEZ performance revealed that growth rates of aggregate exports, foreign exchange earnings and employment have been falling over the years since the late 1980s.

Furthermore, it is also found that the share of EPZ/SEZ exports in total exports has been almost stagnant since 1990. The study therefore undertakes to examine some of the factors responsible for the unimpressive performance of the zones in India. While doing so, it analyses the data generated through a primary survey of zone units and zone offices across all the 8 operational zones. Finally, it outlines a set of policies that the country needs to pursue for making the EPZ/SEZ scheme a success.

- ***Brief History of the EPZ Policy in India***

Attempts to promote the EPZ as an export platform on the basis of economic incentives, such as the free provision of infrastructural services and tax holidays, has been a feature of Indian development thinking since the 1960s. The country has had four phases in the evolution of the EPZ policy. Following is an overview of the evolution of the EPZ policy in India through these four phases.

Initial Phase: (1964-1985)

The first zone was set up in Kandla as early as 1965. It was followed by the Santacruz export processing zone which came into operation in 1973. There was however no clarity of objectives that the government wanted to achieve. Kandla and Santacruz EPZs were set up with multiple objectives (Tondon Committee, 1980). Operationally, an overall inward looking trade policy with many controls and regulations influenced the EPZ policy also (Kundra, 2000). The policies were rigid and the package of incentives and facilities was not attractive. Zone authorities had limited powers. There was no single window facility within the zone. Entrepreneurs had to acquire individual clearances from various State governments and Central government departments. Day-to-day operations were subjected to rigorous controls. Custom procedures for bonding, bank guarantees and movement of goods were rigid. FDI policy was also highly restrictive. According to the business environment rating index which rated investment climate in 43 countries on the basis of 18 independent factors, Indian, zones were placed at the bottom for FDI (TCS, 1976). Three committees were appointed by the Government of India during this period to review the working of the zones. Kandla and Santacruz were the only zones which were operational during the period. Kandla was reviewed by the Kaul Committee in 1978 while Santacruz was reviewed by the Review Committee on Electronics in 1979. Tondon Committee (1981) reviewed both these zones. These committees pointed out that the growth of EPZs in this phase was hampered by several handicaps including:

- The absence of a policy,
- Absence of implementation authority to centrally coordinate and control,
- Procedural constraints,
- Infrastructural deficiencies,
- Limited concessions and limited powers of the zone authorities to take actions on the spot resulting in inordinate delays.

The committees made several concrete recommendations to improve the performance of these zones. The policy regime however remained virtually static.

The Expansionary Phase: (1985-1991)

In its report, the Tondon Committee strongly recommended to locate 4 to 5 more zones in the country to provide a fillip to the country's export promotion efforts. It argued that the excessive protectionism had imparted a significant bias against exports. At the same time, the high cost of production structure created by heavy protection reduced the competitiveness of Indian exports. It suggested that free trade zones, which insulated the export sector from various controls and regulations could be a useful instrument of export promotion. Following the report, the government decided to establish four more zones in 1984. These were at Noida (Uttar Pradesh), Falta (West Bengal), Cochin (Kerala) and Chennai (Tamil Nadu). Visakhapatnam EPZ in Andhra Pradesh was established in 1989. Thus, this phase witnessed the establishment of 5 zones. There were however no significant changes in other laws and procedures pertaining to the EPZs.

The Consolidating Phase: (1991-2000)

In 1991, a massive dose of liberalization was administered in the Indian economy. In this phase of new policy initiatives, wide-ranging measures were initiated by the government for revamping and restructuring EPZs (Kundra, 2000). This phase was thus marked by progressive liberalization of policy provisions and relaxation in the severity of controls and simplification of procedures. Arora (2003) shows that there were in all 146 circulars on EPZs/EOUs issued by the Central Board of Excise and Custom, DGFT and RBI during this period of 10 years. These constituted over 62 per cent of total circulars issued on EPZs/EOUs till 2003.

The focus had been on—

- Delegating powers to zone authorities,
- Providing additional fiscal incentives,
- Simplifying policy provisions, and
- Providing greater facilities.

The scope and coverage of the EPZ/EOU scheme was also enlarged in 1992 by permitting the agriculture, horticulture and aqua-culture sector unit also. In 1994, trading, reengineering and re-conditioning units were also permitted to be set up.

The Emergence Phase: (2000 onwards)

This period has witnessed a major shift in direction, thrust and approach. The EXIM Policy (1997-2002) has introduced a new scheme from April 1, 2000 for establishment of the Special Economic Zones (SEZs) in different parts of the country. SEZs will be permitted to be set up in the public, private, joint sector or by the State Governments with a minimum size of not less than 1000 hectares. SEZ is an almost self contained area with high class infrastructure for commercial as well as residential inhabitation. The units operating in these zones are to be deemed as outside the country's customs territory and will have full flexibility of operations. Several measures have been adopted to improve the quality of governance of the zones. In what follows we list some of these measures.

- Conditions for automatic approvals are relaxed considerably. All proposals which do not meet any or all of the parameters for automatic approval will be considered and approved by the Board of Approval of EOU/EPZ/SEZ set up in the Department of Commerce. The earlier system of an inter-ministerial committee for approving SEZs is dispensed with and a combined board of approval has been set up for both the EOU and SEZ units. All proposals for FDI/NRI/OCB investments in EOU/SEZ units qualify for approval through automatic route subject to sectoral norms. Proposals not covered under the automatic route would be considered and approved by FIPB.

- Furthermore, custom procedures are considerably simplified. There would be no routine examination of export and import cargo by Customs and all imports would be on self-certification basis and no separate documentation is required for customs and EXIM Policy.
- More recently, Development Commissioners are given the labour commissioner's powers. The number of incentives has also been extended to the units operating in SEZs. These include fiscal and non-fiscal incentives.

Non-fiscal Incentives

- Exemption from industrial licensing for manufacture of items reserved for SSIs.
- 100 per cent FDI investment through automatic route to manufacturing SEZ units barring a handful of sensitive industries.
- FDI up to 100 per cent is allowed for: the ISPs not providing gateways (both for satellite and Submarine cables), Infrastructure Providers providing dark fiber (IP Category I), electronic Mail and Voice Mail in the telecom sector.
- Facility to retain 100 per cent foreign exchange receipts in EEFC Account.

5.8.2 Special Economic Zone (SEZ)

A special Economic Zone (SEZ) is considered the sensitive outer skin of its host country; it is also regarded a barometer to anticipate impending macroeconomic trends. SEZs have generated interest in developing countries; for instance, countries pursuing an export-led growth strategy expect SEZs to stimulate external trade and encourage economic activity in the domestic market. In India, specially, SEZ success is expected to translate into exponential growth in manufacturing sectors.

The Indian government has granted several initiatives, such as tax initiatives and world class physical infrastructure, to SEZ units to bolster the production of manufactured goods. With this initiative, the government expects SEZs to achieve the following basic objectives:

- Provide a fillip to the manufacturing sector, especially exports of manufacturing goods.
- Duty free movement of goods and services.
- Attract substantial foreign investment by allowing 100 per cent Foreign Direct Investment (FDI) in the manufacturing sector.
- Boost infrastructure development.
- Generate employment.
- Differentiated economic management like relaxations in certain basic restrictions applicable to the rest of the economy.
- It is often a controlled economic environment for free trade.

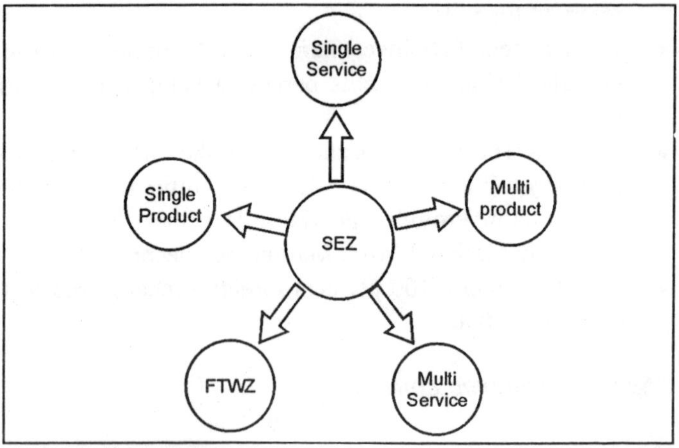

Fig. 5.4: Functions of SEZ

SEZ has not a definitive connotation. It is improper to use SEZ in place of terms like EPZ (Export Promotion Zone) and FTZ (Free Trade Zone).

Historical Perspective

Concept of free economic zones dates back to 300 BC according to Robert C. Haywood, Director, World Economic Processing Zones Association, 2000. Such enclaves were found in the Phoenician city of Tyre in the Greek island of Delos. They city became very wealthy as a result of such politics. The city was viewed as a challenge to the centralism of the Roman Empire. According to the Wepza website, more than 2000 zones are said to exist in over 120 countries. They are in high, low and middle income countries—having capitalist, socialist and communist oriented countries. Such has been irresistible pull of the concept to promote economic growth. China was possibly the most closed and the authoritarian economic system in the world in the 1970s and early 1980s. It could not liberalize its economy as its political system did not allow it. So it created pockets of the economic freedom in the form SEZs which at times exceeded some small countries in their geographical spread. These pockets were a world apart from the rest of the country in terms of the economic system and philosophy. Similar is the example of Dubai, a part of the Emirates that almost exist as SEZ, it has also designated areas like Jebel Ali Zones.

World bodies responsible for administering and advocating global policy initiatives such as the IMF, World Bank, ILO have reservations about the bencfits of such exclusive economic enclaves that liberalize selectively but involves costs for the economics in the form of revenue losses and the regional imbalances and instead advocate across the broad liberalization.

Case Study with special reference to Industrial Resurgence in West Bengal

In West Bengal political stability is considered by the corporate to be the major advantage since the state has some coal reserve but little beyond that by the way of minerals to attract major investment. North

Bengal abounds in fruits making horticulture a lucrative proposition and companies like Dabur have already announced their investment plans. Infrastructure-wise also West Bengal is better placed as compared to some of the other eastern states. Improved infrastructure and industry-friendly image are among the key factors that have made it possible for West Bengal to virtually snatch projects like Tata's small car from other states like Uttarakhand. In West Bengal, efforts are to improve the navigability of the riverine Calcutta port and also to augment facilities by having a deep sea port and a minor port. In respect of power, West Bengal has the highest installed capacity among the eastern states and has been ranked high in terms of power availability and quality. It is in West Bengal that the country's largest BOT project with substantial FDI for developing on infrastructure has come through the second Vivekananda Bridge project providing the connectivity between the city and the rest of the country through NH2. People have begun to take cognizance. A visiting US diplomat recently took note of those new industry-friendly attitudes of the Government in states like West Bengal which seems to be leading the change. The UK minister for trade and industry, visiting India for first time, made Kolkata one of his two stopovers in the country. Global management consultancy from Worbus has set up a corpus of 300 million dollars for investment in emerging companies in this region. A major part of their total fund allocation for India will come to this state and the rest has been set for North India.

Plate 12: SEZ in West Bengal

5.8.3 E-commerce

Electronic commerce (E-commerce) is often thought simply to refer to buying and selling using the internet. But e-commerce involves much more than electronically mediated financial transactions between organizations and customers. Many commentators refer to e-commerce as all electronically mediated transaction between an organization and any third party it deals with. By this definition, non-financial transactions such as customer requests for further information would also be considered to be part of e-commerce. Many disciplines concerned with e-commerce, i.e., economic, marketing, management, finance/accounting, sociology, computer science, and information system etc.

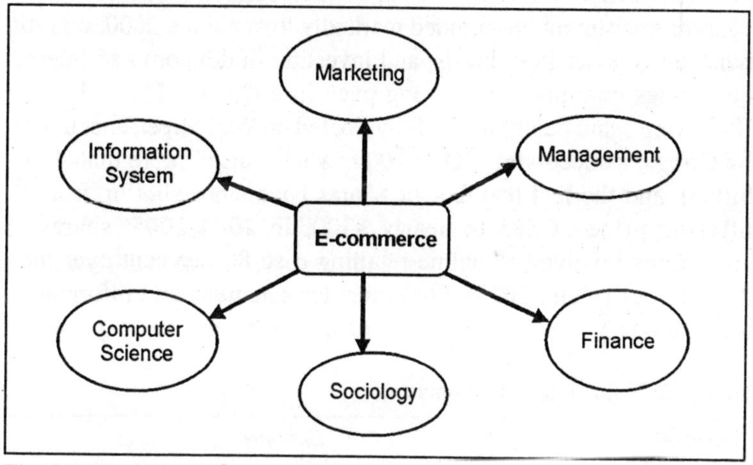

Fig. 5.5: Disciplines of e-commerce

E-commerce—A Brief History

Although e-commerce is a very recent phenomenon of the late 1990s, it already has a brief, tumultuous history. The early years of e-commerce were a period of explosive growth and extraordinary innovation, beginning in 1995 with the first widespread use of the Web to advertise products. This period of explosive growth was capped in March 2000 when stock market valuations for dot.com companies reached their peak and thereafter began to collapse. A serious period of reassessment occurred followed by strong double-digit growth through the current period.

The Visions and Forces behind e-commerce (1995–2000)

The early years of e-commerce were one of the most euphoric of times in American commercial history. It was also a time when key e-commerce concepts were developed and explored. Thousands of dot.com companies were formed, backed by over $125 billion in financial capital, one of the largest out pouring of venture capital in United States history (Price water house Coopers, 2005).The amounts invested by venture capital firms in the period 1995-2005. About 80 per cent of this investment was in Internet-related industries. While venture investment has trended markedly lower since 2000, it is still twice as large as 1995 levels, and investing in dot.com and Internet businesses continues at a strong pace in 2005. By 2004, dot.com IPOs were again being successfully floated on Wall Street, encouraged by Google's successful IPO in 2004, which raised more than $1.67 billion, and the fact that Google shares have since shot up from its offering price of $85 to nearly $300. In 2004-2005, shares of companies involved in online retailing rose 80 per cent over their 2003 prices (Stein, 2005). For computer scientists and information technologists, the early success of e-commerce was a powerful

Table 5.2: Major Types of e-Commerce

Types of e-commerce	*Example*
B2C—Business-to-Consumer	Amazon.com is general merchandise that sells consumer products to retail consumers.
B2B—Business-to-Business	ChemConnect.com is a chemical industry exchange that creates an electronic market for chemical producers and users.
C2C—Consumer-to-Consumer	eBay.com creates a market space where consumers can auction or sell goods directly to other consumers.
P2P—Peer-to-Peer	Gnutella is a software application that permits consumers to share music with one another directly, without the intervention of a market maker as in C2C e-commerce.
M-commerce—Mobile commerce	Wireless mobile devices such as PDAs (personal digital assistants) or cell phones can be used to conduct commercial transactions.

vindication of a set of information technologies that had developed over a period of forty years extending from the development of the early Internet to the PC, to local area networks. The vision was of a universal communications and computing environment that everyone on earth could access with cheap, inexpensive computers—a worldwide universe of knowledge stored on HTML pages created by hundreds of millions of individuals and thousands of libraries, governments, and scientific institutes. Technologists celebrated the fact that the Internet was not controlled by anyone or any nation, but was free to all. They believed the Internet—and the e-commerce that rose on this infrastructure should remain a self-governed, self-regulated environment. For economists, the early years of e-commerce raised the realistic prospect of a perfect *Bertrand market*: where price, cost, and quality information is equally distributed, a nearly infinite set of suppliers compete against one another, and customers have access to all relevant market information worldwide. The Internet would spawn digital markets where information would be nearly perfect; something that is rarely true in other real-world markets. Merchants in turn would have equal direct access to hundreds of millions of customers. In this near perfect information market space, transaction costs would drop sharply because search costs, the cost of searching for prices, product descriptions, payment settlement, and order fulfillment would all fall drastically (Bakos, 1997). New shopping programs would automatically search the entire Web for the best prices and delivery times. For merchants, the cost of searching for customers would also fall, reducing the need for wasteful advertising. At the same time, advertisements could be personalized to the needs of every customer. Prices and even costs would be increasingly transparent to the consumer, who could now know exactly, and instantly the worldwide best price, quality, and availability of most products. Information asymmetry would be greatly reduced. Given the instant nature of Internet communications, the availability of powerful sales information systems, and the low cost involved in changing prices on a Web site (low menu costs), producers could dynamically price their products to reflect actual demand, ending the idea of one national price, or one suggested manufacturer's list price. In turn, market middlemen—the distributors, wholesalers, and other factors in the marketplace who are intermediates between producers and consumers, each demanding a payment and raising costs while adding little value would disappear. Manufacturers and content originators would develop direct market relationships with their customers. The resulting intense competition, the decline of intermediaries and the lower transaction costs would eliminate product brands, and along with it, the possibility of monopoly profits based on brands, geography, or special access to factors of production. Prices for products and services would fall to the point where prices covered costs of production plus a fair, "market rate" of return on capital, plus additional small payments for entrepreneurial effort (that would not last long). Unfair competitive advantages (which occur when one competitor has an advantage others cannot purchase) would be eliminated, as would extraordinary returns on invested capital. This vision was called friction-free commerce. For real-world entrepreneurs, their financial backers, and marketing professionals, the idea of friction-free commerce was far from their own visions. For these players, e-commerce represented an extraordinary opportunity to earn far above normal returns on investment, far above the cost of borrowing capital. The e-commerce market space represented access to millions of consumers worldwide that used the Internet and a set of marketing communications technologies (e-mail and Web pages) that was universal, inexpensive, and powerful. These new technologies would permit marketers to practice what they always had done—segmenting the market into groups with different needs and price sensitivity, targeting the segments with branding and promotional messages, and positioning the product and pricing for each group but with even more precision. In this new market space, extraordinary profits would go to first movers those firms who were first to market in a particular area and who moved quickly to gather market share. First movers could establish a large customer base quickly, build brand name recognition early, create an entirely new distribution channel, and then inhibit competitors (new entrants) by building in switching costs for their customers through proprietary interface designs and features available only at one site. Online businesses using the new technology could create informative, community-like features unavailable to traditional merchants. These "communities of consumption" also would add value and be difficult for traditional merchants to imitate. The thinking was that once customers became accustomed to using a company's unique Web interface and feature set, they could not easily be switched to competitors. In the best case, the entrepreneurial firm would invent proprietary technologies and techniques that almost everyone adopted, creating a network effect. A network effect occurs where all participants receive value from the fact that everyone else uses the same tool or product like example, a common operating system, telephone system, or software application such as instant messaging, all of which increase in value as more people adopt them. Successful first movers would become the new intermediaries of e-commerce, displacing traditional retail merchants and suppliers of content, and becoming profitable by charging fees of one sort or another for the value customers perceived in their services and products. To initiate this process, entrepreneurs argued that prices would have to be very low to attract customers and fend off potential competitors. E-commerce was, after all, a totally new way of shopping that would have to offer some immediate cost benefits to consumers. However, because doing business on the Web was supposedly so much more efficient when compared to traditional "bricks-and-mortar" businesses (even when compared to the direct mail catalog business) and because the costs of customer acquisition and retention would supposedly be so much lower, profits would inevitably materialize out of these efficiencies. Given these dynamics, market share, the number of visitors to a site ('eyeballs'), and gross revenue became far more important in the earlier stages of an online firm than earnings or profits. Entrepreneurs and their financial backers in the early years of e-commerce expected that extraordinary profitability would come, but only after several years of losses. Thus, the early years of e-commerce were driven largely by visions of profiting from new technology, with the emphasis on quickly achieving very high market visibility. The source of financing was venture capital funds. The ideology of the period emphasized the ungoverned "Wild West" character of the Web and the feeling that governments and courts could not possibly limit or regulate the Internet; there was a general belief that traditional corporations were too slow and bureaucratic, too stuck in the old ways of doing business, to 'get it' to be competitive in e-commerce. Young entrepreneurs were therefore the driving force behind e-commerce, backed by huge amounts of money invested by venture capitalists. The emphasis was on deconstructing (destroying) traditional distribution channels and disintermediation existing channels, using new pure online companies who aimed to achieve impregnable first mover advantages. Overall, this period of e-commerce was characterized by experimentation, capitalization, and hypercompetition.

Table 5.3: Seven features of e-commerce technology

Dimension of e-commerce technology	*Business significance*
Ubiquity—Internet/Web technology is available everywhere: at work, at home, and elsewhere via mobile devices, anytime.	The marketplace is extended beyond traditional boundaries and is removed from a temporal and geographic location. "Market space" is created; shopping can take place anywhere. Customer convenience is enhanced, and shopping costs are reduced.
Global reach—The technology reaches across national boundaries, around the earth.	Commerce is enabled across cultural and national boundaries seamlessly and without modification. "Market space" includes potentially billions of consumers and millions of businesses worldwide.
Universal standards—There is one set of technology standards, namely Internet standards.	There is one set of technical media standards across the globe.
Richness—Video, audio, and text messages are possible.	Video, audio, and text marketing messages are integrated into a single marketing message and consuming experience.
Interactivity—The technology works through interaction with the user.	Consumers are engaged in a dialog that dynamically adjusts the experience to the individual, and makes the consumer a co-participant in the process of delivering goods to the market.
Information density—The technology reduces information costs and raises quality.	Information processing, storage, and communication costs drop dramatically, while currency, accuracy, and timeliness improve greatly. Information becomes plentiful, cheap, and accurate.
Personalization/Customization—The technology allows personalized messages to be delivered to individuals as well as groups.	Personalization of marketing messages and customization of products and services are based on individual characteristics.

Major Trends in e-commerce

Business

- Retail consumer e-commerce continues to grow at double-digit rates.
- The online demographics of shoppers continue to broaden.
- Online sites continue to strengthen profitability by refining their business models and leveraging the capabilities of the Internet.
- The first wave of e-commerce transformed the business world of books, music, and air travel. In the second wave, eight new industries are facing a similar transformation: telephones, movies, television, jewelry, real estate, hotels, bill payments, and software.
- The breadth of e-commerce offerings grows, especially in travel, information clearinghouses, entertainment, retail apparel, appliances, and home furnishings.
- Small businesses and entrepreneurs continue to flood into the e-commerce marketplace, often riding on the infrastructures created by industry giants such as Amazon, eBay, and Overture.
- Brand extension through the Internet grows as large firms such as Sears, J.C. Penney, L.L. Bean, and Wal-Mart pursue integrated, multi-channel bricks-and-clicks strategies.
- B2B supply chain transactions and collaborative commerce continue to strengthen and grow beyond the $1.5 trillion mark.

Technology

- Wireless Internet connections (Wi-Fi, Wi-Max, and 3G telephone) grow rapidly.
- Podcasting takes off as a new media format for distribution of radio and user-generated commentary.
- The Internet broadband foundation becomes stronger in households and businesses.

Bandwidth prices fall as telecommunications companies re-capitalize their debts.

- RSS (Really Simple Syndication) grows to become a major new form of user-controlled information distribution that rivals e-mail in some applications.
- Computing and networking component prices continue to fall dramatically.
- New Internet-based models of computing such as NET and Web services expand B2B opportunities.

Society

- Self-publishing (user-generated content) and syndication in the form of blogs, wikis and social networks grow to form an entirely new self-publishing forum.
- Newspapers and other traditional media adopt online, interactive models.
- Conflicts over copyright management and control grow in significance.
- Over half the Internet user population (about 80 million adults) joins a social group on the Internet.
- Taxation of Internet sales becomes more widespread and accepted by large online merchants.
- Controversy over content regulation and controls increases.
- Surveillance of Internet communications grows in significance.
- Concerns over commercial and governmental privacy invasion grow.
- Internet fraud and abuse occurrences increase.
- First Amendment rights of free speech and association on the Internet are challenged.
- Spam grows despite new laws and promised technology fixes.
- Invasion of personal privacy on the Web expands as marketers find new ways to track users.

CHAPTER 6

Economic Geography and Multifold Aspects

6.1 Changing Nature of Economic Activities

The history of Economic Geography is ever-changing and may be divided into four distinct periods; each provided a different approach to the subject.

I. In the first period Economic Geography traced its roots from commercial geography which had grown up as the Western European nation expanded their trading relationships and empires across the globe. Commercial geography reached its zenith in the work of G.G. Chisholm who founded the school of geography at the University of Edinburg in 1908 and published a book "Handbook of Commercial Geography" in 1925. This book provided a precise account of world production and trade. Chisholm also identified forces of concentration and de-concentration. The forces of de-concentration or decentralization would ultimately lead to a more equal worldwide distribution of industrial activity.

II. The search for better explanations led next to a more theoretical Economic Geography in the United States where it focused on the study of the relationship between economic activity and the physical environment. By the 1920s, the field was well established and a journal "Economic Geography" appeared in 1925. This new economic geography was concerned with "environmentalism" or "environmental determinism"—the theory that economic differences were caused by environmental factors, failed to explain the diversity of economics in similar physical environments, and ignored the freedom of individuals to make their own choices, within limits of what they produced.

This environmentalist idea was clearly expressed by W.M.Davis in 1906. To him society was an organism that survived by adjustment to physical environment, the nature of its growth was environmentally prescribed. E. Huntington in his book "Civilization and Climate" published in 1915 argued that climate was the decisive factor in health, physical and mental efficiency, and that since a civilization is the result of the energy, efficiency, intelligence, and genius of the population, ergo, climate is the "mainspring" factors in the progress or regress of civilizations. J.Russel, Smith (USA) and G.Taylor (Australia) were all determinists and maintained an active correspondence with Huntington. They believed that it is the duty of geographers to study nature's plan, and to see how best their national area may be developed in accord with temperature, rainfall, soil etc. whose bounds are quite beyond our control in any general sense. The idea of the interdependence of culture and nature was also developed by the French Geographers Vidal-de-la-Blache in his book "Principle of Human Geography" in 1942 also indicated that "differences in productive activities are often results of difference in environment".

III. A third Economic Geography emerged that concerned itself with areal variation in production and the economic regions that resulted. Environmental determinism was also abandoned by economic geographers and the American geographers became concerned with resources and the conservation of the environment and the majority of economic geographers from 1930 to 1960 returned once again to a very descriptive approach. Economic Geography according to R.S. Thomas became "an inquiry into similarities, differences and linkages within and between areas in the production, exchange, transfer and consumption of goods and services". To J.W. Alexander, Economic Geography became 'the study of the aerial variation of the earth's surface in mans' activities related to producing, exchanging and consuming wealth". In aerial differentiation, definition and mapping of economic regions became an end in itself, the ultimate in descriptive generalization.

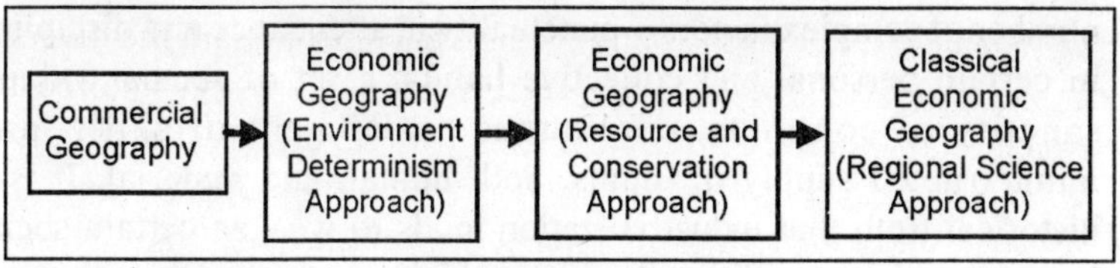

Fig. 6.1: Changes of economic activities

IV. After World War II Economic Geography took new different directions. The search for theoretical approach intensified. Social sciences became interdisciplinary. At this time, the computer technology began to revolutionize quantitative analysis and governments subsidized research particularly for planning and policy-oriented studies. Geographers rediscovered the classical economic theories of location of J.H. Von Thunen, A. Weber, W. Christaller and A. Losch. The locational analysis of Walter Isard called for the creation of a new discipline, "Regional Science". Location theory sought to describe economic landscapes created by "economic person" in whom areal differentiation results not from differences in climate, soils or physiography, but instead from accessibility, transportation costs and economics of scale. This new image of humanity (economic person) has perfect knowledge of present circumstance and future events so that he or she powers of perfect prediction, the goal being maximization of profits. Most location decisions with which this economic person must grapple involve trade-offs which are a function of accessibility, rents and transportation costs.

But this image of "economic person" no longer satisfies economist or economic geographers. In reality, human behaviour displays "bounded rationality" in which profit maximizing must be weighed against competing objectives. Hence, a new image of the decision-maker is being developed—the "satisfier image" with decisions based on limited knowledge and bounded rationality. Thus, the changing nature of economic geography is very much associated with the lessons and contributions of each of these four periods.

6.2 Transition from Agricultural to Industrial Economy

Transition from a predominantly agricultural to industrial economy is never easy. A reasonably good health of industries depends on a number of complex factors—punctuality in attendance and discipline in certain personal and collective habits, a set of secular values, sanctity of contracts, continuous enrichment of skills, and uninterrupted supply of inputs, both human and material. It is a historical truth that industrialization tends to weaken certain social bonds found in a traditional society which creates an atmosphere of psychological stress and insecurity.

Industrial advancement depends in large measure upon the accumulation of capital. In early phase of industrialization, transfer of surplus labour in huge numbers from traditional agricultural sector provided the necessary support system for this accumulation of capital. In holding the society together, the role of the state became very important in this protracted period of transition—from agriculture to industry.

It is a fact that industrial revolution did not take place over all parts of the world at the same time. The countries all-over the world are different stages industrial transition as they are with the stages of demographic transition. There are many countries where it is yet to come. The circumstance that helped of withheld this transition has indeed been dissimilar. Many of the countries which are considered industrial giants today had carried out this transition through harsh authoritarian measures. It is fact that in larger countries (on number count), the early phase of industrialization unfolds not under a truly democratic setup (in Europe or elsewhere). Even Stalin's Russia and China's single partly dictatorships were ruthless in acquiring farm land for infrastructural development for rapid growth of industries. This is not admitting that some kind of authoritarianism is necessary to create an environment so that the transition can take place relatively smoothly.

The rural economy prior to rise in free private enterprises or capitalism was generally poor but it was rather free from mass unemployment. Mass unemployment was unknown in the Middle except when there was war, natural catastrophe and visitation of famine and epidemics. It is a historical truth that industrialization at its initial stage did not portray a rosy picture for the common man, especially the rural poor. Labour surplus and intensity of unemployment therefore has to be seen relative to the technology we are employing and the nature of commodities that are brought to the market for the consumption of the common man. Therefore, it is no wonder that the specter of involuntary unemployment continue as long as the transition continues. The economist, Keynes believes that even the rising capital-intensive labour-saving growth of industry would in the long run absorb the surplus labour since the industries and the state would have to undertake programs to enhance the skill of the common people to see that there is no shortage of skilled labour in industries and the industries would be too willing to invest their capital for expansion of existing facilities and/or put their surplus for diversification of their manufactured products.

Most of the developing countries have realized that they too have no option but to embrace capital-intensive industrialization if the support system for their citizens were to be consolidated and life-style of the common man improved. They cannot afford to embrace the labour-intensive technology in this age of global competition and economic liberalization. Since technologies for upgradation of their industries and diversification of products are now readily available from the developed countries, of course at a high premium, the transition from traditional agriculture to industrialization in these countries is to be achieved as smoothly and quickly as possible. The infrastructure development to support industrialization is not going to be easy from them. If huge capital investment is the single most important impediment to augur this infrastructure development programme, the other formidable obstacle comes from farmers whose agricultural land, often their only asset for survival, has to be acquired by the state pushing more people jobless in countries where unemployment rate social unrest are fast mounting because of fast declining land-man ratio. Land acquisition for construction of roads, ports, industrial hubs, housing complexes, Special Economic Zones (SEZs), etc. will have considerable impact on the availability of land for cultivation. Food securities for many countries would be at stake unless massive investments are made on irrigation, crop rotations are introduced to prevent loss of fertility of the soil and soil erosion and better scientific method of cultivation and agricultural management are adopted. These countries are dependent on international funding agencies like World Bank, IMF etc. for most of their developmental activities. Funds by these institutions are released often on the condition of protection of the existing forest land at all costs and protection of environment must be assured.

The Central Government, through advocates 'economic reforms with a human face', cannot afford to go slow on its economic agenda. The existing labour laws often are inadequate to push forward the productivity of the capital-intensive industries. The government could not go ahead with 'labour reforms' because of strong opposition from different political parties, labour unions and even from its own treasury bench numbers. To achieve a sustainable double digit GDP growth, 'labour reforms', withdrawal/reduction of subsidies (in power, irrigation and fertilizer in agriculture) and provisioning of huge fund for social infrastructure (health, education, population control) are urgently needed. The government needs to review the Land Reforms Act of 1894 in order to make land acquisition and its transfer more transparent. Opinions abound that the investors must be asked to directly negotiate with the landowners and government's role would ensure that the landowners are paid adequate compensation.

The population pressure on land in India is incomparably more adverse than what it was in most developed and developing countries. India has no substantial outlets for its surplus population. The globalization has only created routes for 'brain drain'. Its impact is likely to be felt in hi-tech industries; biotechnology sector, and even in universities, research institutions, higher level of civil services. It is true that the service sector is currently absorbing a large number of educated and skilled workers and it has the potential to absorb many more at an accelerated rate. But the supply side is unlikely to meet their demands since there is shortage of educational and training institutes to equip the educated youths with the necessary skill. Many such institutes at the initiative of private enterprises have come up, but the quality of teaching and training imparted in these institutes at a very high cost often is miserable. In view of rupee getting stronger in relation to dollar, there is some decline in India's export earnings. To maintain the growth momentum in industrial production, expansion of domestic market obtains vital importance.

Most of the newly established industries make use of labour saving technology. Unless very many such industries come up quickly in all regions, it is unlikely that these industries can help in a big way in reduction of unemployment. The pressure of unemployment may lead to acute social problems, even civic strife. The declaration by some regional political parties—"we shall ruthlessly oppose establishment of industries on agricultural land"—does not portray a rosy picture for the smooth transition; both rightist and leftist extremist forces are appearing as destabilizing factor. A democratically elected government cannot remain ambivalent to rising unemployment in the country and the social tension mounting in consequence. The disruptive forces will take advantage of the brewing discontent among the masses. India cannot solve the unemployment problem overnight through lop-sided capital-intensive industrial-urban development. Along with urban-centric industrial development, India needs to pursue village level small-scale industries and dispersed growth centres to offer employment to educated rural youth. Billions of tax payers' money is spent on the development of cities neglecting the countryside. We often used our natural resources for manufacturing of products which are meant only for the consumption of our rich people or for export. Unless employment-poverty is addressed sincerely, serious attention is given to improvement of the social sector, the domestic consumer base for various products and utilities will not expand in spite of high GDP growth.

6.3 Industrial Processes and Urbanization

The proponents of urban growth theories often try to link urbanization process with industrialization and even endeavour to explain the former one with the help of the latter process and extend such explanations to most of the countries irrespective of distorted history of urban or industrial development. These twin processes have also been conceived as having cumulative, casual or circular relationship; obviously urbanization, metropolitanization and megalopolitanisation are conceived as serial stages of industrial agglomeration and employment opportunities with the improvement of infrastructural facilities for spatial integration of the twin processes. Such relationship even if holds good at the national aggregate level, definitely would have variation at the sub-national level because of regional factors. Besides, the urbanization-industrialization interrelationship although holds good at the initial stages, and continues until diseconomies starts in any of them, it is growth of tertiary and quaternary functions which explains the modifications of urban structure and form, and causes horizontal expansion of the metropolitan agglomerations. If such relationship shows any spatial variation in the intra-national or cross-country situation we get concerned about it.

A hasty generalization of urbanization as a demographic counterpart of industrialization is over-simplification of both the processes particularly in case of India.

Although relatively rapid industrialization has undoubtedly accelerated urbanization particularly in and around large metropolises and new emerging industrial complexes and both of them are getting specially polarized. We do expect strong spatial linkage between them. Industrial location policies were accordingly formulated for decentralized urban industrial growth. Small and medium size towns and cities have failed to have a significant positive response. Our expectations for rapid urban growth analogous with industrial growth in independent India have been belied to a great extent although both the processes are simultaneous but they not only lack in spatial integration, there is wide variation in space. Massive investment in capital goods industries in the resource reach but relatively backward region seemingly decentralized the industrial location but not in the urbanization fronts; the reasons lie on the vary pattern of industrialization. On the other hand, various incentives and subsidies programme have failed to counter the urban-industrial polarization process towards small and medium size towns and the intervening backwards areas. Under this circumstance, it is desirable to identify the sub-processes of urbanization and industrialization at sub-national levels and look for a pattern of spatial integration between them. "In India as in other developing countries, the sub-processes operate independently or function with disproportionate mix, this result in a disjointed and primate system. This system is integrated with metropolitan system at the apex, sub-standard rural-urban base, and weak intermediary links through 'subsistence' urban commercialization" (Prakasa Rao and Tiwari, 1978).

6.4 Poverty—A Misery of Society

Unemployment is a major cause of primary (or income) poverty. Poverty resulting from unemployment was thus temporary for most of those who experienced it and the numbers affected were in any case relatively small. The level of the unemployment benefit is generally below the poverty line, all of the unemployed should, by definition, be poor. It is important to recognize that while poverty is generally measured using income (which is a flow variable, normally measured on an annual basis in poverty studies), unemployment is a stock variable that records labour force status at a point in time. There is the important point that the unit of analysis used to determine labour force status is the individual, whereas poverty research focuses on the incomes of income units, who are assumed to share resources (including income) for the benefit of all members. Thus, an individual can have a low (or zero) income and still not be poor, as long as other members of the family unit have an income which, when shared, is sufficient to raise the family above the poverty line even after accounting for the family's needs. The significance of this last point has grown along with the growth in the number of dual-earner families, since this has further widened the gap between the incomes of individuals and the potential poverty status of the families in which they live. It follows directly from these definitions of unemployment and poverty that becoming unemployed does not necessarily involve a movement from above to below the poverty line. The relationship between unemployment and poverty, the relationship is now examined empirically. In undertaking such an exercise, it should be noted that there is a vigorous debate. Single-adult income units, being unemployed is associated with an increased risk of poverty, but that the relationship is weak (in the sense that not all of the unemployed are poor, while many of the poor are not unemployed) particularly when poverty is measured on an annual income basis. The relationship between unemployment and poverty is weaker still among income units with two adults, but the importance of having at least one adult in full-time work is reinforced. What really reduces the risk of poverty is thus not (paid) work itself, but full-time work, and it is only when there is at least one full-time earner that poverty rates fall. It is access to full-time work that is needed to protect people from the risk of poverty. With part-time work growing in importance, coupled with increase of work and a trend to lower wages that is creating a new class of 'working poor', finding a job may change the employment status of many of the unemployed without changing their poverty status.

- ***Urge to Remove Poverty***

Poverty alleviation has been, and rightly so, one of the guiding principles of the Indian planning process right from the beginning. However, there are two alternative ways of attacking poverty by laying the foundations for sustainable poverty eradication by providing better education and health facilities to the poor, and better physical infrastructure such as rural roads to improve the poor's income-earning capacity; or by providing handouts such as free or heavily subsidized food, or old-age pension for immediate succour. Until the Fourth Five-Year Plan in the 1970s, poverty programmes were mainly of the first variety, with initiatives such as the Community Development Programme initiated in 1952, the Green Revolution to increase the production and availability of food grains at affordable prices, and land reforms to get rid of the intermediaries, then came the more targeted programmes to provide immediate income to the poor, by "employing" them to construct village-level infrastructure such as roads or irrigation channels. There were also programmes to provide support to the poor through free or subsidized housing (such as under the Indira Awaas Yojana from 1985-86), or help to poor households in case of old age, death of the primary bread earner, or maternity (through the National Social Assistance Programme from 1995). The programmes proliferated in number, and while allocations were limited because of an insufficiency of fiscal resources, practically every programme continued under the original name or some mutation thereof. For example, the Integrated Rural Development Programme (IRDP) was introduced in 1976 on a pilot basis for generating self-employment for the poor, and rapidly extended to large parts of the country. From 1960, starting with the Rural Manpower Programme (RMP), there have also been various schemes for rural wage employment, such as the Crash Scheme for Rural Employment and Drought Prone Area Programme around 1971, which culminated in the Food for Work Programme in April 1977. These programmes were further refined and implemented as the National Rural Employment Programme from October 1980, and the National Rural Landless Employment Guarantee Programme from August 1983. These two were in turn consolidated and transformed into the Jawahar Rozgar Yojana from April 1989, and supplemented by the

Employment Assurance Scheme from October 1993. Once again, the latter two were transformed into the Jawahar Gram Samriddhi Yojana in 1999. The fundamental question is of the timing and scope of intervention. From the theory of social justice and the so-called Rawlsian max-min principle, there is undeniable force in the argument that the focus should be on the poorest of the poor. But the issue is one of sustainability. Lifting a poor person above the poverty line requires an income transfer that is equal to the "poverty gap", which is the difference between the poor person's income and the poverty line. The total "poverty gap" in a developing country such as India may be too high to allow the government to maintain fiscal sustainability and macroeconomic balance, and transfer the required amount to all the poor to remove poverty. Furthermore, the question needs to be asked: Will this transfer have to be made every year, or with the transfer, will some of the poor become economically viable and remain above poverty without any government support in future years? Thus comes the choice between how much to allocate for the poor for immediate succour, and how much to allocate for building the foundations for removing poverty on a sustained basis in the medium term.

- ***Provision of Basic Public Goods vs. Subsidies***

How does one make helping the somewhat poor an ethically viable policy strategy vis-à-vis helping the poorest of the poor? How does one justify helping the needy versus helping the super needy? There is a stark choice between: (i) helping the "somewhat poor", making them escape the shackles of poverty and contribute to helping those left behind in poverty in the medium term, and (ii) helping only the "poorest of the poor" year after year. Pragmatic policies pursued by east Asian countries demonstrate that what works, and works fairly quickly in removing poverty in a few decades, is helping the "somewhat poor" through improved physical infrastructure such as "*bijli, sadak, pani*" (power, roads and water supply), and social infrastructure such as education and health, and some targeted interventions for "*roti, kapda, makan*" (food, clothing and shelter) for the poorest of the poor. It is possible to argue that, while providing some support to the poorest of the poor, it is better to focus on instruments such as education, health and physical infrastructure, which will allow the poor just below the poverty line to help themselves, escape poverty, and join the middle class. It appears that too much emphasis may have been placed on "roti, kapda, makan" for the poor than on "bijli, sadak, pani". "Bijli, sadak, pani" are public goods that everyone needs, and while "sadak" cannot be bought by the rich as a private good, it is possible to have private arrangements for the supply of the other two. After six decades of planning, "bijli and pani" are available in sufficient quantity only to the rich, who can buy them at considerably higher private and social cost as private goods. Investing in the production of these public goods will strengthen the stability of the existing middle-class households and help the poor at the margin of the poverty line to join the middle class. The middle class can save, invest and provide entrepreneurship, but it cannot build power plants or transmission lines, or roads or water supply systems on its own. It needs the government for that. The lack of emphasis on the development of infrastructure in government policies has seriously hampered the growth of the Indian middle class. The emphasis on trying to set up a wide-ranging welfare state before meeting the basic provision of essential public goods has been a bit premature in India. This has impeded an even more robust growth of the Indian middle class. Middle-class formation is facilitated by a virtuous cycle—as the class starts consuming new and modern goods (such as refrigerators and other consumer durables), the production of such goods leads to the employment of more people in quality jobs, and a swelling in the ranks of the middle class itself. The lack of emphasis on physical infrastructure in public-sector policies has prevented the virtuous cycle of middleclass formation from taking effect. With inadequate roads and an insufficient power supply and other industrial infrastructure, when the Indian middle class consumed modern goods, production capacity expanded not in India, but in countries that could supply these goods at competitive prices. Obsession with Inequality Growth helps in poverty reduction, unless the distribution of income deteriorates dramatically and all the benefits of growth accrue to the rich. Growth with less inequality or what is called "inclusive growth", is more effective in reducing poverty and is superior to growth with increasing inequality. However, higher growth with mildly increasing inequality may be more conducive to reducing poverty than lower, but more equitable growth. It is a fact that inequality of income has increased in India, but there is nothing to suggest that it has deteriorated so much as to result in growth without poverty reduction. Yet, much of public discourse in India has turned on "deteriorating income distribution", rather than "how to promote growth" or "how to reduce poverty". Public discourse is increasingly focused on the income share of the top 10 per cent versus the income share of the bottom 10 per cent. Among the 79 countries for which data on the Gini index of inequality for any year after 2008 is available on the World Bank website (World Bank, 2013), only 21 had less income inequality than India. Of these 21, as many as five and seven were former socialist countries of Eastern Europe and the former Soviet Union, respectively. Furthermore, in Asia, except for the Republic of Korea, all countries in a comparable group Hong Kong, Indonesia, Malaysia, and People's Republic of China, Singapore, Thailand, and Vietnam had higher income inequality than India in the recent period. While it is true that inequality, as measured by the Gini index, has risen in India from 30.8 in 1994 to 33.9 in 2010, it is interesting to note that the corresponding increase in People's Republic of China has been from 35.5 in 1993 to 42.1 in 2009. As Arthur Lewis (1983) has cogently argued: "Development must be in egalitarian because it does not start in every part of an economy at the same time. Somebody develops a mine, and employs a thousand people. Or farmers in one province start planting cocoa, which grows in only 10 per cent of the country. Or the Green Revolution arrives to benefit those farmers who have plenty of rain or access to irrigation, while offering nothing to the other 50 per cent in the drier regions (cited in Bhagwati 1982: 21)." Indeed, Korea and Taiwan have managed to grow fast without rising inequality even during their phase of fast growth, but they are exceptions rather than the rule. There may be merit in focusing on inequality in the medium to long-term, rather than fixating on short-term discrepancies. Inequality has increased in India, and the blame for the increase has been squarely put on the shoulders of the neo-liberal policies pursued from 1991. No economic policy, however, could have assuaged the disastrous effects of our educational inequalities: inequalities which render it impossible for most citizens to participate in the economy, regardless of how that economy is structured. The slow spread of education and the slow growth of the manufacturing sector may be the two most important reasons for growth being less inclusive than what it could have been.

- ***Growth and the Importance of Education***

As the experience of Korea demonstrates, rapid improvements in education and fast growth reinforce each other, and lead to inclusive growth. In Korea, the successful expansion of education, with the number of elementary school students expanding "...from two-three million in 1950 to five-six million in the 1970s...with their enrolment rate exceeding 90 per cent in 1970" was a key ingredient of inclusive growth. Government policies along with cultural traditions contributed to this outcome. The Basic Education Act was promulgated in 1949, and after the Korean War, a six-year programme of compulsory primary education was successfully implemented, with the advancement rate to primary education rising to 96 per cent by 1959. Illiteracy fell dramatically from 78.2 per cent in 1948 to 4.1 per cent in 1958. The Korean government was active in promoting middle school, high school, and tertiary and vocational education through the 1960s, 1970s, and beyond. For example, the Private School Act

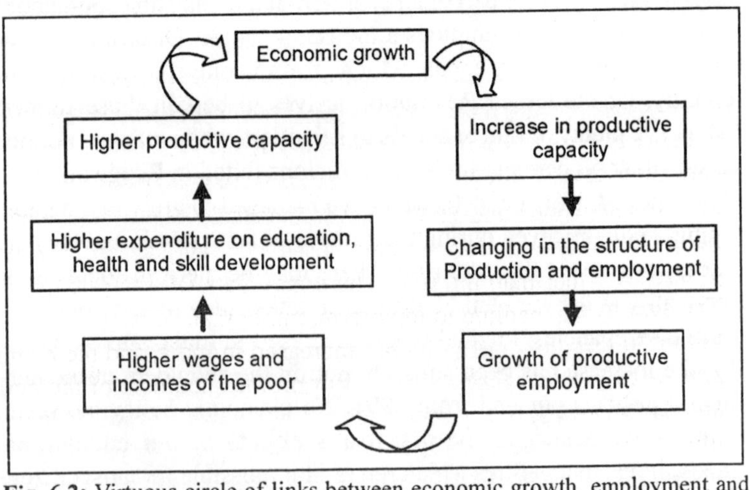

Fig. 6.2: Virtuous circle of links between economic growth, employment and poverty reduction

Source: Islam, 2006.

was passed in 1963, the high school equalization policy introduced in 1973, and private tutoring outlawed in 1980. Compared to Korea, the progress of education has been slow in India, with the adult literacy rate at 62.8 per cent in 2006, compared to 95.9 per cent in Korea in 1958. Perhaps it reflects the two governments' priorities – in India, public spending on education as a proportion of government expenditure was 10.5 per cent in 2010, compared to 15.8 per cent in Korea in 2009. The pre-emption of fiscal resources by subsidies on food, fuel and fertilizer, and interest payments in India leaves little for other purposes. The inadequate education of many in India results in only a limited few being able to take advantage of the opportunities unleashed by the reform process. In India, along with the widening gap between the top and bottom deciles of wage earners, as already mentioned, inequality of income distribution as measured by the Gini index has also gone up from 30.8 in 1994 to 33.5 in 2005, and further to 33.9 in 2010. Evidence suggests that after remaining fairly stable during 1983-93, inequality increased in the subsequent period. The underlying reasons behind increasing inequality are interesting. As pointed out by Cain *et al.* (2010: 283):...increases in 'returns to education' account for a fairly large part of the increases in urban inequality... The increases in returns to education have been particularly pronounced in education intensive services (such as communications, finance, insurance, real estate, and other business services) and education intensive occupations (professional/technical, managerial/administrative, and clerical occupations). Furthermore, with the progress of science and technology, while higher returns to education may continue to exacerbate the wage gap between skill intensive and unskilled or semi-skilled occupations, the persistent failure to industrialize aggressively will result in the low employment of unskilled and semi-skilled workers and higher income inequality. The slow progress in manufacturing so far continues to reflect the failure to provide adequate infrastructure such as "*bijli*, *sadak* and *pani*". The preoccupation with rising inequality, an overriding concern about whether growth is "inclusive" enough or not, and a misdiagnosis of why growth is not inclusive enough may have distracted the focus of policymakers from growth itself, and stultified the growth of the Indian middle class.

6.5 Growth, Employment and Industrial Policy

Creating more jobs and better livelihoods for India's large and youthful population must be a principal goal of the country's economic development. It is the best way to ensure inclusion in economic growth, which the country has not been doing well enough. Solutions, such as the drive to teach skills to millions of people and to change labour laws to make it easier to fire workers in the expectation that this will lead to more employment, are inadequate and can even have unintended negative consequences. A systemic, and less ideological, examination of issues has become imperative to find the root causes of India's insufficient progress towards the goal of more jobs and respectable livelihoods.

- ***Growth and Employment***

The National Commission for Enterprises in the Unorganized Sector (NCEUS), chaired by the late Arjun Sengupta, submitted its report in April 2009. The chairman said in his introductory summary, the most important conclusion that follows from the findings of the Commission is that all these efforts to improve the quantity and quality of employment in the unorganized sector would require a new approach to economic planning in India. The objective of our planning process from now on should be 'maximizing employment', in terms of quantity and quality and social development. India's economic planners must make maximization of employment the objective of planning rather than the maximization of gross domestic product (GDP). What matters to the *aam aadmi* most of all is a regular income, whether as wages or income from ownership of an enterprise. The GDP is an abstract number to him. The income is his reality. In 2010, as a prelude to preparing the Twelfth Five-Year Plan, all officers of the Planning Commission worked in cross divisional teams for three months, culminating in a two-day off-site workshop, to distil the systemic challenges of the country. This was the first time such a systemic exercise was done in the Planning Commission, which is organized in sectoral silos and where officers mostly exchange notes with each other on files. At the end of the workshop, the officers collectively prioritized the nation's challenges. Employment and jobs were at the top. Yet, when they went back to write the plan, the opening chapter discussed rates of growth of GDP, and the subsequent chapters were divided into sectors corresponding to their internal organizational silos. Employment and jobs faded into the background. By 2014, four years later, with economic growth declining and inflation persisting, there was a realization in the Planning Commission once again that what matters most of all is good quality employment and rising incomes for citizens. Therefore, it has recommended to the next Planning Commission, which, if and when formed, will conduct the mid-term appraisal of the Twelfth Plan, that the principal lens through which it should measure the country's economic development is employment. There is speculation about what form a new planning body will take, or if there will be one at all. Therefore, what a mid-term appraisal by it, if done, will reveal is even more speculative. Nevertheless, Planning Commission or not, some facts must be considered. The first is that the Indian economy has not been translating GDP growth into jobs as fast as it should, and as fast as other countries have. With the largest population of young people in the world, which we advertise as the source of our expected demographic dividend, we should be the fastest generator of jobs. Otherwise, not only will we not have an economic dividend, we will also have severe social and political problems. Between 1983-84 and 1992-93, employment increased by a little more than 2 per cent per annum. Then, from 1993-94 to 2004-05, the economy grew faster, but employment growth decreased to 1.85 per cent per annum. After 2004-05, matters became worse. Employment elasticity, which is a measure of the jobs that economic growth produces, had been 0.44 between 1999-2000 and 2004-05, but it decreased to only 0.01 between 2004-05 and 2009-10, reports Onkar Goswami in a chapter on jobs in *Getting India Back on Track* (2014). Other countries are doing much better at translating growth into jobs. The International Labour Organization (ILO) and the Asian Development Bank (ADB) estimate that India has been converting GDP to job at only two-thirds the rate that other Asian countries have been since 2001. India's rate of conversion is only half that of Vietnam's (*The Economic Times*, 14 November, 2012). Clearly, we must focus more on creating jobs with growth. We must make jobs the goal, and growth a means for creating them. For example, we have been saying the goal of our national manufacturing policy is an increase in the manufacturing sector's share in GDP from the 15 per cent it is today to 25 per cent. But the principal goal must be to create 100 million additional jobs in the manufacturing sector by 2022. Large, capital-intensive processing plants that employ very few people can add a lot to the manufacturing sector's output and we can achieve our goal of 25 per cent of GDP that way. Therefore, unless we focus on the goal, which is employment we will choose the wrong growth strategy, as, seems to have been the case since the early 1990s. Jobs and Skills from the connection between growth and jobs let us turn to the connection between skills and jobs. It has been accepted that a principal reason why more Indians are not employed is that they do not have the skills required. Therefore, the country has set itself a "big, hairy, audacious goal" to skill 500 million persons by 2022, the 75th year of its independence. If the purpose of an education is to prepare a young person for life and to earn an income, India's education system has clearly failed. The National Sample Survey Office (NSSO) data reveals that the unemployment rate of youth (between 15 and 29 years) with graduate degrees was 19 per cent in 2011-12. The unemployment rate of persons with a secondary education was 4.6 per cent. And, surprisingly, the unemployment rate of non-literates was only 2.3 per cent. It seems that a young person's chance of getting a job does not increase with more education. In a way, they may be better off not getting an education because they will frustratingly find they cannot obtain jobs commensurate with the effort put in to get educated. The picture in European countries is different. Unemployment levels decline with more education, as one would expect. In Germany, unemployment among people with less than upper secondary education is 14 per cent, whereas it drops to 2 per cent for people with tertiary-level education. In Sweden, unemployment drops from 11 per cent to 4 per cent with higher education. Even in Spain, where unemployment is notoriously high now, youth are better off if educated. Unemployment of youth with less than upper secondary education is 28 per cent in Spain, but falls to 12 per cent with tertiary-level education. There is a huge mismatch between the products of India's education system and the requirements of the job market. Sufficient numbers of skilled persons are not being produced, and their knowledge and skills do not match what the market wants.

Therefore, the national skills mission is trying hard to get the demand side connected with the supply side by involving employers, not only in defining what skills are required, but also in training young people so that their skills will fit the jobs to be done. India's education system needs a revamp. Consider this. Only 19 per cent of India's working-age people have a secondary education, according to the McKinsey Global Institute. In China, 61 per cent do. In Brazil, 48 per cent. And in Indonesia, 46 per cent. At the tertiary level, India compares favourably with the others, with 8 per cent of the working-age population with college degrees, the same as in China, Brazil, and Indonesia. The much lower numbers with secondary education in India, if accurate, suggest that we have a serious problem with the quality and quantity of useful secondary education imparted to our youth. This is an opportunity to revamp the secondary education system and introduce more vocational content to make young people more employable when they finish school. Going on to college does not make them more employable. The NSSO numbers showed that the unemployment level among college graduates is higher than that among illiterates in India, unlike the rest of the world.

- ***Enterprises and Jobs***

We must remain steadfastly focused on jobs and livelihoods. What young people want, and what the country must provide them to ensure its social and political stability, are jobs and livelihoods. Jobs are created by successful enterprises. Therefore, policymakers must turn their attention to the conditions required for enterprises to form and grow more rapidly. This was the subject of the NCEUS report, which has insights and recommendations that have not got the attention they deserve. What policymakers pay attention to is an outcome of political processes and of the public discourse in the media? Thus, some things become politically correct to say, even fashionable. But they may not be the solutions required. They may not even address the real problems. For example, right now, there is pressure from some quarters to reform labour laws to make it easier for enterprise owners to fire people in the belief that this will create more jobs. But this does not address the root causes of why enterprises do not grow easily in India. To sense what these root causes may be let us do a

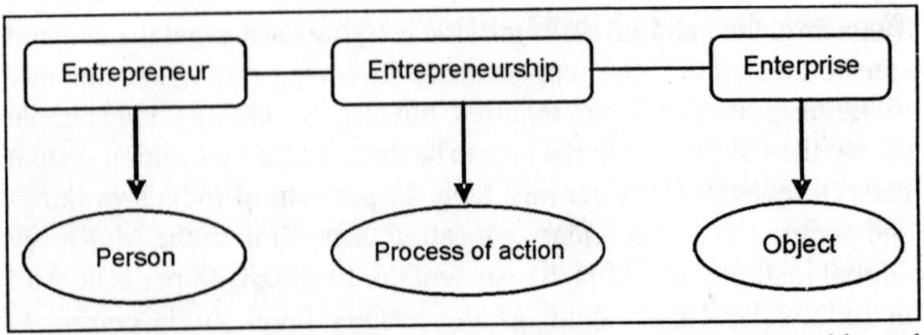

Fig. 6.3: Understanding the concepts Entrepreneur, Entrepreneurship and Enterprise

thought experiment. The informal and unorganized sectors have 90 per cent of Indian enterprises. Overall, these enterprises, with lower capital employment ratios than larger organized enterprises, provide more employment. Such small enterprises are in the principal employment generation sectors manufacturing (overall employment of 60 million in 2011-12, according to the NSSO); construction (50 million); and trade and hospitality (53 million). The largest employment sector is of course agriculture (224 million), but we should be expecting employment in agriculture to fall and those in other sectors to grow. Imagine you are the owner of a small enterprise in one of these sectors. You are told that you are now legally free to fire people whenever you want, and you are asked how many more people you will therefore employ access to finance when required and at a reasonable cost are the biggest constraint that micro, small, and medium enterprises (MSMEs) face. The organized financial system has not been helping them. In 1990, according to the NSSO, 15 per cent of gross bank credit went to unorganized sector manufacturing enterprises. By 2005-06, this had fallen to 3.6 per cent. Another big constraint owners of small enterprises complain about is the quality of the power and transportation infrastructure. It adds to their costs and to uncertainties in keeping up with delivery commitments. Yet another huge burden on owners of small enterprises is the manner in which a plethora of regulations applying to their operations, covering safety matters, labour matters, and environmental matters are applied. Contradictions among some of them, the number of forms to be filled, the inspections that must be endured, and corruption—all these divert the time and energy of owners from running their businesses. The burden of following the regulations, including labour regulations, which must be reduced urgently, should not be confused with the restrictions some laws place on firing permanent employees. Indeed, an owner of a small enterprise may say that the laws on firing and hiring do not affect him. His employees are on contract, often informal ones. The legal freedom to hire and fire is an irrelevant sop. If he is not employing more people, it is because he has other constraints on the growth of his enterprise, such as finance and poor infrastructure. It is simplistic, and wrong, to gauge "labour market rigidities" by the legal freedom to employers to fire workers. Many other constraints affect the hiring of labour, and in the Indian context these other constraints are much greater.

- ***Understanding the Constraints***

The conclusions of these thought experiments have been validated by many surveys of enterprise owners, both large and small ones. The binding constraints on their growth lie not in laws restricting firing of employees, but in the messy, time-consuming, and corrupt administration of the various laws that apply to enterprises, and in the poor quality of transportation and energy infrastructure in the country. Therefore, if we want larger number of persons to find employment in these enterprises, we must ensure that the primary constraints on the growth of enterprises are removed even more rapidly than the upgrading of skills the country is pursuing. If not, there will be no jobs for the millions of skilled people who aim to develop. Many constraints lie in the physical reality of enterprises—the infrastructure around them, and the institutional realities (government, financial services, and so on) they operate in. There are constraints in the mind too, which must be removed to find correct solutions. For example, owners are reluctant to pay more to contract employees, even when they choose and follow the need for fairness in their enterprises (equal pay for equal work), because they say they cannot afford it. A study commissioned by the Planning Commission on the relationship between industrial relations' practices and the growth and profits of enterprises, conducted for it by Bain and Company, revealed that total employee costs (including salaries of management personnel) to total revenues did not exceed 10 per cent in any manufacturing enterprise. It further revealed that if these enterprises were to pay their contract workers the same as permanent employees doing the same work, their net profits would decline by less than 1 per cent. Therefore, the cost burden of being fair is not as much as it is assumed to be. Larger questions of fairness arise from examining the returns to owners and employees, and the differences between managerial and workers' emoluments. The Annual Survey of Industries (ASI) reports that the share of wages to net value in Indian enterprises fell from 25.6 per cent in 1990-91 to 11.9 per cent in 2011-12. Moreover, whereas in 1990-91 workers' wages constituted 64 per cent of total emoluments, they fell to 46.5 per cent of total emoluments in 2011-12, with a much faster rise in management emoluments. Over the same period, the average rate of workers' wage increase has been 7.5 per cent per annum, whereas the consumer price index (CPI) for industrial workers rose by 7.3 per cent per annum, which means the real earnings of workers have barely increased. These issues have an ideological side to them too. Underlying them is an attitude towards the human side of the enterprise. Unlike machines and buildings, human beings can learn and improve their own capabilities when the right conditions are created and thereby improve the competitiveness of enterprises. *The Economist* (27 April, 2013) reports that the UK and US have more flexible labour markets than countries such as Germany and Sweden, and yet they have higher levels of youth unemployment. A report by Accenture is cited, pointing out those firms in the UK and US spend much less on training. Only 8 per cent of British employers trained apprentices, compared to 32 per cent in Germany and a similar proportion in Sweden. And only 21 per cent of American workers were given any training in new skills in the previous five years. Germany and Sweden also have strong traditions of union-management collaboration to maintain industrial harmony, unlike the confrontational attitudes in the UK and the US. Industrial relations practices in Japan, with an orientation towards long-term employment; worker participation in quality and process improvements; and strong unions, are more similar to Germany and Sweden than the UK and US. It is worth noting that Germany, Sweden, and Japan have sustainably competitive industrial sectors, whereas the US, and especially the UK, has been losing their competitiveness. One may conclude that the orientation of employers in India is towards the human side of their enterprises (should it be the German way or the British way?), and with this orientation, the changes in laws they lobby for will determine whether the country will be able to create the jobs required to gainfully employ its burgeoning population of youth.

- ***Enterprises and Industrial Policy***

Industrial policy got a bad rap in the 1990s in India and elsewhere. The way industrial policy was developed and applied in India until the 1980s, as a matrix of controls on what and how much could be produced by whom, stifled entrepreneurship. The collapse of the Soviet Union, at the end of the 1980s, led to a dumping of the idea of Soviet-style central planning, which India's industrial planning process had followed. A new "Washington Consensus" emerged in the early 1990s, promoted by the International Monetary Fund (IMF) and the World Bank, espousing a free-market ideology in which the role of the government in the economy would be very limited. In this, there was no place for any government-supported industrial policy. India was compelled to take the IMF's financial support in 1991, and with it came the ideology of the Washington Consensus. Though Soviet-style planning was consigned to history's dustbin, the baby was also thrown out with the bathwater; the idea of any industrial policy promoted by the government was brushed aside. India has paid a heavy price for muddling along on industrial policy since then. Its manufacturing sector has languished at around 15 per cent of GDP, which is much less than China's or any other country's at India's stage of economic development. The urgent need to stimulate the creation of more jobs in the manufacturing sector spurred the Planning Commission, in the run-up to preparing the Twelfth Five-Year Plan in 2010 and 2011, to set aside ideology and to explore, with the help of the international experts on the development of nations' industrial sectors such as Dani Rodrik, Ricardo Hausmann, Ha-Joon Chang, and Justin Lin, how the Indian government should go about facilitating the growth of the industrial sector. It is ironic that the US has also felt the need for an industrial policy (which it chooses to call an innovation policy) because the government is under pressure to stimulate the growth of more jobs for the youth. The Planning Commission's study revealed what the essence of industry policy is. It is a process of learning in action that is very well expressed in Deng Xiao Ping's image of "crossing the river by feeling the stones underfoot". Industrialization is a process whereby a nation's enterprises learn to do what they were not able to before produce complex products for which they did not have the skills before; manage complex systems for which they did not have the management capabilities earlier; and learn to perform these complex tasks better than their competitors can. Enterprises are the feet that encounter constraints as they move along the ground. The government's policymakers are in the head, and they must receive signals from the ground quickly and accurately, and adjust the weight of the body to support the movement of the feet. The transmission of signals back and forth happens along the spinal cord, which coordinates the system. Rodrik's study and those by others explain how the quality of the process of interaction between producers and policymakers determines whether a country will rapidly cross the stream and develop a competitive industrial sector. The structure and conduct of the process must be fitted to the political-economy institutions of each country. Consensus building in Japan Inc (a combination of industrial associations and government ministries) was facilitated by a process led by the Ministry of International Trade and Industry (MITI)—and it continues, except MITI is now the Ministry of Economy, Trade and Industry (METI). Germany and Sweden have even older traditions of industrial policy consensus between employers' federations, unions, and their governments. In South Korea, the *chaebol* (business families) and the government were partners in the rapid development of industry. In China, the process of consultation between producers and policymakers is enabled by the National Development and Reforms Commission, and also by close links between state-owned enterprises and government policymakers. Whatever be the structures of government and industry, it is the quality of the consultations between them; the speed of learning; and rapid policy adjustments that enable faster improvement of competitiveness of enterprises, increasing the numbers of jobs. The conclusion is that India must improve the process of collaboration and learning between industry and government. Since several constraints on industry in India arise from concerns about the environment and the rights of local communities, these stakeholders must also be engaged in the process for finding solutions that meet not only their needs but also the needs of industry (small and big enterprises), on whom they rely for more jobs and better livelihoods. Investments in enterprises that can create jobs in the manufacturing, construction, and hospitality and trade sectors have been lagging in the past five years because projects are stalled by contentions over land and environment issues and protests from local communities over the tolls and prices for services they are expected to pay. The approach has been to pass more legislation, and to mandate bureaucratic procedures for obtaining the views of stakeholders, which often conflict and have to be resolved through time-consuming processes by an overburdened legal system. What India needs to create and grow more rapidly is a better way of converting these contentions into collaboration, through a process that is less confrontational and more consensual; a Method C. Method A is the inherently adversarial approach in the legal system and on the streets that is now being overused by stakeholders. Method B is the bureaucratic approach in which government functionaries take upon themselves the responsibility to meet stakeholders and find solutions that will be acceptable to all. The failures of Method B make stakeholders turn to Method A, protesting on the streets, or go to court. Other countries that have adopted Method C processes, such as Sweden, Germany, and Japan, are able to produce win-win solutions more easily than India. More countries, such as Malaysia and Brazil, are deliberately applying Method C processes for stakeholders to listen to each other; understand the system as a whole; and find solutions that will be supported by all key stakeholders, and hence will be implementable. India too must use better Method C processes. The Twelfth Five-Year Plan's lengthy document has buried in it, in the chapter on industry, the seeds of the process we need for stakeholders to collaboratively address the root causes of difficulties in forming and growing enterprises. It is the India Backbone Implementation Network, the purpose of which is to make stakeholders concentrate on better processes for collaborative solutions, and to guide them to techniques that may be applied and facilitators whom they can turn to. This seed is producing little shoots already. Among the most encouraging of these is the dialogue under way between central unions and employers' federations to build trust in each other; to get off ideological high horses during dialogues; and get to the root causes of poor skills, industrial tensions, and slow growth of enterprises. The concept of the India Backbone Implementation Network provides a consultation mechanism between the feet and the head that Deng's metaphor suggests is critical to accelerate economic growth and generate more employment.

In fine, (1) India's economic policymakers and India Inc must stay focused very clearheadedly on the creation of more opportunities for employment and livelihoods. (2) Opportunities for employment and livelihoods must arise from the formation and growth of more enterprises, especially in the MSME sector. (3) The process of consultation between policymakers and producers (especially MSMEs) must be improved with more systemic analyses and less ideology based arguments. (4) Multi-stakeholder dialogues must be strengthened to convert contentions into collaboration and confusion into coordination so that agreements can be reached and implementation of policies and projects expedited. This is the way for the country to create jobs and livelihoods faster.

6.6 Top 10 Economic and Development Challenges for India

LSE's Ruth Kattumuri highlights some economic challenges that are of priority for India's development in the coming years. List of the Top 10 foreign policy challenges facing India in recent years is as follows:

1. Sustainable growth: The United Nations describes sustainable growth as a process that "fulfils the needs of the present without compromising the ability of future generations to meet their own needs." This year, academics working on India questioned whether Indian growth was truly sustainable, or whether the country had failed to utilize resources generated by recent economic growth by investing much more in education and healthcare and developing infrastructure in an environmentally responsible way. India must better assess how to enhance economic growth together with low-carbon development initiatives including ways to improve food and water security.

2. Inclusive growth: For Indian growth to be sustainable, it must be inclusive to cover issues related to inequalities between castes (including tribal children and elderly people living in remote areas), colour (dark and fair), disability, gender, regions (rural-urban as well as differences between states), and more. While the gender gap in employment and political participation has been narrowing, there is much more to be done for the health and safety of girls and women. India needs to do more to ensure inclusive growth, particularly by improving social protection policies. Good examples such as 'Amma'sunavagam/canteen', which was recently introduced in Tamil Nadu and sells highly subsidized nutritious meals, are worth expanding to other states to help address problems related to high malnutrition levels.

3. Demographic dividend: Approximately 200 million Indians are between the ages of 15 and 24 and India is well positioned to make the most of a growing population of working age. However, to reap the demographic dividend, India will have to manage the demand and supply of skills and labour carefully. While the government has introduced policies to improve access to education, much more needs to be done to improve the quality of education, standards of teaching, methods of examination, development of skills, vocational programmes, etc. In order to make Right to Education policy effective, the country should also address the challenges of bridging the gaps between children from disadvantaged and advantaged backgrounds being able to study together and better understand, respect and befriend each other. India should look to develop public-private partnerships and social entrepreneurship programmes that can ensure livelihoods for its young population.

4. Inflation: The issue of high inflation is uppermost in the minds of politicians, policymakers and the people. Consumer prices in India have risen at an average annual pace of 10 per cent during the past five years, and Indian households are bracing for another 13 per cent increase next year. To check inflation, the Reserve Bank of India has raised interest rates and will review India's monetary policy framework in line with recommendations by the Urjit Patel Committee, which is expected to submit its report at the end of the year. It is also essential to manage artificially induced national and international mechanisms. The central bank and Ministry of Finance are working together to analyze and understand the reasons and find ways to encourage investment and curb inflation.

5. Rapid urbanization: Indian cities are growing at an unprecedented rate; the country's urban population is expected to grow to 590 million people by 2030. This rapid urbanization is also expected to drive economic growth: according to some estimates, cities could generate up to 70 per cent of new jobs created until 2030 and produce 70 per cent of Indian GDP. To reap the economic advantages of urbanization, the Indian government must develop better policies to meet urban infrastructure needs through sustainable means and address growing urban poverty and inequality.

6. Land reforms: The Land Acquisition Act passed this year received mixed reviews. There are concerns that the new law will drive up costs across the economy and make several industrial and real estate projects unviable, without necessarily delivering justice to farmers and landowners whose lands are acquired. These and other challenges related to land reform particularly in the context of urbanization and the growing need for low-income urban housing mean that India will have to continue drafting land-related legislation to ensure sustainable and equitable growth.

7. Centre-state dynamics: The evident role of states in influencing economic growth, governance and policies has increasing become more prominent. States are driving localized growth, enhancing their own investments, and developing models that are being replicated across the country. But the centre needs to do more to facilitate state-state interaction and the states should also be proactive in sharing of knowledge of best practices among themselves. The Central Government should also seek to do more to balance the uneven growth between states.

8. Older citizens: While India seeks to harness its young population to drive growth, it must also start planning for increased expenditure on health and welfare services for the elderly. Fertility rates in India are declining as life expectancy increases: there will be more than 300 million Indians over the age of 60 by 2050. 'Indians never seem to retire' has been said of people in various sectors, particularly in urban areas, as many continue to work for several years after retirement. Nevertheless, the shifting demographics will add to the burden of inadequate healthcare, welfare services, and families. Elderly women, who will outnumber men, are expected to be the most vulnerable. In addition, there are interesting opportunities and challenges of elderly parents remaining in India while their children have migrated. To tackle these challenges, India must develop policies to ensure that its older citizens too have healthy and happy lives.

9. India-China trade: Despite various diplomatic standoffs this year, the governments of both India and China remain eager to boost bilateral trade to US$100 billion in the next few years. No doubt, trade with China is a significant component of India's economy. But trade relations remain one-way, with more Indian consumers buying Chinese goods than the other way around. India will have to address this trade deficit by improving its export competitiveness and identifying more goods, services and policies to enhance balanced trade with China.

10. India-Pakistan trade: In the past decade, India-Pakistan trade has increased from US$ 370 million per year to US$ 2.4 billion. But this is just a start: according to some estimates, the volume of a normalized bilateral trade regime could be as high as US$ 40 billion. The onus for progress on bilateral trade relations currently rests with Pakistan: despite repeated calls for improved India-Pakistan ties, Pakistan has yet to grant India Most Favoured Nation status. While there is little India can do to boost trade until Pakistan takes this key step, New Delhi should continue its support for increased bilateral trade, as it would be for the benefit of the economies of both India and Pakistan while also helping to improve the political relations between the two countries.

Bibliography

Aggarwal, A. (2004), Export Processing Zones in India: Analysis of the Export Performance, Working paper No. 48, Indian Council for Research on International Economic Relations, New Delhi, pp. 8-13. http://www.icrier.org

Alexander, J.W. (1977), *Economic Geography*, Prentice Hall of India Pvt. Ltd., New Delhi.

Álvarez-Albelo, C.D. *et al.* "The International Trade as the Sole Engine of Growth for an Economy" published on line journal. Spain, calbelo@ull.es.

Barnes, T.J. and Gertler, M. (eds) (1999), *The New Industrial Geography—Regions, Regulation and Institutions*, Routledge, New York.

Batra, G.S. and Dangwal, R.S. (2004), *Globalization and Liberalization: New Development*, Deep and Deep Publication, New Delhi.

Berry, B.J.L. (1967), *Geography of Market Centers and Retail Distribution*, Prentice Hall, INC.

Brown, L. (1978), *The Global Economic Prospect: New Sources of Economic Stress*, Washington, DC. Worldwatch Institute.

Chorley, R.J. and Haggett, P. (1970), *Socio-Economic Models in Geography*, Methuen.

Crowley, M.A. (2013), *An introduction to the WTO and GATT*, Federal Reserve Bank of Chicago, U.S.A., pp. 1-3.

Das, P.S. (2005), *Decentralized Planning and Participatory Rural Development*, Concept Publishing Company, New Delhi.

Dutta, R. and Sundaram, K.P.M. (1999), *Indian Economy*, S.Chand & Company Ltd., New Delhi.

Garnier, B.J. and Delobez, A. (1979). *Geography of Marketing*, Longman.

Guha, J.L. and Chattaraj, P.R. (2002), *A New Approach to Economic Geography*, The Worl Press Pvt. Ltd., Kolkata.

Hanik, D.M. (1997), *Principles and Applications of Economic Geography*, John Wiley & Sons, Inc., New York.

Hazra, A. (2013), *India's Social Sector and Millennium Development Goals*, Rawat Publication, Jaipur.

Jayanthakumaran, K. (2000), *Industrialisation: Import Substitution to Export Promotion*, Faculty Business-Economics Work Paper, University of Wollongong, pp. 6-14.

Khandela, M. (2006), *Globalization and Economic Realities*, Aavishkar Publication, Jaipur.

Khandela, M. (2006), *Globalization and Foreign Trade*, Pointer Pub., Jaipur.

Khullar, D.R. (2006), *India—A Comprehenisve Geography,* Kalyani Publishers, Kolkata, pp. 798-804.

Kotwal, A. *et al.* (2011), *Economic Liberalization and Indian Economic Growth: What's the Evidence*? Discussion Papers in Economics, Indian Statistical Institute, Delhi Planning Unit, New Delhi, pp. 3-5.

Kousadikar, A. and Singh, T.K. (2013), Advantages and Disadvantages of Privatization in India, *International Journal of Advanced System and Social Engineering Research*, ISSN 2278-6031, Vol. 3, Issue 1, 2013, pp. 18-22 http://www.bipublication.com

Lahiri, A.K. (2014), 'The Middle Class and Economic Reforms', *Economic & Political Weekly*, Vol. XLIX, No. 11, pp. 40-42.

Leong, G.C. and Mongon G.C. (1972), *Human and Economic Geography*, Oxford University Press, Oxford.

Maira, A. (2014), Jobs, Growth, and Industrial Policy, *Economic & Political Weekly*, Vol. XLIX, No. 34, pp. 35-39.

Majumdar, P.K. (2013), *India's Demography—Changing Demographic Scenario in India*, Rawat Publication, Jaipur, pp. 347-352.

Miller, A.E. *et al.* (2007), A Review of TRIPS and TRIMs Enforcement Issues In the People's Republic of China: Background and Analysis of the Intellectual Property Protection and Enforcement Crisis Facing U.S. Industry, China's Laws, Regulations and Ractices in the Areas of Technology Transfer, Trade-Related Investment Measures, Subsidies and Intellectual Property Protection Which Raise WTO Compliance Concerns, Silverbrook Associates, Inc. China.

Mccarty, H.H. and Lindberg, J.B. (1966), *A Preface to Economic Geography*, Englewood Cliffs, N, Prentice Hall, INC.

Mitra, A. (2002), *Resource Studies*, Sreedhar Publishers, Kolkata.

Randers, J. (2010), *What was the message of the Limits to Growth?*, Club of Rome, Switzerland, www.clubofrome.org

Ray, P.K. (1997), *Economic Geography: A Study of Resources*, New Central Book Agency (P) Ltd., Calcutta.

Saxena, H.M. (2004), *Marketing Geography*, Rawat Publication, Jaipur.

Sen, S. (2010), *International Trade Theory and Policy: A Review of the Literature*, Levy Economics Institute of Bard College, http://www.levyinstitute.org

Seshadri B. (2013), *Industrialization and Regional Development*, Concept Publishing Company (P) Ltd., New Delhi, pp. 43-44.

Sethi, N. and Sucharita, S. (2013), *FDI and Economic Growth In India*, Rawat Publications, Jaipur.

Sharma, T.C. (2013), *Economic Geography of India*, Rawat Publications, Jaipur.

Smith, D.M. (1981), *Industrial Location*.

Singh, J. and Dhillon S.S. (2005), *Agricultural Geography*, Tata McGraw-Hill Publishing Company Limited, New Delhi.

Sundaram, K.V. (2012), *Development Planning at the Grassroots*, Concept Publishing Company (P) Ltd., New Delhi.

Taaffe, E.J. and Gauthier, H.L. (1973), *Geography of Transportation*, Prentice-Hall of India Private Limited, New Delhi.

Thakur, B. *et al.* (2012), "Changing face of India's Industrial Policies—A Look", *International Journal of Scientific and Research Publications*, Volume 2, Issue 12, December 2012 1 ISSN 2250-3153 pp. 1-7.

Thoman, R.S. *et al.* (1968), *The Geography of Economic Activities*, McGraw-Hill Book Co., New York.

Tussie, D. and Aggio, C., "Economic and social impacts of trade liberalization", a online published journal.

Wang, N. (2010), "The Relationship between Regional Trading Blocs and Globalization", *International Journal of Economics and Finance*, Vol. 2, No. 01, University of Architecture and Technology, China, pp. 1-3. www.ccsenet.org/ijef

World Resources: A Guide to the Global Environment, (1994-95), A Report by the World Resources Institute, Oxford University Press, Calcutta.

Zimmerman, E.W. (1950), *World Resources and Industries*, Harper & Row, New York.

Website: 1. www.amazon.com
2. www.wikipedia.com
3. www.eoearth.org
4. www.epw.in

Index